_To: To_

# MUST
# LABOUR
# ALWAYS
# LOSE?

By
Denis MacShane

# CLARET PRESS

Copyright ©Denis MacShane
The moral right of the author has been asserted.

ISBN paperback: 978-1-910461-53-2
ISBN ebook: 978-1-910461-54-9

A CIP catalogue record for this book is available from the British Library.

This paperback can be ordered from all bookstores as well as from Amazon, and the ebook is available on online platforms such as Amazon and iBooks.

Cover and Interior Design by Petya Tsankova

Claret Press

**www.claretpress.com**

# TABLE OF CONTENTS

# Introduction

This is the book I wish I'd read when I joined the Labour Party in 1970 and embarked on a half century of political activity. In those fifty years Labour has won elections in just four of them so only eighteen were lived under a Labour government. This book tries to explain why and what lessons Labour needs to learn to stop being a losers' party.

In 1960, the political scientist and polling expert Mark Abrams co-authored a book *Must Labour Lose* after the Conservatives won their third consecutive election in 1959. It quickly became out of date as the new Labour leader, Harold Wilson, a cynical moderniser, dropped nuclear disarmament and nudged Labour to accepting the reality of European partnership and cooperation. He faced a caricatural Tory prime minister, a grouse-shooting Scottish aristocratic. It was like scoring on an open goal. In 1964, Wilson won 43 Labour seats in Scotland. (In comparison, Labour has currently just one MP in Scotland.) As a result, the Tories were out of power from 1964 to 1979, apart from a forty-month interlude. So Abrams' 1960 question – Must Labour Lose? – seemed to have been answered. No one would be happier than me if my very different argument six decades later also foreshadows a new Labour government. In the third decade of this century the Tories will ruthlessly dispose of their current leader, the populist fabulator Boris Johnson if he looks like losing. But supposing he isn't a loser?

The jury is out. The Tories lost a safe seat to the Liberal Democrats in a by-election in Amersham in June 2021. The previous month Labour lost a safe seat Hartlepool to the Tories in a by-election. In the 2017 general election there were 11,734 Labour voters in Amersham. Four years later in the by-election only 622 voters supported Labour. Neither party leader could draw comfort from the by-election results of summer 2021.

This was confirmed in a third by-election held in the Labour seat of Batley and Spen in West Yorkshire in July 2021. Its Labour MP Jo Cox was killed in a political murder by an English nationalist during the Brexit campaign in 2016. It remained Labour in subsequent general elections, but the sitting Labour MP stood down in 2021 as she wanted a career in local politics. Jo Cox's sister, Kim Leadbetter, narrowly held the seat with a 323 majority in the by-election. This represented a swing to the Tories of 2.9 per cent. Liberal Democrats failed to turn out for their candidate. Labour's tiny margin of victory, far below previous majorities, was possibly due to tactical voting by LibDem voters rather than a surge of support for Sir Keir Starmer. Many voters wanted to protest the Johnson government, which was plagued with poor handling of the Covid pandemic and by a scandal over the resignation of the Health Secretary, Matt Hancock. So as he entered his second year as Labour leader, Sir Keir Starmer looked like his three immediate predecessors – Jeremey Corbyn, Ed Miliband and Gordon Brown – as a Labour leader not obviously destined to be a winner.

Sixty years ago the Tories had already enjoyed more than a decade in power by the time of Harold Wilson's election as Labour leader in 1963. In 1951 the Conservatives were handed power following a serious blunder by the Labour prime minister Clement Attlee. He called in an unnecessary election in which nearly two million Liberal voters turned to the Tories. Once back in charge the Conservatives ditched all of their policies and nostrums in place prior to 1940 and ruthlessly adopted many of the Labour and statist policies put in place after 1945. Money was poured into council housing, into state education and free health care. Using the Covid Pandemic as a reason, Prime Minister Boris Johnson, is also stealing many of the Labour policies advocated in the previous decade. Extra spending is promised from state coffers to implement policies which are classic centre-left social democracy.

It is a modern update of Benjamin Disraeli's jibe in 1845 that his great rival, Robert Peel, had 'caught the Whigs bathing and walked away with their clothes'. Then Disraeli's complaint was that Peel was embracing liberal free trade ideas in place of Tory protectionism. Johnson is implementing old Labour anti-European demands for closed borders and more support for workers in the north of England through infrastructure investment and vocational training. Johnson is indifferent to Thatcherite nostrums of an ultra-liberal free market. He just wants to stay in power. Labour dreams of winning elections but has little idea of what to do once in office. The Tories don't care what they do in office as long as they stay in power.

My question 'Must Labour Always Lose' is not a prophecy. And this book is not an autobiography, still less a history or political theory book. If it must be something, then I suppose it's a how-to guide, a manual of how not to lose. I have sought to tell the story of the Labour Party's life between losing the election in 1970, losing the general election in 2019 and losing a key Labour seat in a by-election in 2021. Always tell a story through an individual is an old newspaper adage. I'm that individual. I've been a player on the side of the biggest political activities of the past fifty years, never quite close enough to the centre but never far from it. One foot in each camp. This gives me a unique insight. Starting in 1996 I kept a daily record of the politics of Labour as it approached power in 1997 and then during all its years in power and after.

Under Tony Blair Labour managed to win three elections, though the final five years in office after 2005 were not happy ones. Except for relatively brief periods like that, Labour has been a party of losers in terms of forming a national government. Labour won control of local government councils and for a few years the Scottish parliament. But the question that nags, nags, nags at me is why is has Labour been so poor in my political lifetime at winning and then keeping national governing power?

It is not just the fifty years since 1970. Labour won in 1929 but was swiftly out of office and had to wait sixteen years to govern. Labour won in 1950 but then lost in 1951 and was out of power for thirteen years. Even when Labour did win elections, as in 1974 when I first stood for Parliament, the ministerial cars and red boxes were treated with disdain by so many Labour Party members who were unhappy with the government. Confidence and élan drained from the party. Even when Labour won it struggled to inspire people, to nudge the nation in the direction of progressive values and social justice, to celebrate the better Britain that Labour was created to bring about. Being in power I learnt early on was not an end in itself.

Political activity is a noble calling. I sympathise with those who see it merely as a mechanism by which some lucky sods get the chance to sink their snouts into the trough and snuffle up as much as possible before being pushed out of the way. That does happen. And we need a strong oversight system to make politics an unappealing way to self-enrich.

Yet the hard truth remains: no change happens in democracies except via political engagement and collective organising. It was once said that the gap between a right-wing and a progressive-left government may only be an inch but it is an inch worth living in and fighting for. That remains my view. I can't be bothered with crude 'lower than vermin' language about Conservatives or other political rivals. Having said that, I do believe the worst Labour government is probably better than the best Tory government, though to be honest I have not experienced a Tory government in my lifetime that managed to serve all of the nation and not just its better-off majority.

Two decades into the 21$^{st}$ century, as I look at friends in Labour's sister parties in Europe, I see once great parties verging on extinction, poised on the edge of the dustbin of history. Is extinction Labour's fate? I do not know. But the adage remains valid: those who fail to learn from history are condemned to repeat it. So I just hope my successors starting out on their own political journey for Labour may earn the right to be granted governing power by the people of Britain – or perhaps it will soon be just England – for longer periods than my generation managed.

My fears this may not happen are as strong as my hopes that it will. This book explains why.

Denis MacShane, July 2021

**Part 1:**
THE 20$^{TH}$ CENTURY

# The 1970s

## 1970

Politics began for me as I took part in my first general election campaign and watched Labour lose. I went on to watch Labour lose (or fail to win) an overall majority in ten more elections. After each defeat there were earnest post-mortems – the latest being the endless literature on so-called 'red wall' seats – that were soon forgotten. Hope must always spring eternal in the political breast: this time we will win.

We didn't. Repetitively so. Was it because Labour refused to learn from defeats? Or couldn't learn? Or believed that a new leader or new faces and policies would be enough? Stay with me, dear reader, as I work through these decades of Labour losing and, when we had won, not knowing how to convert winning into a permanent change in the political life of Britain.

Politics is about the personalities, about the people who do it. It's utter nonsense that there are immanent forces which carry along political deciders from the party activist voting in a local meeting to members of the cabinet deciding big policy who have no choice but to bow to a destiny they cannot control. Politics is done and made by the human beings who commit themselves in political and public life. If they, we, I get it wrong, real people are to blame. So first a little about me.

All political life should start with a bang. Mine did with a whimper. Born in Glasgow to a Polish immigrant (as the *Daily Mail* would call him) and an Irish-Scottish woman, politics meant nothing to me for the first two decades of my life. At the outbreak of the Second World War my father, Jan Matyjaszek, was a newly commissioned second lieutenant from a poor farming family in a remote corner of Poland. He took a bullet in the shoulder leading his men against a nationalist army from Germany. The bullet went on to kill his corporal behind him. German efficiency: one bullet, two Poles knocked out of the war.

He arrived in Britain with Polish soldiers via Romania and France. The Polish army reformed itself and was stationed in Scotland. There he met my mother, Isabel McShane, whose mother came from Donegal. The Irish Catholic families of Lanarkshire welcomed the arrival of all these dashing officers, who always kissed the hand of a woman of every age, could dance with a devil-may-care brio, and were such devout mass-going Catholics that mothers thought their virginal daughters were safe with these sex-starved Polish officers. At any rate it was proof that the ill-winds of war could blow some good.

My father died when I was ten and holidays into my teenage years were spent with family in Lanarkshire, Ireland or Manchester. I had political history of a sort as boy but the history I picked up had little connection to British politics in the 1960s London where I was growing up.

At my catholic school, St Benedict's in Ealing, where I was sent on a Middlesex County Council scholarship after passing the eleven plus exam, the head boy was Chris Patten. The school became famous for Benedictine buggery and as a global paedophile centre. None of this came my way. I assume the dirty old monks picked on the more vulnerable, shall we say, less cocky boys. Chris Patten and I, or friends like Colin MacCabe, later a controversial English professor at Cambridge, or Peter Ackroyd, the writer, were all cocks of the walk.

At Oxford where I threw myself into student journalism, sex, drugs and rock 'n roll, I did politics in the sense of endless demonstrations against the Vietnam war and against visits by all-white cricket and rugby teams from South Africa. But party politics passed me by.

My 1968 generation held Labour PM Wilson in high contempt. He refused to intervene to stop the white racists in Rhodesia, now Zimbabwe, create a breakaway state, backed by the white apartheid supremacists in South Africa with their close links to Tory elites in London. Wilson failed to grasp the nettle of civil liberties and the need to end to Ulster unionist protestant supremacy in Northern Ireland.

His mandate was too much a matter of luck and he knew it. So Wilson was hostile to claims by workers for fair pay. He refused any reform of the absurd House of Lords. He was terrified at the idea of hard-working, brilliant, East African Asian British citizens being allowed into Britain. While he refused to send any British troops to fight in the Vietnam war he did not show the courage of Olof Plame, the Swedish social democrat leader, who marched in a torch-lit rally in Stockholm against the Vietnam war or Willy Brandt in West Berlin who also protested against President Johnson's folly in pursuing the war.

Palme and Brandt kept the support of the 1968 generation and won elections. Wilson did not. Nor did any Labour ministers. And the 1968 generation was lost to Labour.

> **Lesson 1.** *It is the trickiest problem in democratic politics. It has never been properly answered during my 50 years in Labour. How to not only keep the support of your own generation but also have a feel for the new demands and priorities of rising generations. Very few political leaders manage this high-wire art. Wilson and Callaghan did not, nor in later years did Brown and Miliband. Here is a solution that might help. Labour should bring in retirement age limits thus forcing the party constantly to bring in younger people to leadership positions. It is crude and mechanical perhaps but the moment Labour starts to look and sound middle-aged it neither convinces retirees nor enthuses younger voters cynical about politics. It was absurd that Labour in 2019 was led by a man in his eighth decade with a Labour MP like Dennis Skinner seeking re-election aged nearly 90.*

Politics for me began in Birmingham in the 1970s when I joined the Labour Party in response to the racism of Enoch Powell and his attacks on immigrants. I know for younger readers Enoch Powell is probably unknown. He created a racist shit-storm about immigrants – literally so as he told lies about Afro-Caribbeans pushing shit through the letter box of a widowed pensioner – as big a lie as anything said in the Brexit campaign. If it had just been offensive lies, then it could have been shrugged off. But Powell had the uncanny ability to suss out people's ugliest fears and then state them eloquently and reasonably. With his education and his flat Brummie accent, he gave this nastiness a sheen of acceptability. I was a BBC news trainee. For the first time, I heard and saw casual racism in the streets, while canvassing for Labour or just a having a drink after reporting on Wolverhampton Wanderers

In the 1970 election, I spent most of the time in the BBC West Midlands counting the number of times Labour or Conservative had appeared in the regional TV bulletins. If one bulletin said "Conservative" more than "Labour" I would quickly write a line or two for a later news bulletin to balance out the mentions. It was clunky and clumsy and made for boring news bulletins. But the BBC had a world reputation for accuracy and avoiding party politics, which justified the regressive tax levied on the British people to pay for my and many other salaries.

At weekends I was in London moonlighting doing Sunday shifts on the *Daily Mirror* where I learned two things: the art of writing for the masses and journalism's capacity for drinking. Lunch consisted of three hours in El Vino's, a Fleet Street bar, owned by the Tory MP, Sir David Mitchell. Later as Europe Minister I had to appoint a new private secretary – a post reserved for Foreign Office high-flyers – I set them a test to write a *Sun* editorial in favour of Europe. (The *Sun* was then as it is now hostile to Europe.) I told them I and most MPs could knock off a *Guardian* or *Times* comment piece but the real art of political communication was to write very short, punchy, simple-to-read stories or leaders in best tabloid style. Alas, as the years went by, Labour, the left, my political community, thought that writing a turgid *New Statesman* article was the highest form of political communication.

Harold Wilson's Labour majority in 1966 – bigger than Boris Johnson's in 2019 – was won just before England beat Germany at Wembley in the 1966 World Cup final. Briefly 1966 seemed a good summer for Labour. But tensions soon flared. Seafarers led by the charismatic John Prescott went on strike. Wilson was forced to devalue the pound. Enoch Powell unleashed the first round of xenophobic hate against immigrants which over the years was fine tuned by Nigel Farage and Boris Johnson into the Brexit victory. The 1968 student and militant workers' upheavals showed the gulf between young idealism and the tired 1940s statist administrative style of Wilson and the Labour cabinet. Wilson's 1966 majority of 98 was not enough and so he was voted out in 1970.

At the time, I was living in a poor part of Birmingham called Small Heath with its large Pakistani immigrant population. The racism about "Pakis" was flagrant in pubs and in the casual remarks made by Brummies. The housing was of poor quality, rented out by private landlords for whatever they could get.

I joined the National Union of Journalists as I was approached by the NUJ 'Father of the Chapel' (shop steward) in the BBC newsroom. I'd made a BBC film on Ken Coates, who in 1970, had published *Poverty: The Forgotten Englishmen* about the endemic poverty still to be found in Nottingham. The existence of such desperate poverty in rich England was a revealing shock. Even now when I listen to romantic folk-lore about how Labour governments after 1945 abolished poverty I remember Ken Coates' anger about what his research revealed.

My early years in Birmingham pushed me into politics and into the Labour Party, the only party I ever belonged to and which today for all its faults remains the most important agent for social justice ever seen in Britain.

# 1971

Politics quickly became febrile and confrontational as the new Tory government headed by Edward Heath took over. Heath's government brought in a big bill to try and force trade unions to submit themselves to new laws aimed at allowing the state to exercise more control over trade unions and workers.

There were giant 'Kill the Bill' demonstrations on which I marched. The political atmosphere was getting tense. The new Education Secretary, Margaret Thatcher, announced the abolition of free milk in primary schools. I hated being forced to drink small bottles of milk in the playground. Labour denounced 'Thatcher – the Milk-Snatcher' but children, future Tory voters in the 1980s, couldn't care less.

I campaigned in a by-election held in Bromsgrove where the Labour candidate, a car industry manager, Terry Davis, won the seat in an early sign of Ted Heath's unpopularity. A by-election meeting was held in a local school hall. The speaker's table was as usual up on the stage with the chairs ranged in rows below. The speaker was Labour MP Anthony Wedgwood Benn, as he then was still called, who'd run an impressive campaign to stay an MP when his father, a peer, died.

Tony came in, took one look at the set up and said: 'No, no, this won't do at all. We cannot have Terry and myself up on a stage talking down to people. No, let's get the table down to same level as ordinary people.' The speakers' table was duly taken off the stage. I am not sure who Tony was trying to impress and he certainly did not need a stage or platform to deliver an effective speech full of bromides about Europe.

In his diary in April 1970 just before the election Tony Benn noted, 'If we have to have some sort of organisation to control international companies, the Common Market is probably the right one. I think that decision-making is on the move and some decisions have to be taken in Europe, some in London, and an awful lot more at regional and local level.'

Tony's common sense on Europe died fast after Labour went into opposition and the left across the board from communists to Trotskyists to Tribuneites decided Europe was the enemy. *Tribune* headlines in May 1971 THE BIGGEST SELL-OUT SINCE MUNICH and a month later UNCONDITIONAL SURRENDER captured the mood.

Birmingham Labour Party sent me to a special Labour conference on Europe held at Westminster Central Hall in July 1971. I listened to a parade of the finest Labour speakers – from Michael Foot to the twenty-nine-year-old new Welsh MP, Neil Kinnock. The mild centrist, Keynesian economist MP, Peter Shore flipped his long forelock left and right as he turned himself into a new Churchill with rhetoric against Europe that got delegates cheering. I'd like to say I knew it was false but that would be dishonest. To be on the left of Labour in 1971 was to be anti-European. It was one our shibboleths. We believed the

Common Market was the bastion of capitalism oppressing the working class in the name of profit. All big organisations were, by sheer dint of being big. Except of course for trade unions and the Labour Party. It was common sense, too obvious to debate. There were no comrades from European sister parties to gently paint a different picture. This was British Labour talking to itself.

There is no point in stating the lesson: Beware the Shibboleths. You can't see them because they're both all-encompassing and yet not at all obvious. It's like asking fish to describe water. I'm not sure that Labour suffers from them any less than the Conservatives.

Sixty-nine Labour MPs saved the honour of Labour later that year by voting to join Europe. Birmingham MPs were prominent amongst them: Roy Jenkins, Roy Hattersley, Denis Howell or Brian Walden. The problem was that, other than Denis Howell who lived in my ward, the others were all London-based fashionable intellectuals or journalists who we never saw at any Birmingham-wide Labour event. They did not live in their constituencies and stayed in hotels for elections. It was the way politics was done but it meant MPs, especially leading MPs, lost touch with the base of the party.

**Lesson 2.** *Populist nationalism is the easiest way to get cheers. It works for the right. For Labour the political reward is less certain and is very difficult to square with most progressive centre-left internationalism. Many in Labour infected themselves with anti-European populism in the 1970s and 1980s. It was a gift to the Tories and Liberal Democrats.*

All politics is local is an old adage. Labour MPs are not super councillors. Rightly they are not required to have been born and bred in their constituencies as no Labour leader or prime minister has been. But politics is education, education, education. An MP has a duty to both listen to what his fellow party members are saying but also to explain the reality of political choice in both opposition and in government.

My 1968 generation entered into Labour politics after 1970 and met up with the 1945 generation. The background and social formation of the Vera Lynn generation who were born or who grew up before 1939 and saw war or national service after 1945, and those of Beatles and Rolling Stones baby boomers who enjoyed warm homes, parents in good jobs, enjoyable university years and then rewarding properly paid work were so very different. There was little meeting of minds.

## 1972

There was plenty of politics to go round. The miners went on strike and Arthur Scargill invented the concept of flying pickets. He would send down squads of miners from the South Yorkshire region he controlled to picket power stations or anywhere coal and coke was delivered. Scargill also believed in a little muscle.

And nowhere more so than in north east Birmingham at a giant coke depot next to a gas works. Up to 300 lorries a day would enter the depot to pick up fuel. Scargill, like a good general, concentrated his men. Militant trade unionists from all over Birmingham went down to the so-called Saltley Gates to create by sheer weight of numbers a complete blockage on lorries delivering or picking up coke to keep power stations going.

It was like scene of Roman warfare, a rugby scrum with thousands, as two giant blocks of men, workers on one side, the police representing the state on the other side, pushed and shoved against each other. In the end the chief constable of Birmingham decided in the interests of safety to order the plant to close down for lorries.

As fuel stopped flowing to power stations and electricity supplies were threatened, Ted Heath was forced to declare a state of emergency. The workers had been united and defeated this anti-union reactionary government. Scargill was a national trade union superstar – the first workers' leader to win that status without being a big cheese general secretary. It seemed as if the workers were on the march.

The trade unions were keen on more state ownership and control. They reckoned, not without reason, that their privileged access to Labour ministers via the Labour Party they financed and whose main committees they dominated would give them an inside edge. However no trade union suggested any reform or modernization, any merger, any proper consultation with workers via secret ballots before big decisions on major strikes were taken, let alone ideas like workers sitting on boards of companies or works councils elected by all employees not nominated and controlled by external trade unions.

The main continental economies had outperformed Britain since 1950 – often growing twice as fast as the poorly managed and under-invested British network of firms. It was the main reason the Conservative Party, or at least the Ted Heath wing of it, and the Confederation of British Industry were so keen on joining the European Economic Community (EEC), more commonly known as the Common Market. They saw it as a modernisation project and a great leap forward in productivity and competition. They did not understand that it was not just a Common Market that made European economies better performers than their British equivalents. It was the better training, higher investment, social partnership, and greater depth of research and development that made the Common Market have such a superior economic profile than Britain.

That knowledge was not widespread or accepted. Left academics weren't pushing for it. If Labour MPs did know about it, they acted like they didn't. The Left media wasn't informing its readers of that option. All cities and many big towns had a "socialist" bookshop. But they were full of facile denunciations of efforts to build down European nationalism and build up European partnership. In Britain the left allowed the right to become the standard bearer for European construction. In Germany, Willy Brandt, who had fled Nazi Germany to struggle against Franco in the Spanish civil war, or in Portugal, young socialist leaders like Mario Soares, saw Europe as their route to a new progressive politics. In Britain we refused to play that card. I'd say that with the exception of a few Europhiles, most of us on the left didn't even know that card existed. As a journalist, I would say that this is one instance where our media let us down, and as a journalist I hold myself as part of the problem.

Tony Benn, who was chair of the NEC and a former BBC journalist, told the Labour Party conference in October that 'I sometimes wish the trade unionists who work in the mass media, those who are writers and broadcasters and secretaries and printers and lift operators of Thomson House would remember that they too are members of our working class movement and have a responsibility to see that what is said about us is true.'

Good comrade and socialist as I thought I was, I wasn't quite sure the lift operators of the building housing the newsrooms of the *Sunday Times*, then much admired for its radical, investigative journalism under Harold Evans, should be put in charge. But I welcomed Benn at least putting the issue of ownership and purpose of the press on the national political agenda.

**Lesson 3.** *Getting media politics is tricky. Right or wrong any proposals to bring balance or stop lies or allow a right of reply can be presented as political censorship. Better to try and enlarge news media like Channel 4 News or LBC or support transparency so that lies and defamation cannot be hidden under a cloak of anonymity.*

I had been offered a traineeship on the *Sunday Times* then under its finest editor, Harold Evans, before Rupert Murdoch bought it and appointed right-wing loyalists to senior jobs on his papers. The *Sunday Times* NUJ chapel blocked me taking up the dream offer as the journalists' union had a rule stipulating an initial minimum two years' work in the regions before accessing Fleet Street. I was annoyed but in fact, the NUJ was right. I was an insufferably cocky young man and going straight on to a national newspaper would have been a disaster. Instead I discovered Birmingham, a different world I did not know existed. I found friends. I found politics. I found purpose in life. I think of myself as a Londoner but in truth I have spent the large majority of days in my life sleeping in another part of Britain or further afield in Europe.

Who knows Britain who only London knows?

# 1973

By dint of turning out for street stalls, door knocking and always having a forceful view at ward and constituency meetings, I found myself chair of the Moseley Ward branch and secretary of the Selly Oak constituency Labour Party. The old pre-1970 guard of councillors and party officers had been deselected as younger militants like myself moved in and up.

Was I an example of the legendary infiltration of a leftist so much denounced by MPs who took their constituency parties for granted and the national newspaper political reporters who never got out of Westminster? I don't think so. I got outside speakers to come along, set up Saturday morning street stalls with petitions to sign, or organised an outing for pensioners to Buxton, a lovely occasion. Were we loony lefties? Maybe. But more and more people joined the local Labour Party and began creating a ground swell of energy that led Labour to win the hitherto safe Tory seat of Selly Oak in 1974.

Political enthusiasm and energy are necessary but not sufficient to win an election. There was plenty of energy and enthusiasm under Neil Kinnock's early left, anti-European, pro-nuclear disarmament leadership just as there was under Jeremy Corbyn. But neither man was seen as a prime minister thanks to a past record of political positioning that could not be shaken off or was not seen as necessary to shake off. Just as fatal is blandness, a leadership that shuts down discussion and dodges the difficult issues of the day, like the effects of Brexit on jobs and exports, as they are seen as divisive.

Everywhere one turned there seemed to an injustice to combat. The foul stench of Enoch Powell's racism pervaded the West Midlands. I lived in a district in Birmingham with a large Kashmiri community. Handsworth was one of the biggest Afro-Caribbean communities outside London. They faced discrimination in jobs and housing, and were expected to remain in their quasi ghettos.

I argued at Labour Party meetings for the need to outlaw racial discrimination and to make racist speech a crime. There was casual racism in headlines in the 1970s and, with the arrival of naked women in the *Sun*, a masturbatory misogyny in so much of the national press. As an NUJ activist I began arguing against using the word 'coloured', or 'Asian' to describe someone in the news unless it was germane to the story. After all, journalists had stopped describing someone as a Jew or Jewish, which was common in pre-1939 news reports. We wouldn't dream of using the adjective 'yellow' for a Chinese person in the news. Later the right-wing commentariat sneered at this effort as 'politically correct' or 'woke'.

I was reading as much left theory as I could, gobbling up Gramsci or getting stuck on long words in the *New Left Review*. I had EH Carr's interminable volumes on the USSR and set about reading them. My favourite labour historians were all communists or ex-communists of different sorts: Christopher Hill, Edward – EP – Thompson and above all Eric Hobsbawm. His book *Revolutionaries* came out in 1973 and began with the argument that the Bolshevik 'October revolution ... was the first proletarian revolution, the first regime in history to set about the construction of the socialist order, the proof both of the contradictions of capitalism, which produced wars and slumps, and of the possibility – the certainty – that socialist revolution would succeed.'

Indeed.

I heard Hobsbawm speak many times in different countries. I later had the honour of being elected an Honorary Fellow of Birkbeck College, a wonderful unique British invention that allows adults to do university degrees to all levels on a part-time basis while keeping their jobs. Hobsbawm had taught at Birkbeck since 1947 and became its president. After his retirement I talked to him at Hay Festival parties and no one has come along since with his international width of knowledge of the left, shaped by the European languages he read and spoke.

Another key text was Ralph Miliband's *Parliamentary Socialism* which proved to his complete satisfaction that using electoral politics would never deliver socialism. It was a council of despair.

Yet, the more I read the more I was repelled by the blind religious faith of these leading British left intellectuals in a truly monstrous and evil regime led by utterly wicked men who had nothing to do with the socialism I wanted to see come into being.

The fact, the inescapable and awkward fact remains that this generation of historians had a deep-rooted contempt for social democracy and its necessary compromises. They distanced themselves from the Kremlin's invasions of Hungary in 1956 and Czechoslovakia in 1968. They quietly turned pictures of Stalin to the wall as they reached out for any other form of communism, most notably the cul de sac of modish Eurocommunism from Italy. They kept a distance from Moscow and attacked Trotskyism with ideological mountaineering ice picks in their hand.

The communist historians of the Hobsbawm generation and their younger intellectual followers disliked social democracy more than they objected to the conditions of privation and oppression under which men and women still suffered in a rich country like Britain sixty years after the power grab by Lenin, Trotsky and Stalin. In his 1920 book, *The Social Worker*, Clement Attlee chastised what he called the 'revolutionary idealist' who gets up to 'criticize and condemn all methods of social advance that do not directly square with his formulae and will repeat these shibboleths without any attempts to work out their practical application.'

This insight, scorned as milk-and-water reformism, actually requires much harder thinking and tougher decisions than the knee-jerk denunciations that have filled the pages of the *New Statesman*, *Tribune* or comment pages of the *Guardian* – and I was a contributor to all three of those fine papers for most of my political life.

I preferred Leszek Kołakowski's definition that social democracy is 'an obstinate will to erode by inches the conditions which produce avoidable suffering, oppression, hunger, wars, racial and national hatred, insatiable greed and vindictive envy.' The politics of trying to do what one can to achieve those goals was more worthwhile than all the communist and Trotskyist denunciations of 'bourgeois' democracy or the excusing of the crimes of Stalinism.

> **Lesson 4.** *The research and insights of academics and intellectuals contribute to progressive politics. They help develop fresh policies to deal with new (and old) ills. But there is also a huge lived experience in Labour Party members and voters against which all theory should be tested.*

I was selected to be a Selly Oak delegate to the 1973 Labour conference in Blackpool. It was my first time at the High Mass of the Labour Movement. I wandered about proud of my delegate's badge which declared me one of the initiates.

My jaw dropped as I heard Denis Healey, who had a reputation as a right-wing, anti-communist, pro-American Defence secretary, bellow out calls for state ownership and high taxes that would have done justice to Jeremy Corbyn and John McDonnell nearly half a century later. Healey told us: 'I warn you, there are going to be howls of anguish from the rich!'

How we clapped and cheered. Just below the platform rostrum there was a block of seats reserved for MPs. In

1973, there were all the famous names, the future ministers, crammed together just under the speaker's rostrum. Then he turned and addressed the MPs and Labour peers directly telling them: 'Before you cheer too loudly let me warn you that a lot of you will pay extra taxes too.'

MPs paying higher taxes! Sheer bliss to my young leftie ears. We rose as one to hurrah and cheer the Shadow Chancellor, Denis Healey, as he promised to make Labour MPs pay for Labour policies. It sounded great.

Somehow I had no problem reconciling my antipathy to the anti-democratic ideology espoused by writers like Carr, Hobsbawm and Miliband while endorsing many of the policies that their ideas spawned. To quote Whitman, I contain multitudes. We all do.


# 1974

The year of two elections. Or rather three – two general elections, in which one I stood for Parliament – and my own election in my early twenties on to the National Executive Council (NEC) of the National Union of Journalists (NUJ). It was the moment when I moved from a career in the BBC and journalism into a life of political activism.

The incompetence of the Conservative Edward Heath government came home to roost when sudden rises in prices in energy affected every corner of the economy: heating a home, putting petrol to the tank or buying food in supermarkets for children. Workers, not unreasonably, asked for compensation. It was not their fault their wages bought less and less.

Coal miners, once the proud aristocrats of labour, had seen their wages fall behind other workers in industries like car-making or power-generation. The miners opened talks with the government – their employers as coal was nationalised – while younger miners mounted pressure, having been inspired by the militant leadership of Arthur Scargill. He had been groomed by the Communist Party and was one of the finest orators I'd ever heard speak.

Now Heath declared a state of emergency at the end of 1973 as both railway drivers and mineworkers voted for strike action. Heath decided only an election under the slogan 'Who governs?' – pitching as if it were the elected government versus unelected trade unionists.

**Lesson 5.** *Don't call early elections. Attlee in 1951, Heath in 1974, Theresa May in 2017 all went back to ask voters for a new mandate well before the end of the usual parliamentary terms. Voters don't like constantly being asked to endorse a government. Attlee's blunder was a major error as Britain was leaving post-war austerity but the Tories profited 1951-1964.*

The election in February 1974 decided that Heath would not govern. Labour leader Wilson won 301 seats, 4 more than Heath but far short of a majority. Wilson formed a government and handed out generous pay increases to miners to buy industrial peace.

I went to Portugal and Cyprus to show solidarity with the democratic left parties and journalists' unions along with Christopher Hitchens, already making a name for himself with his incisive thinking. It was the beginning of a life-long commitment to internationalism and a life-long regret that conservatives in charge of Britain's international policy were so reluctant to support democracy and progressive social change in other countries.

In the spring I was elected to the NUJ Executive representing journalists in broadcasting. The 1968 generation had gone into the new radio stations both BBC local radio and news and talk stations like LBC. In addition to pay and conditions questions, there were new debates about the ethics of journalism and why so few women and almost no black or Asian (today's BAME) journalists employed. I had a platform to be as portentous, pretentious and political as I could wish for.

When I turned up for my first National Executive Council meeting, the left faction on the NUJ Executive took me as one of theirs. The organiser of the left group was James Cox, a BBC political journalist, later the presenter of 'The World This Weekend'. He took me to one side. He told me I would serve on the finance committee of the NEC because 'if you know where the money is coming from and where it is going you have real power.' Excellent advice and not just for union work. 'We've also decided you can go on the International Committee,' Jim said. 'You'll like that. We call it the "Outings Committee."'

I owe thanks to Jim and the NUJ NEC comrades who started me down the path of political internationalism. I took to trade union international work as if it were my vocation and more so international political activity. I still get as much of a buzz trying to disentangle what's happening in politics in faraway and nearby nations as I do in fretting who's up and who's down in the Labour Party.

I did as Jim Cox requested and learnt early on a key political lesson. Very little political activity is disconnected from factional alignment within a party or a trade union. There are some lone rangers but most of us belonged to a grouping, a tribe, a network where we know, try to like and occasionally even trust fellow members of the group. I, for example, was only ever a member of the Labour Party. But there were Trotskyists in the International Socialists, later the Socialist Workers' Party like my great friend from Birmingham NUJ days, Aidan White, a true radical. Others were in other Trot groups like the International Marxist Group or the Workers Revolutionary Party which organised left-wing actors like Vanessa and Corin Redgrave, though it was hard to follow or even understand the ideological differences.

It was clear another election in 1974 would be called. I decided to contest a seat and went for the very safe Tory seat of Solihull, the Birmingham suburb to the south of the City. It's where wealthier Brummies, who had money and wanted big houses with big gardens, nearby to tennis and golf clubs, liked to live and pretend they were not part of greater Brummagem.

I chose Solihull because I wanted to shake things up. The paradox of constituency Labour Parties in safe Tory seats is that its rank and file members, usually in well-paid jobs or retired on a good pension, with the degrees or qualifications of the wider middle class, were far to the left of the trade unionist or public sector or metal-bashing workers in the safer Labour seats across the border in Birmingham. By then I was a fluent, aggressive speaker with a line in caustic wit, sarcasm, and above all, the skill of speaking without notes. Put that together with my enthusiastic leftism and I won the nomination.

The campaign was fun. My Tory opponent was Percy Grieve, whose son, Dominic also became a QC and Tory MP. Another MP I got to know in the Commons, Andrew MacKay, was chair of the Young Conservatives in Solihull. He and his team were fed up with their absentee MP and covered Solihull with large posters' asking 'WHERE'S PERCY?' I handed out leaflets in the first-class dining car at breakfast time of the Birmingham to London train, getting off not far from Solihull. It provided a good front page photo for the *Birmingham Post*. Christopher Hitchens came to do a loudspeaker tour in a car urging passers-by to 'Vote Labour and Vote for the Socialist candidate, Denis MacShane. Vote Socialism for Solihull.'

I got the biggest swing to Labour of any safe Tory seat but it wasn't enough. I was never going to win. On the other hand, I had stood for Parliament at the tender age of twenty six. I was an executive member of one of Britain's high-profile trade unions. The world was my political oyster.

# 1975

Standing for Labour in Solihull in October 1974 gave me a taste to be an MP. I would bump into friends like Chris Mullin or Tony

Banks as they sought nominations for Labour seats. The BBC then made a life-changing decision.

I was not fired but removed from Birmingham. I went to work in Broadcasting House writing news bulletins for Radio 4. It was an easy-going atmosphere. Without a family I volunteered for night shifts. In the small hours with other young BBC journalists on their way to become household names we smoked endless amounts of dope.

I did six months on Radio 4's World Tonight. I carried out my own poll of the twenty-three editorial staff on the programme to see how they'd voted in the 1974 election. Twenty-two had voted Liberal. Tories believe the BBC is run by a conspiracy of Labour left-wingers. If so I never met any unless Sir Robin Day then or Andrew Neil and Laura Kuenssberg now are secret Labour Party members.

We watched in awe as Richard Nixon was booted out of the White House about the same time as the North Vietnamese army's tanks rolled into Saigon. The Labour government was a long way off. It seemed to be run by dull men and women who had begun political life before the war – it might as well have been the last century.

**Lesson 6.** *The generation problem bedevils left politics. Long service, loyalty, experience count but if all the bigwigs at the top of the party or a government are grey beards, new generations of voters and possible party members feel left out. There seemed no Labour leader – Callaghan, Jenkins, Benn, Williams – who seemed to link to my 1968 generation.*

As a young Labour Party activist, candidate and trade union organizer I wanted change and I wanted it now. In the 1970s it was easy to mobilise as so many aspects of life seemed so unfair. When I began work for the BBC in 1969 inflation was 5.7 per cent. In 1975 it was twenty-five per cent. The numbers of BBC journalists had been swollen by new current affairs output, more personality reporters, and a large increase in local and BBC news journalists.

They were younger, irreverent and wanted fair pay. All other costs were rising rapidly with inflation but not their pay. They wanted as a matter of day-to-day necessity to increase pay to match the cost-of-living increases. I went quietly from BBC newsroom to newsroom to make the case. The Director General and the BBC Board ignored us. As a consequence BBC journalists voted to go on strike for the first time ever.

ITN took pleasure in leading its news with the story that, for the first time in its history, BBC news both in Britain and on its revered World Service was off air. What Hitler failed to do, the NUJ under my leadership achieved. There was no sense of accomplishment. Most if not all pay strikes can be laid at the door of stupid managers.

In the BBC club bar across Portland Place the BBC journalists gathered to swap gossip and the personality failings of any absent friend. The main subject of BBC club chat was the mammoth fiddling of expenses. Everyone boasted or swapped tips.

The most admired figures were BBC overseas correspondents. One who worked in Africa was a legend for inventing a film production company which he claimed to use to shoot, edit and send back his TV reports. It was reckoned he was claiming

£100 a week in fiddled expenses at a time when a BBC journalist's salary was around £2,000 a year. I found it hilarious thirty-five years later to listen to big name TV and radio presenters castigate MPs for expense fiddling when some of them in their day had helped themselves to licence fee-payers' money as liberally and as illegally as possible.

Much later some details emerged of arrangements made to pay senior BBC journalists and on-screen presenters via trust funds in tax havens like Jersey. It wasn't illegal but the pensioner paying the compulsory licence fee, in effect a TV or radio poll tax, was paying for these lavish salaries. It is one reason why the wider population has so little faith in many of our publicly financed institutions, even the good ones like the BBC.

# 1976

By the middle 1970s it was clear that the centralised World War 2 or post-1945 welfare state Britain, ever obedient to Whitehall decrees, had disappeared.

The employers and secretive anti-union and anti-Labour organisations like the Freedom Association were promoting a strategy of tension by whipping up a press campaign over Labour's industrial strategy or modest employment law reforms. Jim Callaghan easily beat Michael Foot to succeed Harold Wilson as leader of the Labour Party and Prime Minister. Only 300 odd MPs took part in the choice. The rest of the Labour Party was excluded. This was seen as the natural order of things.

Labour was as inspiring as a British Railways sandwich. My big political interest was the media. The new generation of 1968 journalists now active in Labour wanted to create a fairer, more accurate, more honest, more radical media. It was a worthy ambition but how to achieve it?

There was no sense that the Callaghan government had much idea what to do. For the city council elections in Birmingham I worked with journalist friends sympathetic to Labour to produce thirty-nine tabloid-style newspapers, tailored to each ward and its Labour candidate. It was a waste of time. Labour ward after Labour ward fell to the Tories or Liberals, and Birmingham became a Conservative city.

The writing was thus on the wall for the Labour Callaghan government a bare month after Jim had become Prime Minister. Something similar happened soon after Gordon Brown became prime minister in 2007. The 2008 local government election saw Labour slump to third place in its worst-ever local government performance. Both the Callaghan and Brown Labour governments operated against a background of economic difficulties – the oil-shock inflation after 1973 and the financial crisis after 2008.

**Lesson 7.** *MPs see themselves as far superior beings to local councillors. Labour in power always focused on national parliamentary politics. Local elections were left to fend for themselves. But losing local government seats especially to new upstart parties like UKIP, the BNP or nationalists in Scotland and Wales demoralises party workers and voters wake up to the dark pleasure of voting against Labour.*

More than anything else, the sense that a government has lost control of the nation's money in the broadest sense of pay, prices, pensions, investment and spending on public services, is the single most damaging threat to chances of re-election of a ruling party of the left. A beleaguered prime minister and chancellor hunker down in Downing Street, surrounded by aides and officials, and try to work out what to do. The result may make sense in theory but in practice the Downing Street bubble insulates its occupants from the street, workplaces, pubs and homes.

There is no easy answer. The Tories were ruthless in pushing aside a prime minister or leader who was losing support amongst the public. Soft, friendly Labour keeps their leaders forever. Attlee stayed on until 1955 and Kinnock stayed on until 1992 when it was clear neither could win an election. The local elections of 1976 told us everything we needed to know about the chances of Callaghan keeping Labour in office when the term ran out. But no one moved against him. Nor was there the slightest chance of unity coalescing around an alternative. Today it is far from clear that Sir Keir Starmer can get Labour into power. Fast-forward forty-five years and has anything much changed?

The far right was circling. There was a by-election in Rotherham. A friend and head of the NUJ branch there, Stan Crowther, was chosen as Labour's candidate. The racist National Front put up a candidate calling for repatriation of immigrant citizens. They organised a march through the town centre that attracted 7,000 participants. The Enoch Powell poison of blaming problems on foreign incomers for poverty, poor housing and fewer and fewer well-paid jobs was already winning over workers. In 2019 the predominately white working-class seat of Rother Valley voted in a Tory MP.

The National Front was too toxic in 1976 but when softer variations of the same xenophobe theme emerged in the 21st century, especially on the question of Europe, the working-class vote in Rotherham was drawn to the BNP and UKIP. Xenophobia handed 'red wall' seats to Boris Johnson in 2019. Denouncing voters as xenophobes is no answer. What restores their faith in the system will be jobs, training, homes, good schools, support for families, improved health care, controlling foreigners in the UK by knowing who is in the country, more police on the streets. Labour started so well after 1997 in delivering these desirables for working class voters but after 2005 the energy petered out.

In 1976, elements of the working class, especially in 'red wall' seats, were already making it clear they had had enough of being taken for granted by Labour and were ready to be seduced by nationalist identity politics, No one in Labour wanted to listen and start re-thinking politics and policy. Labour has yet to begin the process.

# 1977

The 1970s was the decade of an endless discussion by the Labour left on what to do about the media. It was one of the early signs of Labour moving from a party oriented towards the working class or trade unions to a party grappling with broader societal groupings and their questions, what later would be known as cultural and identity politics.

It always seemed to me that left politics is about bread and roses, about pounds in pockets and poetry, music, culture, about class and what kind of people we are. Much as I have argued all my Labour life for attention and care to be paid to the material conditions of existence – pay, worker rights, investment in public goods – I did not want to live in a country or a world where people face discrimination on account of their skin colour, gender, sexuality or self-identification. The left is about embracing, not hating.

I produced the first NUJ guidelines on race reporting and did surveys for the union on the (non)existence of black or Asian journalists in the national media. This produced the usual denunciations from right-wing pontificators, of whom there seemed to be battalions in the press. I didn't care. The editor of the *South London Press*, a big weekly, exploded when I called his paper 'The Muggers' Gazette'. But he constantly highlighted skin colour in reporting of crimes as if not a single white criminal operated in his paper's circulation area.

I complained to the editor of the *Daily Telegraph* about a heading: ASIAN FATHER OF 12 ON £5,000 WELFARE PAYMENTS A YEAR. I wrote to the editor pointing out that the facts in the story were not in dispute. The man who was unemployed with a seriously ill wife, children who had disabilities and other difficulties, did indeed obtain a mixture of housing, unemployment, disability and carer benefits of about £100 a week. But why highlight the fact he was "Asian" in the headline, I asked? The managing editor of the *Daily Telegraph* wrote back and said if the paper had not said the man was Asian most of its readers would have assumed he was Irish. I don't think the *Telegraph* executive was joking.

For the first time in my life I was arrested. In June I found myself in a dispute in Dollis Hill, an unprepossessing part of north-west London where a dispute that should have been easy to resolve had turned into a massive confrontation. Low-paid Asian immigrant women workers believed the election of a Labour government would allow them to join a trade union, which could negotiate fair pay, found out this wasn't the case.

They worked for a firm called Grunwick which processed rolls of camera film for holiday and family snaps. The firm's owner started to fire the ladies calling for fair pay. The women came out on the street and a rightist well-funded anti-union organisation called the Freedom Association shipped in strike breakers to destroy the hopes of the Asian women for a fair deal. They were paid £28 a week when the average manual worker's weekly pay was £72. They were ordered to do compulsory overtime with no prior notice. They knew nothing of trade unions or militancy, but everyone has a sense of what's fair.

The picket line in narrow streets outside the plant entrance was swollen by trade unionists and students from all over London, thanks to the energetic organising genius of my friend, Jack Dromey, secretary of the local trades council. As NUJ vice president I led an NUJ delegation and found myself in a crowd of trade unionists trying by peaceful means to stop strike-breaking vans from entering the premises. The strike breakers were protected by the police.

**Lesson 8.** *In any dispute it is better to avoid at all costs any conflict with the police. It's not just that these confrontations can be rough, brutal and one sided. But also that on the screens in voters' homes, the pictures of a punch-up with the police nearly always damages the cause being supported.*

I had always been law abiding. At that point, my only brush with the police was to have been caught speeding at 37 mph in my Fiat 500. I didn't know it could go fast enough to speed. The police sergeant who arrested me at Grunwick was quite adamant that I'd destroyed my career. 'Fucking rabble that's all you are, fucking rabble,' he kept repeating as we entered the green police coach designated for arrestees. I couldn't work out a riposte as the arm lock he had effected around my neck in the forty metres between the picket line scrum and the police vehicle had left me quite breathless.

'Fucking rabble,' he said again as he pushed me into a seat and sat down heavily beside me. 'You probably don't know it but having this on your record will ruin you, you little cunt.'

As peace settled, I took out a pen to click into action when he snatched it away. He looked at the pen, a pricey Parker ballpoint. As I made a half-hearted reach for it he held it between his hands and snapped it in half. 'Oh dear, one broken pen, prisoner's property.'

I ended up in a Wembley police station cell with Arthur Scargill. I'd like to say I discussed with the militant miners' leader my theory that mass picketing had had its day and we in the trade unions needed to find new tactics, learn the politics of leverage and even compromise. Sadly not. We just sat glumly on the floor waiting to be released and said nothing.

Outside in the summer sun a lovely sight greeted me. A very pretty young woman wearing a long muslin almost see-through skirt made popular that summer by the future Princess Diana was there with a clip-board. 'Hello. My name's Harriet Harman. I'm a solicitor with the National Council of Civil Liberties and we will be representing you in court.'

It was my first encounter with Harriet who became and has remained a firm friend ever since. I was given a conditional discharge and when I met my serjeant he turned out to be just an ordinary Joe chatting about the problems of bring up a young family with the odd shift patterns of police service which I could talk to him about as I was an expert on doing 24/7 shift rotas for BBC newsrooms.

That summer Labour lost control of the Greater London Council to the Tories. The tom toms were beating that Labour was not going to stay in power much longer.


# 1978

I became the youngest ever president of the NUJ, aged just twenty nine, in the last year of the Labour government. There really seemed little point in the government carrying on. Various wage policies and formulae drawn up by smart young civil servants and government advisors were water off the back of trade unionists. They listened to Labour ministers and MPs who always seemed to get handsome index-linked pay hikes in line with the high inflation telling them to accept wage austerity.

The Labour government had set up the Commission on Racial Equality in response to the growth of Enoch Powell's racism which has sunk roots on the populist right and in some parts of the white working-class unionised community. In a television interview in 1978 Margaret Thatcher said, 'people are really rather afraid that this country might be rather swamped by people with a different culture.' Enoch Powell expressed his 'hope and relief' as Mrs Thatcher used his language.

As a result, the far right organised marches and rallies in immigrant community areas. The police were less than enthusiastic about enforcing the new race relations laws so the Anti-Nazi League was set up as a political and civil society network to show solidarity with minority and ethnic communities. I was there from Labour and the NUJ, Peter Hain was chair of the Young Liberals, Arthur Scargill was close to the Communist Party and there was a good helping of Socialist Worker Party activists. Some friends in Labour didn't want to take on racism and xenophobia. Saying there was racism in Britain and unacceptable sexism (thought the word was not really coined until later) implied that British people, our voters, were racist and sexist. Some are, most are not though the casual use of racist or sexist describers was widespread. Does one deny the problem or confront it openly? Do the former and you let down people who turn to Labour for help. Do the latter and you are accused of stirring up trouble, making generalised accusations. Either way the Labour politician loses.

I wrote a pamphlet, my first political writing longer than a *New Statesman* article called 'Black and White. Race Reporting in Britain.' I pointed out the almost complete absence of what we now call BAME journalists in newsrooms or on screen. It suggested creating Community Relations correspondents and set out guideline on how to remove covert racism in news reporting. In *The Times*, Bernard Levin, then the most famous commentator in the land, devoted an entire column to attacking my pamphlet. He denounced its 'Noddy language' and accused me and the NUJ of trying to censor journalists reporting on immigration and the behaviour of black and Asian communities.

It was tired right-wing neurosis. Bernard Levin used all his considerable writing talent to trash me. I'd never felt so proud. If I had upset the spokesperson of the British elite's conventional wisdom in *The Times* then maybe I was on to something.

I was unwittingly part of a larger social transition that we are still coming to terms with. Soon, much faster than I could have hoped for, the presence of by-lines in newspapers or faces and names on the BBC stopped being all white. Community relations issues were properly reported. Racism in housing, employment, in the Metropolitan Police were investigated. The 1970s began with Powellism in the political and media ascendance. The decade ended with a real fight-back that even the Tories and their supporters in the media had to acknowledge, incorporate into journalism and recruitment with today's result that Britain has the most multi-cultural, multi-ethnic media profile of any in Europe, even if institutional racism still pervades the thinking of much of today's establishment.

I stood for Camden Council in May in the Swiss Cottage Ward. I was chair by now of my local ward in Kentish Town. Labour lost a third of its seats in what had been a solid Labour council. No one takes much interest in municipal politics. But they are a training ground for national politics. You learn that political impossibilism doesn't work. But that lesson can take a long time to learn.

**Lesson 9.** *A Labour Party or its trade union allies seen as encouraging endless industrial action fast falls out of favour with voters.*

On the doorstep I heard about voters' dislike of the endless strikes that were linked with the Labour era in office. At a TUC drinks reception, I was in a group chatting to Jim Callaghan. He was a tall, bulky figure, dressed in his conventional middle-class bank manager's two-piece suit. In a lull in the conversation I asked him how he was looking forward to the Labour Party conference in a two weeks' time.

'Oh, I much prefer being here with the trade union delegates who live in the real world not all those loonies and lefties at the Labour conference,' he said. Then he realised he had no idea who this long-haired, well-spoken young man was.

'You're not a journalist, are you?' he snapped. 'That's all completely off the record, you know!' I nodded respectfully though a bit of me wanted to go and find a reporter on a tabloid paper and get a headline, 'Callaghan Attacks Labour as Loonies and Lefties.'

But he had a point. Labour was divided between the trade

unionists and the more middle-class lefties. Callaghan dressed middle class, acted middle class, but actively and publicly disliked that half of it. The result was a divided Labour Party that couldn't lead the nation even though it was in power.

Then two NUJ members, the investigative journalist, Duncan Campbell and the American foreign correspondent, Mark Hosenball, published a story in a small left journal, the *Leveller*, about British eavesdropping activities from a military airfield base in Akrotiri, close to a tourist beach in Cyprus. It wasn't much of a secret. The giant geodesic dome under which the radio scanners scooped up all sorts of communications in the Middle East could be seen from any sun lounger on a southern Cyprus beach. It was about as secret as the prime minister's address in Downing Street.

But the Callaghan government decided to prosecute under the Official Secrets Act, the two journalists and a young British soldier who helped them. And then it kept digging that hole deeper. The NUJ took it to the September congress of the TUC where Jim Callaghan spoke. The TUC leaders thought Callaghan was going to announce the general election and wanted to ward off any criticism of the Labour government from the platform.

Every big TUC general secretary of the time came up to me as the NUJ president and begged me to take the NUJ motion off the agenda so as to avoid any embarrassment to Callaghan. This only got the issue more publicity, which is precisely what we wanted. Our generation was fed up with being told we could not report matters we thought of public interest just because some high functionary pleaded national security was at stake. Especially when it clearly wasn't.

Just before the session at which I would move the motion opened the general secretary of the TUC, a thoughtful Oxford educated TUC functionary Len Murray, beckoned to me to leave my seat and follow him to the back of the Brighton conference centre.

'Denis, if you get up and move your motion two things will happen, I promise you. First, it will be ruled out of order by the chair so you won't get it discussed. Second, your career in the labour movement in this country is over, finished.'

Len was no bully and his words were delivered like a headmaster exasperated with an unruly pupil. But they were clear and the menace was unambiguous. I politely said I was sorry but the cause of journalist freedom was more important. I began my speech and indeed was ruled out of order by the chairman, David Basnett. I left the rostrum. Within twelve months the second of Len's threats came true as I was indeed out of Britain, though my career in the labour movement was undamaged by the episode.

# 1979

Election year as Jim Callaghan limped on to the last possible moment. I made a small contribution to Callaghan's defeat as NUJ provincial newspaper journalists took part in a six-week-long strike December 1978 to January 1979. It was an ordinary pay strike. Provincial daily and weekly newspapers had made handsome profits on the back of holding down journalists' pay.

Even the *Economist* was forced to contrast the low wages of journalists and the high profits of the regional newspaper groups and argue: 'What is at stake... is more than low pay. It us whether the loyalty and the professionalism that employers have relied on for so long can continue...Today the unions feel that loyalty has been a one-way relationship and that the words "relied upon" could be replaced by the word "exploited".'

I did endless picket line visits but there was no militancy. The real problem arose in the law courts. The NUJ executive had required journalists working at the Press Association news agency not to send copy via telex machines to provincial newspapers. Each day an army of PA correspondents, usually superb professionals, sent out enough reports from all over the country, from Parliament and the Royal Courts, to football matches, business and economic news and light features. Enough to fill an evening or weekly provincial paper. So just one or two editors who showed no solidarity with journalists could easily bring out a paper.

To counter this the NUJ asked its members at the Press Association offices in Fleet Street to stop providing this service. We consulted QCs, checked the current state of employment law, and were told we were perfectly in order in requiring our PA members to stand with their colleagues in the provincial presses.

But we reckoned without an anti-union judge called Lord Denning. I found myself in front of him as his small pig-like eyes bored into mine and told me the NUJ had no right to enforce its rule book or request solidarity from its members. In effect, Lord Denning, acted as the strike-breaker-in-chief for the wealthy newspaper establishment. We rushed to the Law Lords (as the Supreme Court was called in those days) and after a short period of examining the case and checking what the existing law stated the Law Lords ruled unanimously against Lord Denning and in my and the NUJ's favour.

Denning however knew what he was doing. The mood shift in the country was palpable. People were fed up with militant trade unions and loud-mouthed trade union bosses swaggering around as if they ruled the land. Denis Healey later told me he had to take two or three calls a day from trade union general secretaries. They thought the unions' control of the Labour Party entitled them to phone up the Chancellor of the Exchequer and tell him what the nation's economic or fiscal policy should be. I was as strong and militant a trade unionist as it was possible to be aged thirty but this seemed to be wrong, undemocratic, and would end in tears. As indeed it did.

The country was heading right. Those long fifteen years between 1964 and 1979 when Labour was the main game in town were now over. I felt and feel now no guilt over my contribution to its demise as a political force. I headed a union that went on strike – and more than once at that. Endless strike action helped Labour to lose. What Labour was doing wasn't working. Everyone knew it. Admittedly I didn't foresee the long tenure of the right. But who did?

**Lesson 10.** *Labour at all levels must be professional at communications – getting out what the party stands for and is doing to as many voters as possible. It is not a question of a celebrity press chief but working into* *all politics the need to communicate effectively to non-activists the what, who, and why of any and all political activity. The American Black poet-thinker, Audre Lorde, once said, 'The master's tools will never dismantle the master's house.' She might well be right. But the left should at least figure out what those tools are and how to use them, if only to build a different kind of house altogether. This was true then and more so now that there's Facebook and Twitter and social media.*

Instead, I brought out a book called *Using the Media*. I put a decade of journalism into a set of guidelines on how to write good press releases, organise a news conference, do good TV or radio interviews and organise events in a way they got media coverage. It was very straightforward and sensible advice; a stating of the obvious. There was nothing left-wing about the content.

Ironically, it was published by the left publishing house, Pluto Press, run by a lively South African Trotskyist called Michael Kidron. He lived in a very big house on the edge of Hampstead Heath. I had never been in such a large, comfortable house looking out over North London's best vista. Where did these revolutionary Trotskyists get all their money from, I wondered? But Kidron was a joy to work with on my book, a brilliant editor and a man of warmth and wit.

Here's the second irony: the first big order came from the Foreign and Commonwealth Office who bought 200 copies for their embassies overseas. I never dreamt that 20 years later I would be an FCO minister.

After years of militant trade unionism in the small incestuous British media world I needed a change. A friend at the TUC told me of some international trade union outfit in Geneva called the International Metalworkers Federation that was looking for a trade union savvy person who could write, help with speeches, do press work or so on. They brought me over to Geneva for a 3-week trial run. It seemed to go OK, so they offered me the job.

The salary in Swiss francs was handsome in terms of British pounds. I would be working with trade unions and on international questions. I could keep writing on politics for the left press. All this suited me. I knew nothing of Geneva except it was close to the Alps where I had recently learnt to ski. Maybe a couple of years in Switzerland would improve my skiing. And by then surely the working class in Britain would have risen up and got rid of Mrs Thatcher. Labour would be back in power with friends like Tony Benn playing a leading role.

# The 1980s

## 1980

1980 was the *annus horribilis* for democratic trade unions in Britain while at the same time the *annus mirabilis* for democratic trades unionism in Poland. It was also the moment when Labour decided to embrace the past with passion and no little emotion but a wilful disregard for what was happening in society and in an increasingly post-national global economy.

I had barely got my feet under the table working for the International Metalworkers Federation in Geneva when I was swept back to Britain for the first giant strike of the Margaret Thatcher era.

Steelworkers around the world were always the nobility of the 20th century industrial working class. Two world wars had been won thanks to arms made from steel melted, rolled and fashioned in the steel plants of South Wales, South Yorkshire, the North East, and Lanarkshire. The reconstruction of Britain after 1945, its new homes, big roads, bridges, ports, motor cars, aeroplanes, and the household appliances like washing machines, fridges, and electric cookers all originated in the steel made in unfashionable towns and regions where Labour ran councils and elected most MPs.

Steelworkers had great power and showed great responsibility. Shutting down a blast furnace is not like walking off a car assembly line or refusing to print a newspaper. Steelworking is hot, arduous, dangerous work.

To go on strike was a big decision. The last time the main UK steel union, the Iron and Steel Trades Confederation (ISTC), later known as Community, went on strike was in 1926 at the time of the General Strike. Globally, the 1980s was a decade of huge strikes by metalworkers (cars, steel, shipbuilding, aerospace, engineering, machinists) in countries like Poland, Brazil, South Africa, South Korea, Germany, to struggle for democratic rights and freedom and for a fairer share of the wealth their labour created – more pay or shorter working hours like the 35 hour week won after 18 months of rolling strikes by four million metalworkers in Germany.

I doubt if the UK steel union, the ISTC thought in 1980 it was kicking off the last great hurrah of the industrial working class in Britain. The union wanted a decent pay hike as their moderation and collaboration with the nationalised British Steel Corporation had seen their wages fall, relative to other industries, during the high inflation 1970s.

The new Thatcher government had different ideas and made it clear to the men running British steel there would be no concessions. The union had to lose, and be seen to lose. The complacency of the Iron and Steel union that the simple act of taking their men off-site would collapse the industry did not last long. They found out that there were 2,000 small steel firms that imported steel from all over the world where workers would not go on strike for their ISTC colleagues. That is, the ISTC and the left discovered globalisation, although we didn't call it that back then.

My job was to try and stop steel coming into Britain from the continent. We identified 143 ports or harbours around the British coast where steel from abroad could be landed. It was mission impossible.

The steel strike early in 1980 was a signal times were changing. The ISTC found that bringing out all their members on a peaceful strike was not enough. With a sympathetic anti-union government, determined employers could now find ways around trade union action. I did not realise it at the time, but this should have been a signal to the left, especially the left that had enjoyed a decade of organising strikes and protests in the 1970s, that the party was over. There were other models to follow to obtain fairer pay, more social justice.

Going on strike, however, seemed more exciting with many more opportunities to make speeches denouncing capitalism and Conservatives. It's also what we did. The relationship between Labour and unions is historic and familial. Reading the times and moving from militancy to social partnership or at times, if necessary, vice versa is a political art Labour never fully mastered.

I went to the Labour Party conference to find it had become anti-European. It was not especially a project of the left. It had been Hugh Gaitskell, the lost leader for the Labour right, who delivered a violent attack on European cooperation worthy of a Nigel Farage in 1962 when he said that to have a common market for goods with other European nations 'would mean the end of Britain as an independent nation state ... an end of a thousand years of island history ... the end of the Commonwealth.' Plenty of Labour right-wingers like Peter Shore, Denzil Davies or John Mills were as anti-European as Neil Kinnock, Dennis Skinner or Robin Cook.

I had by now spent my first year working with European trade unions out of Geneva though I seemed to spend every weekend back home promoting my book, *Using the Media*. Blood curdling denunciations of Europe didn't seem to have any connection to the reality of the European social democracy I was slowly coming to terms with after my first decade as fully paid-up English anti-European leftist.

## 1981

Labour politics was getting ugly. A breakaway group of MPs was set up under the aegis of the Labour grandee Roy Jenkins who had returned from Brussels after a stint as president of the European Commission. Jenkins had been a liberal reforming Home Secretary under Labour PM Harold Wilson: ending capital punishment, allowing women to have legal abortions and abolishing state censorship laws. Jenkins also took on the homophobic and hypocritical British judiciary with a law that decriminalised homosexual sex acts between consenting men over the age of 21.

Jenkins was a strong pro-European. In a differently

structured political economy such as existed in northern European member states of the European Community he might have risen to the top of a humane, fairer politics. But the inflexible traditionalism of British Labourism made him more and more of an outlier in a Labour Party which thought Tony Benn was the man to worship and follow.

Jenkins' comrades in his new political project were David Owen who had been Foreign Secretary under Jim Callaghan, and Shirley Williams, another darling of the London elite liberal intelligentsia who drank chardonnay at their soirées in Notting Hill, Islington and Kentish Town

Ever since the Polish workers had risen up and occupied shipyards in Gdansk, mines in Silesia, and factories everywhere I'd been commuting between Britain and Poland acting as a link person between the Polish union and the network of metal industry trade unions around the world. I published the first book on the Polish union in English in May. More and more old left comrades looked at me suspiciously as they cottoned on to the news that my idea of socialism did not forgive the crimes of Stalinism.

Here was an insurrectionary movement in the form of a trade union taking on a dictatorship and calling for democratic rights in the workplace. My book on Solidarnosc was widely circulated in South Africa where independent black unions were also emerging as the most powerful challenge that apartheid had ever seen. In Brazil, the metalworkers' leader Lula, was challenging the military rulers of Brazil.

But in Britain there was little interest in these remarkable political developments on the global left as the Labour Party turned in on itself. In May an election took place that was as important as the arrival of Margaret Thatcher and Ronald Reagan in the two previous years.

Francois Mitterrand, aged 64, defeated the centrist liberal French President, Valéry Giscard d'Estaing. Just at the moment when the entire world looked as if it was turning hard right, here was one of the world biggest economies, armed with nuclear weapons, going in a very different direction.

I was there in Paris in the Place de la Bastille where the French left has always gathered in times of protest. This time however a million over-excited members of the 1968 generation who in France had lived under rightist governments ever since General de Gaulle took power in 1958, came to celebrate the election of a Socialist president in power – followed by the Socialists winning a majority in the National Assembly.

I decided to write a biography of Mitterrand. Quartet published it in 1982. It was my first book I saw on sale in WHSmith. To my astonishment, the political world outside of France knew nothing of the new French president. In Washington and on rightist papers in London he was seen as a pro-communist leftist because he had been elected on a "common programme" drawn up with the still-powerful French Communist Party.

In fact, Mitterrand was a visceral anti-communist and opponent of Sovietism. He caused an explosion in Moscow in 1984 when he praised Andrei Sakharov, the Russian dissident, at a banquet in front of the Moscow communist elite. Mitterrand supported the installation of cruise missiles in Germany and Britain in response to the stationing of short-range Soviet missiles in East Europe in the early 1980s. Mitterrand went to West Germany's parliament, the Bundestag, and supported the German chancellor, Helmut Kohl, saying: 'The protestors are in the West. The missiles that threaten us are in the East.'

Aligned with socialists like Felipe Gonzalez in Spain, Mario Soares in Portugal and Andreas Papandreou in Greece, Mitterrand loathed the Latin American military juntas who were cuddled and cosseted by Reagan's America. When Argentina invaded and occupied the British Falkland Islands in the south Atlantic, the first call Margaret Thatcher received was from François Mitterrand. He promised details of the French Exocet missiles sold to Argentina. At the same time, the pro-Argentine administration in Washington was trying to broker a deal to save the face of the Jew-hating junta in Buenos Aires.

On the economic front, Mitterrand took France in the opposite direction to the Anglo-Saxon model. Industries were taken into state ownership, the minimum wage was raised, workers were given new powers, public services were reinforced and protectionist measures to try and slow down imports of video recorders from Japan were introduced.

It didn't last long. Mitterrand soon dropped the protectionist aspects of his economic policy at about the same time as he eased the communists out of government and reduced the once mighty French communist party to increasing irrelevance. Instead Mitterrand turned to Europe as a project France could back to restore some *gloire* and economic *puissance*. He sent Jacques Delors to Brussels as Commission president. In one of the paradoxes of history Delors forged an alliance with Margaret Thatcher to force through the abolition of national vetoes on trade policy to create the EU's giant Single European Market with no border checks between its twenty-seven nations to allow their businesses to make money and invest in any corner of the continent.

The debate on the Mitterrand legacy never stops in France. But his fourteen years coincided with the end of communism and the rise of the European Union. It was an alternative to the Reagan-Thatcher world view of a politics turning its back on social obligations. 'There is no such thing as society,' intoned Mrs Thatcher. Instead Mitterrand offered an imperfectly executed attempt to build a partly publicly owned but mainly private enterprise economy in which the people also had a stake. Mitterrand decided France would back to the hilt the construction of Europe, and changed history.

There's an old joke. What do you call someone who speaks three languages? Trilingual. What do you call someone who speaks two languages? Bilingual. What do you call someone who speaks one language? English. But the joke's not entirely fair. Most politicians and editors, not all, but most who rise to prominence in Europe will speak more than one language. The English left's mono-lingualism was depressing and counterproductive.

At a conference once Tony Benn once asked me to be introduced to Jean-Pierre Chevènement who was seen as his equivalent in the French socialist party: a spokesperson of the left, a supporter of statist socialism and opposed to the European construction and partnership save on a purely state-to-state intergovernmental level. I made the introduction and left the two great men to talk to each other. I could see them in the corner of common room of the provincial university where the conference was taking place energetically talking to each other.

When it was over Tony came over to me, sucking on this pipe, and said 'Well, thank you very much, Denis. That was marvellous. Of course I couldn't understand a word Jean-Pierre said but he is clearly a good comrade, a fine socialist, one of us.' Benn in the early 1980s remained the commanding speaker of Labour. He was also unbelievably polite. You can take a boy out of Westminster School, but you cannot take Westminster School manners out of the boy.

**Lesson 11.** *A New Labour education secretary, Estelle Morris, sadly abolished the obligation to teach foreign languages in secondary schools and Boris Johnson abolished the Erasmus programme of the European Union that allowed British students to spend time learning a foreign language. It may be too much to expect many Labour MPs and leaders to speak and read a foreign language. But Labour should strengthen its ability to learn from progressive politics in other countries by encouraging the learning of foreign languages.*

In December, the communist rulers of Poland moved to suppress Solidarnosc, arresting Lech Wałesa and other leaders of the union in Gdansk, Warsaw, Krakow and other centres. I'd passed much of the year in Poland, writing endlessly about what was happening and bringing Polish trade unionists to Western Europe, America and Japan as guests of the International

Metalworkers Federation of industrial unions across the non-communist world.

I spent December days and nights sitting in front of the telex machine in my Geneva office sending out 'Where are you?' messages. There was no communication of any sort. Like Pinochet a few years previously, here were stupid reactionary rulers, egged on by Moscow as Pinochet had been egged on by Washington, ending democracy achieved by working people and a progressive intellectual class.

Miserable as I was at seeing the efforts for freedom and social justice of my Polish friends in Solidarity put in deep freeze, I knew the struggle would restart. Poland would never surrender.

## 1982

Arriving back in April from the National Union of Journalists annual conference very late at Kings Cross with friends like Scarlett Maguire and Anna Coote, we were confronted with an early edition of the *Sun*. IT'S WAR screamed the headline filling the front page. War? War!

A foul military junta in Argentina, obsessed with arresting and torturing socialists, trade unionists and especially Jews, had decided to pander to the passions of nationalist identity politics by occupying the Falkland Islands, a tiny colony in the South Atlantic consisting of two inhabited islands with 1,820 people and 400,000 sheep, 8,000 miles from Britain.

It seemed to me to be a Ruritanian opera. But I was wrong. The passions of nationalism and national pride are the most powerful emotions in politics. Labour's leader, Michael Foot, found himself back in the 1930s denouncing the Argentinian rightists as latter day Nazis marching into Austria or Czechoslovakia.

Both Foot and Mrs Thatcher were on the back foot. Unemployment early in 1982 had risen above three million while the breakaway Labour MPs in the Social Democratic Party were winning by-elections, council seats and adoring publicity from the *Guardian* and BBC.

The Falklands war was a life-line for Mrs Thatcher. She took over Michael Foot's bellicose line. She told Ronald Reagan whose Secretary of State, General Alexander Haig, supported right-wing military governments in Latin America as part of the US global struggle against any left-wing politics, that Britain would take all military action necessary to reconquer the British colony.

Mrs Thatcher was criticised by Labour left-wingers like Neil Kinnock whose lifelong hostility to military power was one of the animating passions that had made him the most popular backbencher with Labour Party members. But the public was with the soldiers and the Royal Navy. When the Argentines surrendered she got a political boost that lasted until the end of the decade.

**Lesson 12.** *Don't mock patriotism, love of country, the union flag or the armed services. Flag-waving nationalist xenophobia in the manner of UKIP or some cruder Tory*

*Europhobes is tedious. But never underestimate the core support for flag, nation, soldiers that is engrained in British identity. By all means call for reform of the military and the royals, but a political price is paid if voters think Labour is unpatriotic*

During the war I was in Poland and China. In Poland I was running money to the communications staff and printers working for the underground Polish Solidarity union. I carried $10,000 of trade union donations in small notes stuffed down my jeans to buy paper or equipment or to arrange transport. The Solidarity leadership knew me so I was a safe courier.

Stupidly, just after I had handed over the money, I was with Polish friends at the National Day events in the middle of Warsaw when they held up pro-Solidarnosc posters. From nowhere, Polish militia troops arrived. We were all rounded up. Luckily, Roger Boyes, a young BBC journalist saw my arrest and broadcast it on the World Service.

I spent two uncomfortable nights on straw bedding before the British embassy official arrived. He gave me a small Harrods bag with two apples, some Ryvita, a small jar of Marmite and a copy of *Country Life* – essential emergency provisions for a British leftie who had got into trouble with the communist authorities.

I appeared in front of a 'Workers' Court', two men in blue overalls with a magistrate in between, and kicked out of Poland not to return until Poles broke free of Soviet communism.

Back home I got Michael Foot to launch my biography of François Mitterrand, the first English language book on a new

French president. Michael loved France and was expelled from Paris for his caustic reporting in 1958 about General de Gaulle's semi-putsch that put him in power as the only man who could solve the Algerian war. Foot was kind and generous. 'It's very good that, Denis, who we all know and like, has written this book of François Mitterrand. He seems a nice chap and he certainly calls himself a socialist. But he seems to be in favour of Europe and I can't see how any socialist can support the Common Market.'

Dear lovely Michael. He wrote once:

'Men of power have no time to read books. Men who do not read books are unfit to hold power.' I was delighted and honoured that he launched my book. However now into my third year working with the European left, the idea that Labour should be hostile to Europe was making less and less sense to me.

My friend, Chris Mullin, had taken over as editor of *Tribune*, Labour's weekly paper which acted as a connecting-rod for the disparate elements of the Labour left. Chris, like many, had decided to link himself with Tony Benn. He edited a collection of Benn's articles, *Arguments for Socialism*, and worked with Jon Lansman, ten years younger than Chris or myself, in Benn's failed effort to be elected as Michael Foot's deputy.

I had been writing for the *New Statesman*, *Tribune* and other left journals. Getting the copy over in the days before the internet or even faxes was a bore. I arranged with Chris Mullin to drop off an article on a weekend in London to see my daughter, Clare. Chris told me to bring it to Tony Benn's large handsome house in Holland Park bought, to be fair, when prices were very low in what was not at all a fashionable area in the years after the war. My brother, Martin, was finishing medical school and offered to drive me to Tony Benn's house before I got the tube out to Heathrow.

It was a Sunday afternoon so we could park right outside the house on Holland Park Avenue. Tony opened the door in his perpetual button-down blue Oxford shirts he must have bought by the dozen when visiting America. The cardigan was on. The pipe as ever between teeth and hand. I said Chris Mullin had told me to call by to hand in my *Tribune* article and introduced my brother.

'Well, you'd getter come in then. Chris is inside,' Tony Benn's ever-courteous style welcomed us but I had a sense he wasn't sure if I should be in his house. Was this because I had been a prominent supporter of the Polish union, Solidardosc which the left in England routinely denounced as an anti-communist Vatican-CIA conspiracy? Was it because I was using examples of clever progressive politics from social democratic parties in Europe that did not share Benn's visceral opposition to European partnership in arguments about Labour's direction of travel? I was uncomfortable about Benn's discomfort.

At any case, Martin and I walked down the corridor behind Tony to the sitting room with its sagging sofas, silver coffee pots, endless piles of book and journals, and years of left memorabilia collected by the remarkable Benn couple.

Chris Mullin looked up in surprise, as did the others there: Jon Lansman; the intellectual left MP Stuart Holland, who had in Labour's opposition years fluently argued in books like *The State as Entrepreneur* a far greater role for state ownership and control; and slumped in the sofa, half smiling, half grimacing, Frances Morrell, a larger-than-life woman, who had become Benn's trusted political adviser when he was a minister 1974-79. Frances was busy promoting Ken Livingstone as leader of the Greater London Council. I quickly thrust my article into Chris's hands, and walked backwards out of the room smiling and bowing to the Labour left royalty we had stumbled across.

As we went into the afternoon sunshine, my brother Martin, who had remained silent, turned and said, 'My God, there is a conspiracy to take over the Labour Party. I have just seen it.' Yes, I wanted to say to him. But there has always been a small group who believe they have a shining path to socialism, and there will be in the future. And so it was with Jon Lansman, who re-emerged after 2015 to form Momentum and help do to Labour under Jeremy Corbyn what he did as Benn's aide to Labour under Michael Foot. The wheel comes around full circle.

Jon is an engaging, likeable activist, a humanist Jewish organizer and mobiliser of young left activists. He was depicted by Denis Healey as an evil genius, organizing Tony Benn's meetings and campaign to try and take over the Labour Party. He faced the same abuse from the same right-wing newspapers 40 years later after 2015. In truth Lansman had the influence he had because the men who opposed and abused him were not up to the job of defining democratic socialism in a manner that would win support from a majority of voters and Labour activists. And intellectuals like Stuart Holland, a serious thoughtful engaging thinker and teacher, preferred to insist on the purity of his ideas than adapt to the art of the possible, otherwise known as democratic politics.

# 1983

The bitterness and infighting in the Labour Party continued unabated. Unemployment soared over three million as Margaret Thatcher pursued her policy of making working people pay for the giant changes in manufacturing. Into political mainstream, Thatcher embedded *globalisation* – the idea that anything could be made anywhere in the world at the cheapest possible cost by workers without decent pay or any right to form unions to secure fair pay.

The Social Democratic Party was popular with the press while poor old Michael Foot just struggled to make any headway. He turned seventy in July 1983 but somehow seemed much older in appearance. Everyone on the left loved him. No one could see him as a prime minister. The manifesto was the fall guy for a wretched campaign. It had goals we'd recognise today: women's rights, infrastructure investment and pollution control. But it also promised to renationalise industries that Mrs Thatcher had privatised. It was dubbed the Longest Suicide Note in History. But really, it was more than that. Foot couldn't sell it to the people, or even to all the Labour Party members. I doubt if there has been a Labour leader as much loved as Michael Foot. But he was yet another loser when it came to winning elections.

I vaguely hoped of finding a seat to fight and would find myself on a cold winter platform in Doncaster or Preston waiting to change a train, having bumped into others of my political generation who were on a seat hunt from their London bases.

I had met Tony Blair through a group of mutual friends who lived around Victoria Park in Hackney – a posting stage for what would be the New Labour generation of rising young lawyers, journalists, academics before they moved to grander homes in Islington or Hampstead. Tony, also a wannabe Labour MP, had been lucky. He had won nomination for the safe Tory seat of Beaconsfield when a by-election was held there in May 1982.

He got a meagre ten per cent of the vote and came a poor third behind the victorious Tory and a Liberal candidate. However he came over as bright, young and middle class, different from the aggressive and cocksure left seeking to control Labour, and at twenty nine, far more attractive than the 1945 generation of Labour MPs who held shadow cabinet posts and seemed not just tired, but well past their sell-by date.

It struck me then and strikes me now that the best way to renew the stock of MPs is for Labour to have a party rule imposing a mandatory retirement age. After all, even the Vatican bans cardinals aged over eighty from voting on a new pope. A retirement age of seventy for Labour MPs or maybe after a maximum of four terms or twenty-five years in the Commons would automatically help renew the party without the efforts to drive out long-serving MPs by any automatic re-selection process.

**Lesson 13.** *Keep rejuvenating the Labour Party. Mandatory retirement ages for MPs should be the norm in law and as a Labour Party rule.*

A good hard-working MP who has a base in the constituency and pays attention to local party activists should on the whole not face too many problems. He or she can spend all the necessary time and money in the constituency with staff seeing off any serious re-selection challenge such as advocated by Chris Mullin and others in the 1980s to make Labour more left-wing. Time and again, however, I saw how debilitating this was, as Labour MPs were reduced to being well-paid local councillors without time to think, act or speak on national and international policy as they spent all their time minding their backs locally and schmoozing their base of party activists.

Blair was luckier. After winning his spurs in Beaconsfield he turned his attention to the North East of England. Here, solid working-class mining, steel-working, and ship-building seats had long guaranteed safe berths for Labour MPs. The trade unions dominated the local constituency parties and kept the hard left at bay. The regional trade unions chieftains had a penchant for supporting the selection of clever younger intellectual Labour would-be MPs from London.

Blair spotted a new seat, Sedgefield, which was being created as part of the endless boundary reviews that change constituency names and geography on a rolling basis. He went up and mentioned his father's years as a law lecturer at Durham University, though perhaps not the fact his dad has been chair of the Durham Conservative Association. The family connection to the region helped but Tony used the boyish charm which served him so well all his political life to sit over endless cups of tea with local Labour Party members, councillors or constituency office holders.

They did not need the help of a head hunter agency to spot a future star. Most constituency Labour Parties like to have an MP who has some profile, makes a splash and appears on TV. In Tony Blair they could see the future. He ticked all the right boxes sporting a Campaign for Nuclear Disarmament badge on his jacket. He campaigned in the 1983 election on Labour's manifesto pledge to negotiate a withdrawal from the European Community. Let us pass over the need to say whatever it takes to be selected for a safe Labour seat.

Hostility to Europe and to nuclear weapons are perfectly legitimate causes. Another Labour MP also elected in 1983, Jeremy Corbyn, made the same promises and still believes in them four decades later. A stellar generation of Labour MPs were elected in 1983: Tony Blair, Gordon Brown, Margaret Beckett, Jack Straw and Clare Short amongst them. They joined my friend, Harriet Harman, who entered the Commons in 1982 in a by-election.

They were young, in their thirties, but even so it took a further 14 years of hard political work and some major adjustments of their personal political profile to get to the point of being trusted by the people to run the nation.

Labour's vote in 1983 shrunk to twenty-seven per cent, just a bit more than the renegade Social Democrats. Mrs Thatcher had a majority of 144. Labour held 209 seats – still more than under Jeremy Corbyn after the 2019 election when again there was no opposition from the shadow cabinet to a rambling wishlist manifesto which guaranteed Boris Johnson his big win.

I watched all this with dismay. Bit by bit I was learning about European left politics. My Labour Party seemed to be on the dark side of a British moon unable to modernise theory or practice. Observing European democratic left politics I had got used to the idea of a party conference or the membership choosing who the party leader would be. The fight within Labour over whether MPs alone should decide the party leader made no sense at all from a European democratic left perspective. Still less was the idea that trade union general secretaries would wield such power within a political party.

The response of the Labour Party after its 1983 defeat was to elect as Leader Neil Kinnock, who'd maintained a solid left profile since his election as young MP from South Wales in 1970. Kinnock was great fun and a wonderful speaker. Christopher Hitchins and I met him more than once in the bars of the House of Commons and the craic between these two witty and 100 per cent political beings was terrific. His campaign manager was Robin Cook, elected in 1974, and also someone who had maintained a left profile based on ideas and policies, not the Bennite infighting that had helped Labour lose the election so badly.

Kinnock and Cook were prominent anti-Europeans, as were the newly elected Jack Straw and re-elected Margaret Beckett. Roy Hattersley who took a progressive line on European construction was firmly on the right of Labour as was John Smith. Hattersley nominally stood for the leadership of the party but simultaneously offered himself as deputy leader, which he duly won. The old 1945 guard of MPs passed the torch. Kinnock's hand was grabbed by Hattersley who held it aloft on the platform at the Labour Party conference. We all cheered.

The TUC annual conference happened just before Labour's conference and the coronation of Kinnock and Hattersley. The TUC president was Frank Chapple, a former communist, who had risen to be general secretary of the electrical workers union. Like many ex-communists, Chapple swung as far to the right as was possible in political terms.

Chapple made a powerful speech in favour of OMOV, One Member One Vote, as the system Labour should use for electing its leader and other internal Labour Party elections or policy decisions. This challenged multiple groups: the old guard of Labour who believed MPs should choose the leader; the 1970s left; and outfits like the Campaign for Labour Party Democracy which wanted a small group of engaged activists to hold power, not to widen key internal elections and choices to every party member.

In the end under Tony Blair, OMOV won the day and was heralded as a mechanism to guarantee Labour would make wise choices in the future. Less than two decades later OMOV produced Jeremy Corbyn not once but twice.

## 1984

Margaret Thatcher seemed to reign all-supreme over politics. She was Ronald Reagan's very best friend. His easy re-election following her 1983 election triumph seemed to confirm an unstoppable right-wing trend in the English-speaking world. Mind you, there was always Bob Hawke in Australia. However much as I liked Oz and its Labor politicians and trade union leaders, it was a very long way away.

In Europe Margaret Thatcher was also dominant. She was powering ahead with her economic liberalisation project called the Single European Act, which massively decreased the power of national government to control trade in goods and services, and handed wide new powers to the European Commission in Brussels.

François Mitterrand and Helmut Kohl played her beautifully. They pretended to play tough with the Iron Lady but in the end came up with a rebate that allowed her to proclaim victory. In exchange she not only agreed to a major transfer of power from national governments to Brussels she agreed to a big increase in the UK's contribution to the overall European Community budget, which went up from £654 million in 1984 to £2.54 billion – a fourfold increase by the time she left office in 1990.

Labour was still trying to absorb lessons from its 1983 election defeat when the party supported withdrawing from Europe. Margaret Thatcher was a convinced pro-European and relished depicting Labour as little Englanders wanting to disconnect from Europe.

A new generation of younger Thatcher devotees who worshipped her was beginning to shift the party much further to the right. While young Tories were enthusing about white apartheid supremacism I was working in South Africa with independent black trade unions, which were staging rolling strikes for an end to apartheid. They were clever with brilliant activist lawyers, union organisers, journalists. They chose

European and American multinationals like Ford, Volkswagen or Volvo for their strike activity. This allowed trade unions and politicians in North America and Europe as well as influential members of the US Congress to send financial support or solidarity delegations.

The white apartheid rulers in South Africa liked to pretend they obeyed the democratic norms of the West so could not stop such solidarity visits or financial help. I wrote a book, *Power! Black workers, their unions and the struggle for freedom in South Africa*, with two friends, the South-African-exiled BBC journalist, Martin Plaut, who had run the Africa Desk in the Labour Party's International Department, and another Labour friend, David Ward of the World Development Movement who later became John Smith's chief of staff.

The South Africa mineworkers' union had a charismatic leader, Cyril Ramaphosa, later the president of South Africa. Cyril avoided strikes for the sake of strikes and instead conducted a series of cat-and-mouse stoppages. These were enough to get the support of black mineworkers and demoralise the apartheid boss class without ever going over the edge into a confrontation that would have invited the kind of repression that led to Steve Biko's death in the previous decade.

They looked with dismay as Arthur Scargill launched an all-out strike to bring down the Thatcher government after the decision to close a mine in South Yorkshire. Scargill defied the new laws which stipulated that workers and trade union members needed to show their support for a strike in secret ballots. To the despair of the TUC and the new Kinnock leadership in Labour, Scargill rejected any idea of consulting the miners. Without that democratic mandate many NUM (National Union of Miners) members refused to follow the strike order. The hopes of bringing the UK to a standstill as power stations ran out of fuel proved illusory.

To be honest, I followed Labour Party politics without much interest. I dutifully attended the TUC and Labour conferences but the miners' strike and the personality of Arthur Scargill overwhelmed absolutely everything.

**Lesson 14.** *Syndicalist quasi-revolutionary calls to topple an elected government are unlikely to work in mature democracies. Labour must always stay close to electoral ballot box democracy.*

In any event, whatever was said at the Labour Party conference was quickly forgotten as the IRA tried to kill Margaret Thatcher the following week. A giant bomb blew up the Grand Hotel in Brighton where I'd often stayed. Thatcher was hated but political assassination was not part of any democratic politics. Two years after taking on and defeating the nationalist junta in the Falklands, Mrs Thatcher had emerged unbowed after a nationalist fascistic terror bomb had sought to kill her. The Argentinian thugs like their IRA comrades doubtless thought violence would defeat Mrs Thatcher and cower the country. The opposite happened. She emerged stronger than ever both in 1982 and now after the Brighton bombing. Mrs Thatcher told Tory MPs in July that her government had to fight the 'enemy without', meaning Soviet communism or a military dictatorship in Argentina, and the 'enemy within' – meaning Scargill and the miners who followed him.

Although I was up to my neck working with industrial trade unions and achieving good results – with the sole exception of my own country – I was more and more sensing that the 20th century model of a mass movement of organised workers physically producing the material needs of society was coming to an end. So much of what I had in my home, my Mazda car, the watch I wore, the trainers on my feet, my jeans and t-shirt were made thousands of miles from Britain and Europe.

I loved going to a wonderful New York event called the 'Socialist Scholars Conference'. It was organised by the Democratic Socialists of America, the more left of the two US parties affiliated (like Labour) to the Socialist International. Every famous name of the New Left that had emerged in the 1960s was present: Noam Chomsky, Barbara Ehrenreich, Britain's Tariq Ali, and even a very young Barack Obama picking up early ideas for his long journey through politics.

Michael Harrington was president of the Democratic Socialists of America. He had trained to be a catholic priest before embracing left politics. His book, *The Other America*, published in 1962, described in clear, non-academic prose, the continuing existence of widespread poverty despite the boom and economic growth of post-war America. John F Kennedy read and it formed the intellectual analytical underpinning for the Great Society attack on poverty, later enacted by President Lyndon Johnson after Kennedy's assassination.

Harrington told us all: 'When I started in politics there were very few socialist scholars and a heck of a lot of socialist workers. Now it's the other way round.' He was right and it's got worse since. Is this all bad? Yes and no. Yes, because there is too great a disconnect between those doing the theory and those doing the reality. And no, because ideas have power. Don't underestimate them. If the left controls or even influences the narrative of what's appropriate, then that gets translated into policy, just perhaps not by the left.

# 1985

The great miners' strike continued in Britain. It was now turning into the Stalingrad of the trade unions. More and more NUM members were going back to work driven by the remorseless pressure of no money, and failure of any effective solidarity.

I organised solidarity trips by German and other metal-workers in Europe.

The visiting delegations from Europe arrived with food parcels for families and money for strikers, and were horrified as armed police stopped their buses or coaches from coming off M1 roundabouts to go to striking pit towns and villages.

German and Nordic unions felt emotional sympathy for British coalminers. But they had long ago agreed on a reformist path to technological change. They sought new investment and jobs on a social partnership basis in coal mining, steel or ship building communities hit by changes in global manufacturing. The steelworkers, miners or shipbuilders of Asia also asserted their right to dig coal, build ships or make steel. These industries could no longer exclusively belong to the workers of the north.

I looked on it from my increasingly European and North

American labour movement knowledge and experience. Scargill and the NUM had been successful a decade ago in helping to remove the Ted Heath Tories. But he forgot the iron rule of generalship: Never fight the same war twice. Scargill was a latter-day Bourbon who had learnt nothing and forgotten nothing. Smart left politics has to be innovative and catch the world by surprise with new ideas.

I tried to get back directly into Labour Party politics by applying for the job of the party's press officer, pompously titled as Director of Communications. The moment I heard Peter Mandelson was in for the job I knew he would get it and deserved to do so. Already Peter was writing and talking about Labour as a challenge of presentation and communication rather than the obsession with who was up or down in Westminster. He was sharp, focused, ready to put in a 24/7 commitment. I worked hard but I was interested in ideas and I was enjoying my international labour work.

I had one daughter already and was aiming at more and in due course four more children arrived over the next decade. Peter had the round-the-clock, seven-day-a-week, every waking moment of the year devotion to politics, either schmoozing or threatening journalists to get good coverage for Kinnock and Labour. I was a political animal but wanted a life of family, reading, writing, skiing, and mountains and sea as well.

I was adding German to my French and fascinated by politics in other countries where I had a ringside seat. I went through the interview process at the Labour Party's grim Walworth Road office just down from the Elephant and Castle. Dennis Skinner came up to me. 'Good luck but it's stitched up for Peter Mandelson.' I had guessed as much and in my pocket had a ticket to Washington DC to meet American leftist friends.

Peter was the right man at the right time and started the job of changing Labour toward electability far more effectively than I could have managed. But it still took a further long twelve years before it happened.

For years the main opposition on the undemocratic left to Labour came from the Communist Party. After the crushing of the Hungarian democratic uprising in 1956 or the Prague Spring in 1968, the new anti-Stalinist left became the main source of opposition for social democratic, socialist and Labour Parties. Trotskyist ideas were part of Labour's make-up after 1968. The Trot papers spoke up for the unfashionable causes of women's and gay and lesbian rights, or against the institutional racism of the police, the prejudices and hypocritical moralising of the judiciary, the lies and distortions of the tabloids. In other words, all that the Labour movement establishment (white, middle-aged, dull and not a little complacent) was uncomfortable with.

The Trots, especially in journalism, were gadflies, endlessly cheeky, and formed a network of like-minded anti-reactionaries. They were brilliant at hard-hitting TV current affairs exposé programmes. The roll call of Trotskyist activists who went on to fame and fortune as media bosses is remarkable. They were never any threat to the ruling elites who watched their calls to revolution with amusement and then pounced to hire the smartest of them and turn them into upholders of the status quo.

**Lesson 15.** *Labour needs a left that challenges and thinks aloud on new issues – but not a left that despises* *the broad mass of Labour voters and activists, elected MPs and councillors. A cocky, arrogant left that insists it alone has the right answers and is keener to promote itself than promote Labour turns off voters.*

For Labour, the Trotskyist Militant Tendency was a party within a party, dedicated to classic entryist techniques advocated by Lenin and Trotsky in their hate of democratic leftism. Together with others on the left in Labour, Militant focused on seeking the de-selection of MPs or councillors they did not like.

MPs who had not voted for Tony Benn were told they would face de-selection. Chris Mullin's pamphlet giving clear instructions on Labour rules about candidate selection was widely read. I watched him outside the Labour Party conference selling his booklet. It became the bible for anyone who wanted to deselect a Labour MP with clear guidance on how to go about the purge.

But even hard-line left MPs were uneasy about allowing Militant to launch an all-out internal party war based on ousting loyal Labour MPs who simply displeased outside bodies like Militant.

In a remarkable act of courage Neil Kinnock, who had been a fellow traveller of the hard left in Labour ever since his election as a twenty-eight-year-old MP in 1970, now denounced them openly at the 1985 party conference. We sat riveted as Neil, rather like Khrushchev in his famous denunciation of Stalinism at the 20th party congress of the Soviet Communist Party in 1956, spelt out the truth about far-left infiltration into Labour.

I sat there transfixed. I had heard the polished professional leadership speeches of Harold Wilson, Jim Callaghan and Michael Foot at Labour Party conferences. But never something so raw and passionate and so truthful. Derek Hatton and some left MPs walked out in protest, but Kinnock won an enormous ovation as Labour –and the country – realised that something momentous had taken place. Democratic politics' raw theatre struck home. I'll go further and say it's the best drama ever, nothing beats it. You want real life real drama, then go into politics. I guarantee you, it'll deliver.

**Lesson 16.** *If Labour wants to galvanise its members and the public, then nothing beats raw theatre. The human species is hard wired to respond to it. The Ancient Greeks knew that and taught it in their lyceums, Willy Brandt knew that and used it to heal a post-war Germany, Bill Clinton was a master of it. And Boris Johnson is only pure theatre. Used wisely, it'll take more of the public further than carefully crafted statements of well-meaning intent. Today's Labour is too earnest and careful, too fearful of putting a foot wrong, to hone the art of raw political theatre.*

# 1986

By 1986, Mrs Thatcher's economic miracle had left 3.4 million out of work. But they were in the forgotten north and midlands in steel, coal-mining, shipbuilding, metal-bashing regions which the *Enrichessez-vous* Tories of the epoch were happy to consign to the dustbin of history.

Now suddenly, there was a strike of newspaper workers in London. Rupert Murdoch transferred the production of his papers, the *Sun, The Times* and *Sunday Times* from age-old Fleet Street buildings to a new industrial estate in Wapping. There journalists would write their stories, design pages, write headlines and chose pictures, then input them automatically to be printed. The electrical workers union refused to support the printworkers who had never shown much interest in broader trade union solidarity. Thus Murdoch had enough technicians to print his papers. It was the end of centuries of craftsmen (there were very few if any women printworkers) whose skill and culture had given the world the printed page.

In America and most of Europe the print unions had cut a deal with newspaper owners and approved a transfer to new technology. I met regularly with print union friends at the TUC. I asked why they could not accept the inevitable and go for a compromise agreement. The answer was blunt: 'We know that, Denis. It's going to be over soon. But for the time being we are still earning three, four, five times what we can get when it's all automated so we'll fight to hang onto that for as long possible.'

Wapping became a by-word for the final great failure of syndicalist trade unionism in Britain in the 1980s.

On Saturdays I went to Wapping where there were calls to all trade unionists in London and beyond to attend peaceful protests to try and block the lorries carrying the *Sunday Times* from leaving. There were 3 million trade union members in London alone. But the numbers who turned out to support the printworkers and journalist rarely if ever got into five figures. The police could easily clear a way for the distribution lorries. Murdoch won his Battle of Wapping. London's workers had had enough of 15 years of Scargillist militancy. No major strike had been won for a decade. The Thatcher government no more brooked compromise than Arthur Scargill did.

I tried to get Labour comrades to look at what this loss of power of workers meant for policy and politics. From 1926 to 1986, the trade unions and with them the Labour Party were a force in the land. Sometimes battered, sometimes wilfully weakened by anti-union legislation. Often rendered impotent by their own sterile internal disputes over personality or degrees of militancy. But nonetheless important and able to reach out to new categories of workers, and pick up new issues and causes that would matter to those without money power. Trade union membership had come down from 13 million in 1979 when I was president of the NUJ to a little over 10 million in 1986. By 2021 only 1 in 10 workers in the private sector was a union member.

**Lesson 17.** *Labour puts up ideas and policy to reform and improve most much economic activity or social policy. But it has been shy of looking at workplace representation and what trade unions needed or need to do to become relevant again. Perhaps it is too late. But Labour should not be unwilling to tell hard truths to union just because of the historic attachments and links. Nowhere in democracies do trade unions sit on the controlling bodies of the main centre-left party and seek to dictate its policy.*

*Links between progressive parties and the unions are stronger as a result. President Joe Biden talks of creating 'union' jobs and is proud to call himself a union man in a way no Labour leader has for decades. Unions should take the lead in proposing a new relationship with Labour but stay out of trying to control the party or manipulate the selection of MPs and the party leader and putative prime minister.*

In 1986, after a decade or more of organised entryism into the Labour Party, Militant's leaders were finally expelled. Left-wing anti-Europeans like Margaret Becket smelt the coffee and in due course converted themselves into  respectable moderate Labour MPs who decided to find favour with Europe and to tuck in behind the Labour modernisers as they emerged a few years later.

Margaret was one of the best chairs of cabinet committees I'd seen in action. But supposing Margaret had been a reformist and not anti-European in the 1970s? The same question might be put to Robin Cook, and to so many others who played to a left anti-European gallery for most of the 1970s and 1980s.

# 1987

The twelfth election of my life. Won six, lost six. So not too bad. But somehow it didn't feel like Labour's year. I was based in Kentish Town where of course everyone was Labour. But no one was winning. The miners had lost. The printworkers had lost. London labour politicians on the Greater London Council not only lost, they'd been abolished by national fiat. Yet the ambience around Kentish Town dinner parties where everyone was a lawyer, an academic, a think-tanker, in media and also a Labour Party member was curiously cheerful as they looked out to distant horizons of Tory rule.

This was the beating heart of the fashionable London left opposition. "Spitting Image" was our TV show. We even had a new newspaper, *News on Sunday*, launched in April. It disparaged tabloid attacks on the 'loony left'. What no one was prepared to say was it was deeply dull.

The left of Labour was slowly falling apart. The principal leaders and devotees of Militant Tendency had been expelled. The Campaign for Labour Party Democracy had achieved many of its goals in breaking the stranglehold of MPs on electing the party leader or assuming they would never be challenged by local activists if they failed to pay heed to their views. Younger Labour MPs like Tony Blair made a point of having a home in their constituencies. They commuted long hours with their children to be present in the Commons and available for national media, while also being seen hard at work in their constituencies.

Ken Livingstone had broken with his protégé John McDonnell who wanted a more aggressive confrontation with Mrs Thatcher. As Ron Todd, a friend I had got to know as chief Ford negotiator for the Transport and General Workers Union, said at the time: 'What do you say to a docker on £400 a week who owns his house, a new car, a microwave, and a video, as well as a small place near Marbella? You do not say "Let me take you out of your misery, brother!"'

This was the lesson that Todd, one of the greatest working-class leaders of his time, who had been a Royal Marine Commando in the Far East in the closing stages of the war and had been on guard duty when Japanese war criminals were hanged, understood instinctively. What we, the pundits and university educated socialist know-alls of Kentish Town, could not.

In Frankfurt I had a friend, Jacob Moneta, a German Jew who had been an active Trotskyist in the SAP (Socialist Workers Party, a German anti-Stalinist party in the 1920s and 1930s). After 1950 he became the chief editor of the giant four-million-strong German metalworkers' union, IG Metall, and provided left intellectual stimulus for its leader, Otto Brenner, the greatest post-war trade union leader in Europe. Moneta had got out of Nazi Germany to Palestine before the full murderous Nazi onslaught on Jews got going. Sitting in his Frankfurt apartment serving me coffee from Nicaragua the veteran leftist made a different and important point. 'Look, if I had said to a German metalworker in a steel works, electrical factory or shipyard in the 1930s that one day they would have a secure job, five weeks holiday a year, a car, a nice house or flat, good schools for their children, guaranteed high quality health care independent of income, decent pensions then they would have thought that was socialism!'

This remains the bleeding wound at the heart of all democratic left politics. The more that is done for Labour's voting base the less there is any impulse to vote left. In 1947, the worker on an average industrial wage in Britain paid no or hardly any income tax. The arrival of the NHS, council homes, schools for all, and all that is associated with the Welfare State massively improved the life chances of working people, but it was paid for by the taxes of the middle and upper classes. We were and remain victims of our own success.

The highest rate of income tax was ninety-nine per cent during the Second World War and it stayed at ninety per cent up to 1971 when it was cut to seventy-five per cent, though Denis Healey as Labour's Chancellor then increased it. Thatcher cut the basic rate to twenty-seven per cent in 1987. Of course, she increased indirect taxation which is always more regressive – that is those on low incomes pay a higher proportion of their income in indirect taxation than the better off. But a worker on average industrial earnings looked at their pay slip and saw a big chunk of their pay going to fund state activities delivered by a growing number of state employees who never faced the threat of job losses or reduced income that in the 1980s had hit three million British workers.

Labour was identified as a high-tax party at a time when voters wanted to keep more of their income in their pockets. Selling council homes to tenants, or mass purchase of shares in the newly privatised and floated companies in telecommunication or airlines gave a sense of prosperity that a Labour Party, rooted in northern industrial culture and led by a man from the South Wales mining communities, seemed at odds with.

**Lesson 18.** *Labour should be very, very careful before committing to higher taxes on average or even better than average wages and salaries. It may sound good at*

*a conference rostrum but most workers and employees*
*resent handing over a good part of their pay to the state*
*bureaucracy. Taxes are needed but the time has come to*
*ask the wealthy not the workers to pay a fair share. Taxes*
*on carbon, excess profits and financial speculation need*
*to be worked up into policy rather than increasing income*
*tax on middle-class working people.*

The Labour campaign was certainly slicker than 1983. The Labour manifesto stressed improved rights for women and BAME citizens. It was worthwhile identity politics but who would pay for the more generous public services Kinnock promised? Rightly or wrongly, the Tory commitment to lower taxes and controlling inflation, which ate into pensioners' fixed incomes, had more traction. Labour was not ready to change. In London, Ken Livingstone entered parliament after his glory years heading the now-abolished Greater London Council.

Ken did not win votes for Labour in London where the Tories won most seats. In the wider south-east Labour had just one seat compared to 107 for the Tories. Labour at least scored more votes than the breakaway Social Democratic Party, now involved in a messy dalliance with the Liberal Party. Labour's vote went up from 27.6 per cent in 1983 to 30.8 per cent in 1987. Mrs Thatcher won nearly four million more votes than Kinnock. She had 376 seats compared to Labour's 229 MPs.

In more recent times there is an almost automatic assumption that a leader who loses an election stands down – Gordon Brown in 2010, Ed Miliband in 2015, Jeremy Corbyn in 2020. Kinnock decided to stay on as Leader. Tony Benn tried to challenge him. His running mate was Eric Heffer, an engaging Liverpool self-taught intellectual leftist who walked around the Labour conference squeezing his not insubstantial beer belly into a Solidarnosc t-shirt.

Luckily for Kinnock, Jon Lansman, with his unerring record of getting Labour Party internal politics wrong, organised the Benn-Heffer campaign. After initial surges of enthusiasm, by the end of the decade the Bennite left – so strong in 1980 – just evaporated. Chris Mullin was now an MP and after years of devotion to Benn he broke with Tony, as did other younger newly elected MPs like Tony Banks and Dawn Primarolo who had been Benn's agent in Bristol. Other high profile left MPs like Margaret Beckett, Joan Ruddock and Clare Short also left the hard-left Socialist Campaign Group to support Kinnock.

That was a comfort for Kinnock who was now winning support from the Labour right as he took on Militant. But his decision to stay on as Leader delayed the necessary renewal Labour needed. It would take a further ten years before the door to a Labour government opened and during that decade a great deal of harm was done to the social fabric of the nation.

In 1979, the wage of a South Yorkshire industrial worker was ninety-four per cent of the European Community average. By 1997, it has been reduced to seventy-five per cent of the EU average industrial wage. Labour's lost decade and a half of the 1980s up to 1997 with election-losing policies was a national tragedy.

# 1988

Tony's defeat marked the end of Tony Benn era, which had begun after 1970 with his move to anti-Europeanism and his rejection of the Gramscian concept of historic compromise – the only way post-1945 non-communist left parties had ever won power. At local party meetings in Kentish Town hardly anyone noticed the challenge by Tony Benn to replace Neil Kinnock was taking place. No one cared.

Kinnock's victory flattered to deceive. In truth Kinnock was not up the job of winning a general election but the idea Tony Benn or a more left-wing Labour leader could was now finally demolished

> **Lesson 19.** *The trickiest lesson of all. Labour has to learn to retire a Leader who won't win an election. Ruthlessly. Unapologetically. Because that's how politics works.*

The Liberal Party and the Social Democratic Party merged, and Paddy Ashdown became leader. We all disliked the Social Democrats more than the Tories. They were seen as renegades, traitors, political thieves in the night who would steal Labour votes. In fact, the opposite happened as the LibDems were soon to begin gauging great chunks out of the Conservative solid block of voters in place since 1979.

Nothing exciting seemed to be happening on the left side of politics in Britain. Then out of the blue something remarkable took place. I was attending as usual the TUC congress when the President of the European Commission, Jacques Delors, made a speech that changed politics and helped turn Labour into an election-winning party.

Mrs Thatcher had supported the appointment of Jacques Delors as Commission President. Many of the symbols of Europeanism – the common passport cover or the directly elected European parliament – were instituted under Mrs Thatcher, as was the final coupling of Britain and the continent with the Channel Tunnel. She supported political Europe, foreign policy Europe, a Europe generous to poorer states and a Europe based on a significant sharing of national sovereignty implicit in the Single European Act.

However, the alpha and omega of Mrs Thatcher's premiership was her attack on British trade union power which she blamed for Conservative defeats in the 1970s. The heart of the platform on which Mrs Thatcher won the election in 1979 and re-election in 1983 and 1987 was her pledge to change trade union practices and reduce syndicalist militant power in British workplaces

Cut to Jacques Delors with his speech to the annual congress of the trade unions in September 1988. The speech was a closely argued explanation of the 1992 single market project. I sat in the Congress hall and listened to Delors' English with its thick French accent as he made a speech that did not sound radical nor was there any criticism of Mrs Thatcher or the British government.

Listening to his speech at the time it seemed to be a standard defence of Delors' 1992 project for the greater integration of European capitalism. The references to trade unions were moderate and based on social partnership, compromise and support for market economics. It could have been made by Conservative ministers in the 1970s as they tried to bring law into workplace relations – the norm in many continental countries. It was light years away from the socialist rhetoric of the confrontational trade unionism that Mrs Thatcher had already crushed. In themselves these were commonplace generalisations, little different from the conventions of the International Labour Organisation and broadly accepted in western democracies. For the British trade unions however Jacques Delors was received like a Joan of Arc saving the British workers and trade unions from the crushing tyranny of Mrs Thatcher.

The TUC delegates and trade union leaders on the platform got up for a standing ovation to cheer Delors as no visiting speaker had been cheered before. They spontaneously began chanting *Frère Jacques* or singing the striking miner's hymn 'Here We Go' to the tune of the French revolutionary song *Ça ira*. Both the left and the right of British trade unions welcomed this hero from across the Channel who put the banned 'Social' back into the vocabulary of British politics.

Thatcher took the Delors speech as a personal insult. If Jacques Delors had thought more carefully about the impact of his speeches in the summer of 1988 and if Margaret Thatcher had praised Delors for giving moderate and useful advice to British trade unions, perhaps history would have been different.

Instead she reacted aggressively and went to Bruges soon after Delors' TUC speech and attacked the idea of a 'European super-state exercising a new dominance from Brussels'. Overnight Thatcher decided Europe was her number one enemy.

Thatcher liked to have enemies. Since defeating the unions and Argentina, she'd been a hunt for another. Enter Europe, stage left. It was logical for Labour to make their enemy's enemy their friend.

One by one Kinnock, Robin Cook, Jack Straw, Margaret Beckett and others who replaced the 1945 generation of Labour leaders in the 1980s did U-turns, and followed a new generation of trade union leaders like John Monks, Brenda Dean, John Edmonds, Bill Jordan and eventually Bill Morris to find favour in European construction. By dint of a decade of working with the European left I had already come to that conclusion, as I saw all around me more progressive politics and government than anything on offer in Britain.

Might the time have come, I wondered, to put my knowledge and experience to use by aiming for the Commons?

## 1989

Ten years of Mrs Thatcher. But the world was changing. At the global level, the progressive values of democracy and freedom made a giant stride forward when the first free elections were held in Poland. Seven years previously I'd been shivering in fear in a communist cell in Warsaw waiting to be taken upstairs for interrogation by the Polish secret police and hoping I could blag my way out.

Now my Polish comrades had pushed communism into the dustbin of history. The excitement was over the Berlin Wall tumbling down but the heavy lifting had been done by the Poles. In China, students and others went on the street demanding democracy. They alas were crushed. There were pious words from Tory ministers but Chinese communism had already worked out how to reduce criticism from western democracies by stuffing the mouths of politicians, bankers, opinion formers and the business community with gold. In South Africa where I'd worked and travelled to support independent black trade unions, a new president, FW de Klerk was elected. He made it clear his task was to dismantle apartheid.

Meanwhile Labour was shedding policies which had made it unelectable for more than a decade. The big change was Neil Kinnock telling us at the Labour Party conference that it was pointless proposing the elimination of nuclear weapons 'without getting anything in return.' This had been the argument of the multilateralists since 1960 and finally Neil after two decades of promoting unilateral disarmament accepted that they were right and that he, Tony Benn, Robin Cook, and all those who lost elections on the altar of disarming Britain, were wrong.

Labour's new shadow employment secretary was Tony Blair. He announced in a letter to his local party chair in Sedgefield that Labour would not seek to bring back the closed shop, that is, an employer could not employ someone who did not already have a union card. In the trade union world this was a dramatic announcement as the closed shop was seen as the crown jewel of trade union power. Tony was a public-school and Oxford-educated lawyer not yet 40. He had no affinity with the labour movement. But unions respect decisive leadership. Blair made that statement without any consultation or clearance with union leaders. They knew in their hearts that the era of the closed shop was over. They were more than impressed that this relatively unknown, young but personable Labour frontbencher was prepared to take the risk of stating that the closed shop emperor was actually naked, and he would no longer pretend otherwise.

> **Lesson 20.** *Progressive politics must be based on permanent reform. Labour failed in government 1966-1979 and in opposition in the 1980s to propose any serious reforms of the labour market as it mean asking trade unions to structure themselves and operate differently. This not only left working people much weaker, it allowed easy propaganda wins for the right that Labour was in the pockets of trade union bosses.*

Blair was a friend of a group of Labour Party intellectuals – like the journalists John Lloyd and Barry Cox, who raised TV current affairs to a new analytical level with Weekend World, and Alan Hawarth, a Labour Party official and his lawyer wife, Maggie Rae. They were all part of the 1968 generation who had started out on the left and spent the last decade in opposition. This was the left that wanted power and in Tony Blair they had spotted a man who might deliver it.

After the party conference I learnt that an old friend, Stan Crowther, had announced he was standing down as Labour MP for Rotherham. My heart leapt. Stan had been a prominent figure at the NUJ annual conference bringing a solid South

Yorkshire trade union and left Labour perspective to debates. He and I had been on the same side of many debates and I could count on him as a friend. All the other likely candidates were local and as is so often in politics the new, younger outsider was attractive. Stan encouraged me to have a go for the seat though he promised he could deliver nothing more than his own union branch.

Rotherham is a steel town. Its main union was the Iron and Steel Trades Confederation. I worked closely with the union, and knew as a friend its president Roger Stone who lived in Rotherham. He helped to open doors. So did my youngest brother, Martin, just starting a career as a surgeon at the Rotherham District General Hospital.

My only serious opponent was called Jimmy Boyce, almost my exact opposite except we were both born in Lanarkshire. Jimmy was an unskilled worker who migrated to Sheffield where his talents as a speaker and Labour activist were recognised and encouraged by the communist-controlled local political committee of the AEEU metalworkers' union. He was a Sheffield City councillor and part-time student in adult education.

He was friendly and we got on very well. Jimmy had a great advantage. The selection of an MP was then based on complicated Labour Party rules. These created a kind of electoral college in the constituency. Votes were divided up with a percentage going to Labour Party members and the rest divided up between affiliated trade unions, Young Socialists, the Trades Council, the Fabian Society or Labour women's groups.

In the end Jimmy Boyce won the nomination with 1.2 per cent more of the votes of the electoral college than I'd won. We crunched all the figures and could not work out where Jimmy's votes came from. We found out that a union branch secretary had refused to abide by his branch meeting's decision to support me and gone home to fill in the ballot paper for Jimmy.

My team sat around miserably. We could have cried scandal and gone to the press but Jimmy had done nothing wrong. He was a very different Labour Party man from me but had every right to be an MP. Labour needed working-class MPs with real industrial experience as it did a multi-lingual PhD candidate like myself.

I decided that God did not want me to an MP and went home to work out the next stages of my life as a Labour activist.

# The 1990s

## 1990

Might the tide be turning for Labour? In one of those classical misjudgements that happens in politics when a policy reads well on paper Margaret Thatcher's attempts to reform local government financing blew up in her face.

It had been a long-standing gripe amongst Tory circles that people who lived in council homes paid far less to help run councils than rate-payers living in their own homes whose worth determined what was paid – the norm in most countries. Taxing property which can't move overseas always makes sense but not to English Tory ideology.

Mrs Thatcher's response was to move the tax that paid for local council services off the value of the property – which of course found favour with wealthier Tory voters who lived in larger or more expensive houses – and make everyone living in an area pay a tax for council services.

This might have been acceptable if it took the form of a local income tax but to please her better-off supporters, she made it a flat-rate tax. The poor would pay a higher share of their income in her tax than those with higher incomes. Highly regressive, it quickly became dubbed the 'poll tax,' a reference to previous – and always failed – attempts in British history to tax per head.

The rage was palpable. The poll tax allowed Labour activists to be out on the streets organising petitions or holding rallies but where the majority of the nation now was. Unlike support for Arthur Scargill strikes or nuclear disarmament or leaving the European Community – which pleased Labour militants but put off voters – pretty much everyone was angry about the poll tax and ready to sign up to oppose it. It was beyond delicious. I went to sleep every night with a smile on my face and woke up with a bounce.

**Lesson 21**. *Mass mobilisation can work as long as it has popular support. The campaign against the Poll Tax was vigorous, noisy and took many radical forms including non-payment and big street protests. Far more than Labour activists were involved. In contrast to the Scargill strikes, it was a nation-wide popular moment.*

It was also a signal of how out-of-touch Thatcher now was. Labour had a seventeen-point lead in February and a twenty-three per cent lead by April. The protests and demonstration continued all summer and early autumn. But then the Tories did what they were always good at and which Labour could never manage: they got rid of a leader who was looking certain to lead them to defeat. They thus changed the political narrative. The Conservative Party is unsentimental in changing a leader when it is clear the existing one is no good.

The Tories turned to a non-Thatcher in the form of John Major, a mild-mannered man who had entered the Commons in 1979. Major had grown up in Brixton, did not go to university, but worked hard, was polite and spoke well. He had a gift, undervalued but so important in politics, of not making enemies. Mrs Thatcher made him Foreign Secretary when she demoted Geoffrey Howe, and then Chancellor of the Exchequer when Nigel Lawson resigned. What he did in these two high posts in government made little impression. For Tories who respected holders of the high offices of state, Major had the formal qualifications to be Prime Minister. It worked as he ditched the poll tax, toned down the excesses of anti-European insults now raging in the Thatcher psyche, and played up his love of cricket and non-university background.

Labour had lost a decade. It was also rapidly moving away from its politics of the 1980s. The shadow cabinet election produced a team in which the only identifiable left-winger was Michael Meacher, but even he had broken with Tony Benn. A new Labour Party was emerging that was now ready to be where voters were. But it was too late. The Tories has been smarter. In dumping Thatcher, they left made Labour look out of touch clinging to a leader who never looked like an election winner.

I had been lucky to spend so much of the sterile decade 1980-90 – fruitless for the left in Britain – outside the country. But I was British, and Labour had been part of me for 20 years. What to do now?

# 1991

There are some years when everything happens in politics and then fallow years when not very much goes on. While John Major had new ministers and the great names of Thatcherism faded away, Labour looked same old, same old. At every level, all of us in Labour were just taking deep breaths trying to imagine a non-Thatcher political world. Kinnock and Hattersley had been fixtures in Labour politics, one on its left and one on its right, for more than two decades. The great political cleansing of Labour continued. Voting for the National Executive Committee now took place with every Labour Party member able to vote. As a result, big name left-wingers lost out.

The rising star of Labour was John Smith. I bumped into him at the TUC Congress in the bar of a hotel where delegates enjoyed a late-night drink after the official receptions and fringe meetings were over. John was endlessly fascinated by European politics and I now had a reputation as a Labour insider who knew about Europe, spoke European languages and enjoyed European social democratic politics. We sank whisky after whisky with John pouring the drink down his throat like the Sahara swallowing a rain shower. I stumbled back to my hotel and woke up at eleven the next morning with the worst hangover of my life.

In comparison, John Smith had been up early for a briefing breakfast with journalists and then caught the train to London to appear in court as a leading QC. I drove back to Manchester to stay with my uncle Joe, a GP and graduate of Glasgow University like John Smith. Uncle Joe was a big fan of his fellow

Glaswegian. He was however dismayed at my report of the drinking session. 'That's bad, very bad. John had a serious heart attack a few years ago. If he is drinking as seriously as you say, he's not long for this world.'

Labour was shaping ambitious plans for social investment and other progressive measures. At last, after ten years in the wilderness, Labour had woken up to the point Franklin Delano Roosevelt had made when he said 'a rising tide lifts all boats.' Redistribution works best when there is something to redistribute. A cake never gets bigger as it gets divided into ever more slices; it upsets those getting smaller helpings without sating the hunger of those finally getting a small slice. Willy Brandt had put it differently in 1960 when renewing the West German Social Democratic Party. He called for 'as much market as possible, as much planning as necessary.' An acceptance of market economics and open competitive borders was axiomatic for Labour's Nordic sister parties. Was Labour was finally on its way to accepting what was the European democratic left norm – that markets and progressive politics were not oxymoronic?

**Lesson 22.** *Markets are not the enemies of progressive left politics. Unfettered markets are. Labour has to get more sophisticated with its analysis of capitalism.*

# 1992

In the thirteenth year of Tory rule Labour and its cheerleaders had high hopes of coming back to power. John Major seemed a very pale shadow of Margaret Thatcher. He was utterly out of touch with new developments in the European Union. Neil Kinnock and Robin Cook were now making speeches extolling the need for Labour engagement with Europe.

Tony Benn as ever remained hostile. He refused to campaign for Labour MEPs, like the innovative left internationalist Glyn Ford, as Benn could not bear to find anything positive to say about Europe. Labour defectors who had stood for the SDP like Roger Liddle or Andrew Adonis were now coming back to Labour.

I went to Labour's 1992 spring conference in Edinburgh which met to discuss local government and European affairs. The only buzz was the general election and a sense that John Major was desperately clinging on to Downing Street at the head of a broken Tory party. The gossip was on the size of the Labour majority and who would get which jobs in a Kinnock administration.

In a taxi with Labour MPs and activists going to the airport I pointed out that Labour had to win nearly ninety seats to get a tiny majority and far more to form an effective government. Maybe because I was watching politics from Swiss mountains, I could see things a bit more clearly. Winning an election is not climbing Mont Blanc. It's more like completing a hundred 10k races or getting to the summits of all the 282 Munros in Scotland. With the best will in the world I could not see how

Kinnock's Labour Party could win all these seats. My Labour friends were horrified; many of them were candidates. They almost threw me out of the cab to walk to the airport.

I wish I was wrong but when a party of government takes the kind of wrong turning Labour took after 1979 or in the lost decade of 2010-20 it takes a long time and a new set of ideas, top figures and policies before the public will again give its confidence to a political party asking for the right to decide taxes, police on the streets, the state of schools and health, as well as scores of identity-issue policies to win back full public endorsement. The Tories won more than 14 million votes – their biggest ever score and 2.5 million more than Labour.

There was still a way to go.

So we replaced Neil Kinnock with John Smith. John had been brave as a centrist pro-European in the 1970s and managed to navigate when the left of the Labour Party was dominant after 1979 without losing his nerve or his constituency. But I wasn't convinced John was the man to reinvent Labour as we headed towards a new century.

**Lesson 23.** *The Covid pandemic introduced a new medical concept: Long Covid, a lingering hard-to-shake-off continuation of the malady. Labour has suffered from the political equivalent. Thatcher and Scargill may have gone, and Tony Benn and Ken Livingstone no longer commanding national figures, but Labour was still associated with its unelectable virus dating back to inner party sectarianism after 1979, the 1983 manifesto to quit Europe, the Scargill and Wapping strikes, and the* *pacificism of unilateral disarmament. It takes years for voters to forget why they could not bring themselves to vote Labour. The poor results for Labour in May 2021 showed that what might be called "Long Corbyn"– the lingering but ineradicable memories of the disastrous lost years for Labour 2015-19.*

In the summer I read that Michael Meacher, a thoughtful left MP friend was doing a house swap holiday on the southern Atlantic coast of France close to the Pyrenees. Meacher was elected in 1970 along with Neil Kinnock and Dennis Skinner. Meacher was of that generation of Labour MPs who were aged around forty when the Thatcher era began. There is nothing more miserable for a politician than to have served an apprenticeship and then find the chance of plying your trade in government is gone as voters elect and re-elect the other party. Meacher trudged through Labour's wilderness 1980s gradually detaching himself from Benn, who, he came to realise, was not going help Labour win elections.

But Michael also could not read the new times. I planned to spend some of my summer holiday in 1992 improving my Spanish just across the Pyrenees in San Sebastian, the seaside Basque city with the best tapas in Europe. I called Michael and suggested we got together for a chat and dinner. I drove up to Saint Jean de Luz and we found a sea-side restaurant.

He had just written a book called *Diffusing Power: the Key to Socialist Revival*, which had been launched by John Smith (memo to anyone hoping to rise in the Labour Party: there is nothing less likely to sell copies than a book with 'Socialism' in its title). Meacher enthused about the new party leader. 'I really like him. Kinnock wasn't interested in ideas. It was all about presentation guided by Mandelson. John is completely different. He reads widely and knows how getting policy right is vital.'

I gently said to him, 'John is a great guy, but the next English Labour prime minister will be Tony Blair.'

He exploded. 'Blair! Blair! I've served with Tony Blair on the front bench, on the NEC, in the shadow cabinet. Tony Blair is nothing! Nothing! Nothing!' he bellowed as other diners in the restaurant wondered why *les rosbifs* were having such a heated discussion.

'Michael,' I said. 'I know exactly what you mean but as a friend of yours let me suggest you find any bit of Blair still sticking out and start sucking now.' He snorted, and we retreated to the safer topic of how Labour and Michael would bring socialism to Britain.

Tony Blair was firmly on my horizon and had been for some time. All political leadership is about telling followers in a party that this or that cherished belief was past its use-by date. One example was the great Labour PM Clement Attlee in the late 1930s telling the Peace Pledge left MPs to grow up and understand that to defeat fascism, petitions and marches were not enough. Another was the post-war Labour PM Harold Wilson forcing Labour's anti-Europeans to come to terms with the existence of the European Community and winning the 1975 referendum on Europe.

Tony Blair seemed braver than Smith or the new rising younger stars of Labour, like Robin Cook and Gordon Brown.

Their higher ability as platform orators was not as important as telling the truth to your own followers and leading them out of dead-end politics.

Meanwhile we were lifted out of our misery by the win for Bill Clinton.

Clinton was at Oxford the same time as me and any number of friends from Christopher Hitchens to Martin Walker, both of whom claimed to have been buddies of his at the time, including one or two women students who were said to have slept with him. If so, they kept their friendships remarkably under wraps for more than 20 years as in all my perambulations through the British and American left in the 1970s and 1980s I don't remember anyone mentioning him.

Clinton had the same political life story as so many of us including Joe Biden. The excitements of the 1968 generation. A 1970s full of passionate opposition to the Vietnam war and Richard Nixon. Working for George McGovern and then disappearing into the deep weeds of American political careerism. He was a keen political fixer, an organizer, and above all a seriously good speaker. His election victory was a joyous moment for progressive politics around the world after the long years of Reagan and Thatcher followed by the boring incompetencies of the first George Bush and John Major.

Soon after Clinton's victory in 1992 I found myself at an autumn Labour European conference in Bournemouth. Standing in line to get a coffee I began enthusing to the Transport and General Workers union general secretary, Bill Morris, about the new US president.

I suggested to Bill Morris that the UK labour movement could take a lead in giving new direction to the Labour Party by organizing a big conference in London to coincide with the US president's inauguration early in 1993 and learn from the architects of the Clinton victory how progressive politics can actually do what Labour was failing to do – win elections and power.

Bill instantly agreed to put up the first tranche of sponsorship money and I went off to help get what we called the 'Clintoneconomics' conference off the ground. I had spent a lot of time in America in the 1980s working with trade unions, getting to know left-wing writers, intellectuals, journalists over drinks in the Tabard Inn in N Street in Washington or at seminars and left political conferences.

I'd learnt so much about the positive and progressive side of America. The one-dimensional view of the United States as a red-in-tooth-and-claw capitalist, war-mongering, racist or red-neck country purveyed by the left in Britain failed or perhaps refused to acknowledge the many reformist, progressive, indeed left (but never use the word 'socialist' in America) policies and ideas on offer in the US.

And now here was a young democratic president inspired by Roosevelt, willing to walk on picket lines, and using the language of aspiration rather than regulation, of empowerment rather than increasing taxes. The Clinton generation was my generation. We wanted a good life for all but never at the expense of curtailing our own appetites and desire for money. After the misery of Labour's fourth defeat here was a political star on the progressive side of US politics who could actually win elections. Britain seemed like Japan or Germany to be permanently under the control of centre-right politicians. Clinton showed this did not need to continue for ever.

# 1993

The New Year started with a bang. The giant Queen Elizabeth conference centre in Westminster was filled for a January weekend with a post-Kinnock Labour gathering to learn how Bill Clinton had become president with a centre-left platform.

It wasn't exactly left by most European standards but after twelve years of conservative protect-the-rich Republican government under Ronald Reagan and the first George Bush, Clinton harnessed all the best and the brightest of 1968 generation economists, educationalists and government thinkers and practitioners. He had a record as an innovator on education in his home state of Arkansas. His big-ticket offer was to extend free medical cover to millions of Americans who did not have any insurance, as most health care provision in America is linked to your job. He also pledged 100,000 new police on the streets – a political offer that appealed to Labour's new shadow Home Secretary, Tony Blair.

Working with the Labour pollster, the ever-energetic and ideas-enthused Philip Gould, I talked to American friends like Bob Kuttner and Don Stillman, the innovative government and international affairs director of the United Autoworkers Union, the most progressive union in America and to the *Guardian's* influential US editor in Washington, Martin Walker. We brought to London key aides who had worked on Clinton's successful campaign to explain in different workshops and plenaries what Clinton had done to shape a progressive platform that won the White House.

John Major had tried to help George Bush by releasing confidential M15 files on Clinton as a Rhodes scholar at Oxford in 1968. There was nothing much to report, but the stupidity of Major abusing his office to send secret information about Clinton caused a stir. The conference was called 'Clintonomics,' a name I'd dreamt up.

We got all sorts of Labour luminaries, trade union leaders like Bill Morris and Margaret Prosser, journalists, academics, think tankers and intellectuals, carefully balanced for gender and ethnic background. Clinton had made a pitch to Afro-Americans. He marched on picket lines with striking workers from Caterpillar. He had hugged AIDS sufferers. He was everything the Tories were not and never could be in the post-Thatcher era. James Carville's slogan 'It's the Economy, Stupid' was now thoroughly embedded as an election winner.

We were helped by John Prescott coming out with a denunciation of the Clintonomics conference with the usual tired metaphor about not importing any of these American ideas into the Labour Party. John's attack was front-page weekend news. It gave the conference a big boost.

Even without Prescott, the two-day conference was packed, with parties going on into Saturday evening. Tony Blair and Gordon Brown and Peter Mandelson walked around in wonderment at this gathering of ideas and energy. Gordon

Brown, the shadow chancellor, who always went on holiday in America as he spoke no European language and read voraciously on US politics had already forged a bond with Clinton when the Governor of Arkansas had come to Europe.

> **Lesson 24.** *Progressive politics exists in many different countries and regions of the world even if complete centre-left control of the legislature and executive in the manner of a majority government in Britain is rare. Labour should be on the permanent look-out for good policy ideas and proven success stories of helping the less well-off from Norway to New Zealand. Labour's continuing insularity and its inability to learn from best democratic left practice in Europe or overseas is a century-old weakness.*

In the summer John Smith led a Labour delegation to Geneva for a Socialist International conference, held at the Palais des Nations, the sprawling UN seat. I took John out for a Sunday afternoon drive along Lake Geneva stopping for a lunch in one of the many lovely lake-side restaurants. Then most Swiss shops selling newspapers sold English papers as well. John spotted a copy of the *News of the World* with the splashy front-page headline 'THE BEAST OF LEGOVER'. The story was silly, a smear and funny all at the same time as it described Dennis Skinner meeting his American researcher at her Chelsea flat. Their London relationship was no secret but John chortled with pleasure at the discomfiture of his fellow Labour MP who was never short of sanctimonious moralising and denunciations of the weakness of any other politician he disliked, including many in Labour.

The next day I helped Gordon Brown find his way out of the labyrinth of the Palais des Nations to meet a friend for lunch. A stunningly beautiful woman appeared and led him away. Clearly in addition to his formidable brain there was considerable wit and charm that had seduced many. That got lost the longer he was in power which was a terrible shame.

I returned to South Yorkshire at the invitation of the main steel union, the Iron and Steel Trades Confederation, to speak at a meeting called to protest yet another shut down of the many steel plants and furnaces in Rotherham. I spoke on a platform with Jimmy Boyce, now the town's MP who was making a name in the Commons by always heckling any statement or answer from John Major.

We shared a train trip back to London. Jimmy looked tired and drawn with his scarf wrapped round his neck against the autumn chill. 'It's not really much fun,' he complained. 'You're just lobby fodder, doing what you're told by the whips.' He really did not sound as if enjoyed being an MP at all. I said nothing and we chatted amiably until Kings Cross.

I went back to Geneva when my doctor brother called from Rotherham. 'It's Jimmy Boyce. He is very seriously ill. He is waiting in hospital for a heart and lung transplant. I'm sorry but as a surgeon and doctor I don't think he's going to make it.' My life was about to change.

# 1994

Jimmy Boyce MP died at the end of January. It meant Rotherham would need to find a candidate for the by-election.

I waited until the funeral attended by the party leader, John Smith, and a crowd of Labour MPs was over. In politics, death opens doors and the way forward to finally becoming an MP stood before me.

I had been visiting Rotherham in the 1990s partly because my brother and sister-in-law were doctors in the region, but also because of my trade union links from the International Metalworkers Federation were with the big industrial trade unions organising steel and engineering workers. They were happy to support my candidature as a bookish, Oxford graduate who had placed his abilities at the service of trade unions for many years. So I became Labour's parliamentary candidate for Rotherham. The first two letters of congratulations were hand-written notes from Tony Blair and Gordon Brown. Both understood the need for a personal touch to win friends amongst MPs.

The campaign was low profile, avoiding anything that might make headlines. My Tory opponent was a mild-mannered but very right-wing anti-European, Nick Gibb, later a Tory education minister. His main policy was the restoration of hanging, once popular with Tory working class voters but no longer salient.

My campaign minder was Kevin Barron, the MP for the neighbouring Rother Valley seat. Kevin was a skilled coal miner electrician and had been Arthur Scargill's far-left aide in enthusing the South Yorkshire miners to go on strike in the 1970s.

We got on well and he gave me plenty of advice. He employed his wife and sister-in-law using parliamentary allowances to pad out the family income. In his office, he showed me the biggest most modern photocopying machine that seemed to fill the office. He explained that he was popular with local party branches as all their papers and leaflets were prepared on this handsome machine which was paid for out of parliamentary allowances. I vaguely thought that MPs allowances were only for parliamentary work not party-political work or employing family members, but Kevin put me right.

On a train I bumped into John Prescott. He explained how to maximise car allowance expenses by buying a car with a large engine as the mileage between London and the constituency was based on the engine size; the bigger the car the more the money flowed in. He waxed lyrical about second hand Jaguars and so enthused me about the profit to be made on mileage I went out and bought for £4000 the first and last Jaguar in my life. God but I loved that car. When baby Benjamin arrived we had to swap it for a people carrier to transport the four young children.

Kevin warned me, 'Don't get your end away in the constituency' but in the middle of a by-election sexual adventures in Rotherham were not a priority. I was introduced to the House of Commons by John Smith early in May. I was staying in London sleeping on the sofa of an old friend, Donald Macintyre, political editor of the *Independent*, as I sorted out the move from working in Geneva and neighbouring France where my family of three girls, soon to be joined by their brother, lived with their French mother. Don woke me early on a Thursday morning with the news of a call from his newsroom that John Smith had been taken to hospital after collapsing at a Labour Party fund-raising dinner. An hour later, it was confirmed that Smith had died of a heart attack.

Without thinking I said to Don: 'It has to be Tony.' I had no idea who else might be a candidate for the Leadership but from far-away Geneva, Tony Blair was the only possible Labour leader who could connect to voters that neither John Smith, good as he was, nor any other Labour personality could reach.

I went into the Commons and the Palace was heaving with talk of succession. Might Gordon Brown run? The front page of the *New Statesman* said, 'No Cook, No Contest' but already it was clear that the two top Labour Scots, Gordon Brown and Robin Cook, were not going to have the same entry into English homes especially those that had not voted Labour for 30 years.

I made my first or maiden speech in the Commons in a Europe debate. Afterwards, Ted Heath came up as we were leaving the Chamber and grunted: 'Good speech.' This was praise indeed from the curmudgeonly Ted who walked around the Commons by himself, like a ghost from the past, as he still could not get over being beaten by Margaret Thatcher for the leadership twenty years previously.

Tory MPs dubbed me the MP for Geneva but this just gave me more profile. Barely in the Commons and I was lucky to get a Prime Minister's question to John Major. PMQs are drawn by ballot and an MP can wait months or even a year or more without being drawn but here I was with a question high on the order paper. It was a sweltering summer's day and I was wearing a lightweight fawn suit. I sat packed into the sardine rows of the crammed Labour benches nervously waiting for my turn.

Suddenly I felt a jabbing tap, tap, tap on my shoulder from the bench behind. I ignored it to concentrate on my question. Being in the Commons when it's full of MPs, whether for a debate or for Prime Minister's Questions, is, I assume, like being on stage at a packed theatre. It does not matter how experienced a public speaker you are, or how much in command of the subject you are, the atmosphere is electric, and it is so easy to stumble.

Again, the irritating tap, tap, on my shoulder. I turned in exasperation to see Diane Abbott grinning at me. 'For fuck's sake I am about to do a PMQ,' I snapped.

'Oh, I'm so sorry, Denis. Yes, of course you are. Sorry. Good luck.'

I rose and instantly had the attention of the Prime Minister and the whole House as the brand-new MP. How would I perform? What on earth would be my question to Major? The theme of the moment was the choice of a new President of the European Commission. John Major had vetoed a Belgian who he judged to be too sympathetic to Social Europe. So I asked Major the question any prime minister dreads – one he cannot answer.

In as soft a voice as possible, forcing MPs to listen closely I asked: 'Could the prime minister name any candidate for the European Commission president who is not in favour of Social Europe.'

Major looked desperately to ministers on his left and right but they, like he, had no answer. Suddenly the House realised

Major was helpless. As a professional he fumbled out some words but for a newby MP on this first confrontation against an experienced Prime Minister it was clear I had scored a point.

**Lesson 25**. *Labour needs to take the House of Commons seriously. Morale is as important for a political party as it is for an army. To sap the morale and weaken the confidence of the Tories Labour needs to have the sharpest MPs whose questions or interventions can trip Ministers and expose them as not up to the job to Tory MPs and via the media to a wider public. Labour MPs think they have mastered the Commons but quickly can appear boring and routine. Labour in Parliament should train up its MPs so they can have real impact.*

Labour MPs hummed their approval and slapped me on the back. Relieved I turned back to Diane.

'I'm so sorry Denis, I hadn't noticed you were on the order paper. You did very well. Congratulations. I just wanted to know if this lovely suit you're wearing is silk.'

It was, but I didn't feel up to discussing my choice of clothes with Diane Abbott, a woman of ability who with a little more focus and self-discipline would have been a star of 21$^{st}$ century politics.

Slowly I played myself in. Much of the summer was taken with finding a home in Rotherham and in London for the recently enlarged family. At the Labour Party conference the BBC put me up with Jeremy Corbyn to react to Tony Blair's first speech as party leader. I keep it in my iPhone. Jeremy and I look so young and despite the efforts of the BBC presenter to goad us into disagreeing with each other we both praised Blair and agree that some of his new policies like the minimum wage were progressive politics all wings of Labour would welcome. In a throwaway line, Jeremy said that Blair seemed to be concentrating on saying things that would appeal to voters as 'Labour is desperate to win the election.'

It was a statement of the obvious. The whole point of the game is to play to win. And it's telling that Labour had to say it aloud.

Since 1970, I had been caught between those keen to win elections and those keen to win internal political fights. That era was over. Finally. The conference, the party's newest MP and the nation could sense that Labour was in business and was serious about power.

## 1995

I threw myself into my work. Labour had adopted as flagship policy a statutory minimum wage law. Instead, I introduced a bill in the Commons to create a statutory maximum wage. The Bill sought 'to fix the emoluments of chairpersons, chief executives and senior managers of private limited companies and public bodies so that their combined annual earnings do not exceed twenty times the average take-home pay of their non-managerial employees save if the said employees agree through a ballot of their non-managerial employees or through their union to permit salaries of their chairpersons, chief executives and senior managers to exceed a 20:1 ratio.'

I gave as examples the starting salary for a cashier at Barclays bank in Rotherham then £7,000 a year; the chief executive of Barclays earned 100 times that amount. At the Rank Hovis plant in Rotherham, the base rate for an operative is £164 a week. Greg Hutchings, the CEO of Tomkins, which owns Rank Hovis, earned £1.2 million a year – 145 times that amount.

The 20-1 ratio would in today's terms mean a top salary of around £600,000 a year which does not seem poverty pay. In 2020 the highest paid CEO of a FTSE 100 firm 'earned' £58.73 million – 1,935 times the median salary of a full-time worker in Britain.

The political scientist, R.H. Tawney wrote of the 'reverence of riches which is the hereditary disease of the English nation. If men are to respect each other for what they are they must cease to respect each other for what they own.'

I linked this to work I was doing on the importance of the family as the biggest factor in social stability. It is in the family that the principle of 'from each according to his or her means, to each according to his or her needs,' can be best seen in operation as family members of different generations try to help each other, extend the arm of financial support or just care for weaker, less fortunate family members.

As I told the Commons in February 1995: 'We need many more jobs for full-time male workers. I know I shall be criticised by leading members of my own party and I must court unpopularity by saying that the inability of the male breadwinner to earn a salary sufficient for a family to grow up on is a labour market problem we have not dealt with. On the contrary, we have made earning such a salary all but impossible for so many of the half of the population who are not women.'

> **Lesson** 26. *Labour for too much of my lifetime has been terrified about talking of family and single-earner households. A Labour Party that wants to win power must support the family and family incomes that allow children to grow up without hunger or poverty.*

Quite soon my Commons and political life was taken over by international issues, foreign policy and above all the Europe question, and more by accident rather than intent, I shunted aside the issue of systemic poverty. It is the biggest failure of my half century in politics. While in power Labour would do a lot to help the poor but do little if anything to tackle the ever-widening pay gap or try to rebalance the labour market in the direction of more fairness. As Labour today turns its interest away from the real existing materiality of social existence to focus on identity questions, it is letting down the nation and the people it should speak for.

It was clear from talking to other like-minded modernising Labour MPs that the Blair-Brown focus was not going to rebalance British capitalism to be a bit less celebratory of greed. Labour arrived in power bang in the middle of a forty-year cycle of excessive economic liberalism which always opposes social justice. Labour ministers lived with the conventional economic wisdom of the *Financial Times*, or the *Economist*. They could not imagine – let alone fashion – an alternative. As I noted in my diary at the time, I was surprised at the extent to which Labour MPs just talked to other Labour.

> I am depressed at the very narrow networking of Labour Party people in the country at large. We had Harriet Harman and Jack Dromey to dinner and also invited Ian Hislop (a banker friend from university not the Private Eye editor) and his wife Minette Marin, who writes a column for the Sunday Telegraph. The evening went well, but the next Monday in the Commons tea-room Harriet said how nice it was to meet people outside the usual circle of friends they saw for dinner parties such as Patricia Hewitt, Tessa Jowell and Margaret Hodge.

> This struck me as being crazy. These are all nice people but are a tiny incestuous circle of Labour Party friends who have been talking to each other for the past twenty years. The Labour Party must have a rayonnement outside its closed circle of mutually admiring chums and be seen and known in other power centres, or at least opinion forming places in London and elsewhere in the country.

In *The State We're In,* the *Guardian's* economic editor, Will Hutton, published an impressive analysis of what was wrong with our economic and social management. Will had worked in Zurich in financial matters and had a much better understanding of how, in some aspects of economic management, the centre-left in some continental European countries had much to teach us.

So I organised a dinner-seminar at my house for all Labour MPs serving on the Commons Financial Standing Committee which examined in detail the proposals made in the annual Finance Bill. Will spoke to us, explaining the ideas in his book. It was an easy evening before we all had to return to the House for a 10 p.m. vote. Alistair Darling, the shadow chief secretary who was close to his fellow Edinburgh politician, Gordon Brown, led the Labour team in the Finance Bill examination in committee. As Labour prepared for power I asked Alistair if Gordon was incorporating any of Will Hutton's thinking.

'I think you'll find we are all post-Hutton now, Denis,' was Darling's reply. He remained the most enjoyably cynical of all Labour ministers, but I regret Hutton's original thinking made so little dent on the carapace of Treasury neoliberal orthodoxy which would survive unscathed for the thirteen years of Labour government.

They say that Blair was Thatcher's greatest creation. I tend to think that actually it was neoliberalism. Frustratingly, its benefits had been disproven since the Budget Director for Ronald Reagan, David Stockton, went on record in 1981 saying it was a load of bollox. Academic study after sociology analysis after economic white paper proved that neoliberalism enriched a tiny proportion of the population at the expense of the whole. But Labour would not hear of it. It had found its golden calf.

There was a wonderful moment of British pageantry and the last outing of the 1945 political generation as the Queen attended by Yeomen of the Guard and Household Brigade trumpeters came to Westminster Hall for a commemoration of the 1945 defeat of nationalist Germany. There were all the great names in politics who had fought in the war. They clanked about with their medals on their lapels: William Whitelaw and Merlyn Rees, Tony Benn and Michael Carrington, Denis Healey and Enoch Powell as thin as a rake, staring rigidly ahead. When he died soon after, he wore his wartime uniform as a Brigadier in his coffin. The Tory and Labour medal wearers greeted each other with warmth, respect and affection. In 1914-18 and 1939-1945, the Old Etonians had shared the risks and fears, and the wounds of war with miners and unemployed labourers with all of them called up in the national interest to serve their country.

Today's Tories and Labour people have no such common bonds. For the most part they have made their way up the political ladder by expressing contempt and loathing for their opposing representatives of the two nations in Britain which still exist as they did in Disraeli's day.

Meanwhile the Conservative John Major cabinet was going from bad to worse. Major and the Foreign Office under Sir Malcolm Rifkind had refused to intervene in the terrible wars of the Balkans. We watched in horror as the beautiful medieval, multi-faith city of Sarajevo was shelled by Serb artillery. I had sat in the White House mess with Clinton's aides early in 1993 to beg them to show leadership to stop the Serb massacres.

'Sorry, Denis. This president will never send a single American soldier to the Balkans. It is Europe's war. You sort it out,' I was told. To our eternal shame, we couldn't. America was once again needed to bail out a genocidal Europe. A decaying Helmut Kohl and a cancer-devoured François Mitterrand and a Jacques Delors who had no interest in defence and security issues sat on their hands. Britain, which did have the military power, turned away much as Tories had done in the 1930s when their doctrine of non-intervention allowed Hitler and Mussolini win Spain for their fellow nationalist authoritarian, Franco. Then news arrived of the cold-blooded slaughter of 8,000 Bosniak men and boys by Serb butchers at a town called Srebrenica. It was like Stalin's massacres of Polish officers, civil servants, judges and teachers at Katyn in 1940.

I listened with disgust to Sir Rifkind explain why, while Britain deplored the genocidal slaughter, it was all too difficult. He did not use the term 'a faraway country of which we know nothing' nor did he have a bowl of water on the Despatch Box in which to wash his hands. Top Tories were working for Milosevic and earning a fortune advising him on privatisation and other fashionable economic nostrums.

I sat in shame and dismay and also swore to myself that when Labour entered office, we would bury modern non-interventionism and take on the dictators of the world. The road to Iraq lay before us.


# 1996

The zombie government of John Major limped on and on. Watching this pathetic sight converted me to the idea of fixed term governments. Most of the democratic world writes into its rulebook that a legislative term should last for a fixed period:

four years in America and most European democracies, three in Australia and five in France.

I'd watched the death agony of the last year of the Callaghan government in 1978-79 and was witnessing the utter pointlessness of the last moments of the Major government. A successful party leader, prime minister and government always sought a new mandate after four years as Macmillan did in 1959, Thatcher did in 1983 and 1987, and Blair did in 2001 and 2005. If you know you only have 4 years to get something done, you go and do it. The fifth year in government is rarely happy as Attlee showed in 1950, Douglas-Home in 1964 or Brown in 2010. The Tory-LibDem coalition made a step towards fixed terms but the present Tory government wants to reverse even that.

When I asked one of Blair's aides, Tim Allen, a smart, friendly, French-speaking press officer, if Tony could do a short video for the conference of the steelworkers union, the ISTC, a founding member of the Labour Party in 1906, Tim asked me: 'What's the ISTC?' It was a genuine question from a young Labour man but showed up the gulf between unions and the Labour high command or at least their staff.

I noted in my diary:

The trade unions in Britain seem incapable of focusing their energies and concentrating their forces to decide what they really want and then putting a lot of effort into trying to achieve it. I think the relationships with trade unions are very important and I dread the development of a Labour Party that is so without roots it floats from one opinion poll to the next or from one charismatic leader to the next without any real compass or idea of where it's going. The Labour Party cannot be simply a party of government management. It needs a vision and a sense of what it exists for and a part of that has to come from a relationship with the trade unions.

I made time to move a short bill to identify employers whose pay was so low their workers all qualified for welfare payments. However hard I tried to make myself a good New Labour moderniser I couldn't turn my back on a life of promoting social justice of the most basic level – a fair day's pay for a fair day's work. Tony Blair liked historical biography but never showed much interest in Labour history. He saw it as a cage to escape from in order to succeed.

**Lesson 27.** *Labour history barely features in contemporary left discussion. But those who won't or don't learn from their history usually repeat all its mistakes.*

At the Labour Party conference, I had dinner with three right-wing anti-EU journalists: Anne Applebaum, Simon Heffer and Boris Johnson. They were all bewitched by Tony Blair. The touted saviour of the Tory Party was a super-market CEO called Archie Norman. I said he would be a disaster in the Chamber of the House of Commons and be easy meat for Labour. Boris protested vigorously and I realised that he did not really understand how the Commons worked or the rhythms of the Chamber. Johnson told us he 'wasn't really interested in becoming an MP and couldn't afford the pay cut it would entail.' He didn't sound convincing.

Europe just could not get off my political agenda. Labour MPs who, until the day before yesterday, were simply anti-European and had endorsed the 1980s policy of quitting Europe, now rebranded themselves as anti the European and Monetary Union, and opposed to Britain swapping the pound for the Euro. Gordon Brown casually announced that any such move would be subject to a referendum. That killed the idea as serious politics. Twenty years before the Brexit vote anyone half awake knew that a plebiscite on any aspect of Europe would ignite every populist, nationalist, anti-immigrant and xenophobic passion in Britain with the Murdoch papers, the *Mail* and *Telegraph* whipping up noxious fervour.

I paid my first visit to the British Embassy on the rue Faubourg St Honoré, one of the poshest addresses in Paris. The building was taken from Napoléon by the Duke of Wellington, and is exquisite inside. The Ambassador, Sir Michael Jay, became a friend, a great Francophile, and in due course, the Permanent Under Secretary of the Foreign Office, the nation's top diplomat. After a perfectly chilled Chablis in the *Salon Jaune*, the two of us passed to a dinner of potted shrimps, guinea fowl and a sort of upside-down spinach pudding, which was quite the most delicious way of serving this boring green vegetable. There was a decent Burgundy to wash it down.

Most of the time I spent with ambassadors as one of Labour's foreign policy wonks in government (in due course becoming an FCO minister myself) the food was much more modest, cooked in nondescript John-Lewis-style kitchens. But diplomacy and fine dining go hand in hand and an invitation to the British Embassy in Paris was much sought after. Michael quizzed me about Robin Cook. I had similar approaches from other British ambassadors. My reply was always to ask them what papers they read, other than the obligatory *Financial Times*. The answer was usually *The Times*, the *Daily Telegraph*, the *Economist* and *Spectator*.

After seventeen years of Tory rule it was natural that government officials should read the same papers as their masters. I told them to try the *Guardian* and the *New Statesman* though to be honest I was far from certain either paper had much influence on the incoming government. The ambassadors, like the nation, would get to know the new ministers once they were installed in office.

# 1997

1997 was the year of Labour's great May Day election victory. Twenty-seven years in the party and here I was, part of a Labour government. It was a thrill but also it wasn't. Now we would have to deliver. The nation was tired of the Tory party, its sleaze, its rank Europhobia, it's white, male, mainly posh-boy style. Yet had the British people really moved to the left? Or had they finally found a leader to fall in love with – Tony Blair? Could he and Gordon Brown remake the economy or just tart up the Tory austerity economics that led to rotting classrooms and shoddy social housing?

Brown's Edinburgh sidekick was Alistair Darling who I noted in my diary 'is a curious bird and the most deeply cynical MP I have come across.' We chatted about a tabloid story about Tony's hair turning grey. 'Ah well, I'm six months younger than he is so at least I can still say that there is a Labour leader who is older than me.' I teased him about going to one of Edinburgh's poshest public schools, Loretto, while Blair had gone to the other one, Fettes. 'You from Loretto and Tony from Fettes make a lovely little pair,' I told him. 'Don't worry, Alistair, I'll maintain the tradition of voting for public schoolboys from Scotland if you're in the running to take over from him.' 'Yes, at least we need to make sure that no comprehensive schoolboy becomes leader of the party,' he replied with a grin.

Again, and again I was being type-cast as a Europhile – as indeed I was. I had to debate with endless Tory Europhobes. Once I was at a City lunch debate with a French banker and John Redwood. He came over as a completely manic, as I noted in my diary. 'He reminds me exactly of Tony Benn 18 years ago. The eyes stare ahead. There is no humour. There is a flow of perfectly formed sentences with an underlying populism and nationalism while busy preaching to the Europeans. The only moment he stumbles is when he seeks to refer to the Frenchman but could not remember his name or work out how to pronounce it when looking down at his notes and so quickly refers to "the Monsieur" in an almost derogatory fashion which sends a frisson around the hall.'

Already there was New Labour elite coming into formation. I felt a sense of it in March when I went to have dinner with Andy Marr, the editor of the *Independent* and recorded in my diary.

He and his lovely wife, Jackie Ashley, live in a nice big suburban house in East Sheen. Richard Rogers, the architect, is there dressed in rather hippy, craft-shop clothes with his nice American wife, Ruthie. Rogers was bitterly contemptuous of Jack Cunningham, the Shadow Culture Secretary. 'I had worked with Mark Fisher on some drafts of a policy for architecture and the arts and we took it in to see Jack and he completely threw it out of the window and put in his own ideas. But the problem is he doesn't have any. He is absolutely useless. There really is no point in voting Labour as far as the arts are concerned. I am an old-fashioned socialist so Labour will get my vote anyway but really it is all too depressing.'

Andy had cooked a wonderful cassoulet and the whole evening was gay and full of good conversation. Polly Toynbee was there with her boyfriend, David Walker. There was also an editor of Newsnight there with his wife, a very pretty woman who edits a nursing magazine. She was fairly exhausted and kept falling asleep. But she did say that they were saving a huge chunk of their income in order to send their three children to private schools after the age of 11.

This makes me so upset. None of this trendy media elite are willing to really campaign for the necessary reforms in our schools so they don't have to beggar themselves. Jackie has taken her son out of the local primary school and put him into a private school where she says he is much happier. If this kind of behaviour continues under a Labour Government, then we will be done for.

The election on May Day 1997 was a foregone conclusion. I spent most of the time in target seats like Bedford and anywhere the Labour Party told me to go. Sir James Goldsmith, an anti-European millionaire businessman and playboy, set up a Referendum Party to campaign for an EU plebiscite. His press officer was a young British Indian woman called Priti Patel who oozed contempt for Europe and Europeans. Goldsmith or perhaps Ms Patel covered Rotherham with giant posters consisting of a very big flattering photograph of me. In rather small letters the posters attacked my pro-Europeanism. But as I drove around the constituency or walked in the town centre all one noticed was a large photo of myself. Most people thought I had paid for these promotional pictures to go up all over the town.

Two weeks after the election victory I went to a *Tribune* lunch at the Gay Hussar. Michael Foot was there along with Ken Livingstone. I noted in my diary.

Ken told us that he thought the Blair project would soon break down and he was waiting to inherit the party. He insisted that having an elected Mayor of London was a 'nonsense and nobody is in favour.' I just thought electing a Mayor of London after the years without any democratic government in the capital was popular and made sense. Ken was as chipper and cheerful as ever and seems badly out of touch.

Going into the Commons and seeing the 431 Labour MPs many with a look of utter astonishment on their faces I could see no political problem for Blair as swathes of Labour MPs owed him for their seats, or their ministerial red boxes. I came across a new fan of Tony Blair in Norman Lamont, the former Tory chancellor, when we shared a train journey to Leeds to debate Europe. He told me how (to paraphrase him):

after Blair was put on the front bench opposite me on Treasury questions Michael Howard and I invited him and Cherie to dinner. It was a kind of test to see what he was like and it was very clear he is as conservative as I am. Once in a debate with me he stressed the need for Britain to have 'competitive tax rates' and I thought to myself, which Labour front bencher would understand the importance of that, or the implications. He is very able, and I think you have a good chance of being in for ten years.

A constant theme of the year was the non-communication between Gordon Brown and Robin Cook. The Treasury and the Foreign Office simply refused to talk to each other as these two great departments of state were overseen by two men who acted like playground rivals. The roots of the feud went back to their rivalry in seeking to be top cock in Scottish Labour, first Edinburgh – both were Edinburgh University graduates – then wider Scottish Labour politics. Cook was elected an MP in 1974 and Brown in 1983, both for East coast Scottish seats.

Political palaeontologists have sought to find out the source of their conflict. There is no clear evidence. Both men were brilliant politicians, captivating speakers and innovative policy writers. I once said to Robin I thought Gordon Brown was one of two intellectuals in the cabinet. 'Oh,' asked Robin innocently, 'who's the other one?' I mumbled my way out of a reply as much as I admired Robin, I did not see him as an intellectual, a man of ideas who can take and organize them into a serious thesis that changes one's understanding of the world.

Robin had been solidly on the left, hostile to the EEC and in favour of nuclear disarmament. Nor was he an admirer of America. He was the politics of the Labour left of the 1970s in its purest form. He never drifted off into Trotskyism or Stalinism though was happy to collaborate with campaigns. He regarded the London left of Ken Livingstone and Ted Knight as not serious and the industrial militant syndicalist left of Arthur Scargill as doomed to failure. If you'd asked him what he believed in, it was a Labour government. After a short period as a leftist MP opposed to the compromises of the 1974-79 government, Cook took turned his fire power on undermining the Tories which he did better than any other Labour MP during the eighteen long years of opposition 1979-97.

Casting a shadow over Robin was Gordon Brown. Together

with pro-European, Atlantacist, reformist and revisionist Scottish Labour MPs like John Smith, George Robertson, Donald Dewar, John Reid, Brian Wilson, Helen Liddell, Calum McDonald, aides like Douglas Alexander and Pat McFadden, and an exceptional cohort of left social democratic political journalists like Andrew Marr, Jim Naughtie and John Lloyd, these Scots formed the core of what became known as New Labour. They were inspired by Bill Clinton and European centre-left reformists like Felipe Gonzalez, Jacques Delors or German social democrats.

As a Scot, Gordon was more aware of the nationalist identity currents that swirl through modern politics. He was nervous of awaking the sleeping beast of English nationalism à la Enoch Powell. Above all, if Robin Cook was making himself into Mr Europe in British politics that was a good enough reason for Gordon to tune down his Europeanism.

If the measure of labour market success was the number of people in employment, then communist Europe might have been seen as the model. In Britain, there became less and less point in improving productivity as firms could give up investment in apprenticeships, training, upskilling and new machinery to increase output as it became much easier to hire cheaper labour, especially from the growing pool of trained and skilled East Europeans. They came as tourists but given that there were no controls, not even basic identity cards, once in the UK they found jobs and often worked harder and more efficiently than their British counterparts.

Brown had decided to import the US Earned Income Tax Credit system, a state subsidy to low-pay employers. It helped create jobs as it did in the US where it was originally a Republican policy; firms could keep up their profits by hiring low-wage labour subsidized by the taxpayer. It was a slight improvement on the Tory government's record but would not eliminate poverty nor encourage training and apprenticeships to improve productivity. Labour was not learning from Europe but instead copying and pasting a twenty-year-old right-wing panacea from America where income inequality had gone up since its introduction.

**Lesson 28.** *A Labour Party without a thought-out labour market policy will before long let down its supporters.*


# 1998

This was the first full year of the Labour government. It was thrilling to be in power. I wrote in *Le Monde* for New Year's Day that Blair was converting the Labour Party into "*Un Rassemblement du Peuple Anglais*" – the Bringing Together of the British People, a translation into English politics of the title General de Gaulle gave his political movement after 1945. It wasn't post-politics as politics never is. But it was a Labour Party prepared to be for more than just ardent Labour Party members. As I noted in my diary 1 January:

They certainly believe the superman, 'leader of destiny stuff' at No 10 but the British people have a long tradition of pulling everybody down to earth. Yet how lucky I am to have not just a ringside seat but a place in the ring itself in this extraordinary national drama.

I was now a parliamentary private secretary in the Foreign Office team though No 10 kept calling me in to discuss what was happening in European politics. Most ambassadors and officials had converted themselves into loyal admirers of Margaret Thatcher and John Major. They had lost interest in and contact with the new centre-left forces rising to government power in a number of European countries, and often my contacts and talks with friends on the European left provided better intelligence than the *Daily Telegraph*- or *Spectator*-reading British diplomats. My FCO pass as a member of Robin Cook's ministerial team at the Foreign Office allowed me to go and wander from office to office to talk to ministers, officials and advisors.

I was sad when the magnificent warrior Indian Prince that filled most of one of the walls in Robin's office as Foreign Secretary was taken down to be replaced by a boring mirror. Cookie said he didn't want the prancing Maharajah waving his sword as it was too redolent of Empire. I thought he was being precious, and it was just a wonderfully colourful 19th century giant portrait and not a soul except previous occupants of the office would notice the politically correct gesture.

The FCO got its revenge as the mirror was positioned high on the wall, just above Robin's rather short head. He wasn't that vain but all politicians have to preen. So as he left the office and checked his tie was properly knotted, he had to stand on tip toes to see himself in the mirror.

I worked hard drafting questions to be tabled by Labour MPs for the monthly Foreign Office questions slot as well as possible supplementaries –follow up questions by Labour MPs – as well the rebuttals to questions tabled by Tory MPs. There were plenty of Labour MPs with a great deal of knowledge about one issue somewhere in the world that mattered to them – Palestine or Israel or Kurds or Chagos Islanders or Nicaragua or the Southern Sahara or between Pakistan and India over Kashmir or the twenty-four-year occupation of northern Cyprus by the Turkish Army. But few had an overall joined-up view of what a Labour Britain's foreign policy and alliances should be.

I continued all my European political networking going to campaign for Gerhard Schröder, speaking on platforms with him in my rocambolesque German as the *Financial Times* journalist and German expert, David Marsh, called it in the *New Statesman*. Schröder won the Chancellorship and so Britain, France under Lionel Jospin, and now Germany all had centre-left prime ministers.

Could this be converted into a new reformist centre-left start for Europe, I wondered in conversation with MPs, think-tankers and journalists who took an interest in Europe. I networked endlessly in France, writing articles for the French press and appearing on French TV and radio selling the idea of a pan-European progressive politics based on the presence of three centre-left leaders heading governments in London, Paris and now Berlin.

**Lesson 29.** *Investing in durable political alliances with progressive reformist governments abroad takes time, money, effort. Prime Ministers think personal chemistry with other leaders is all that counts. It rarely is.*

I think my local constituency party liked me being part of the government team and were just so glad to have a Labour government they forgave the increasing tilt to the right of much of what Blair was doing.

It quickly became clear that of the senior cabinet ministers Robin Cook was the weakest link. His dramatic messy separation from his wife when his affair with his London secretary became public wore him down. Until he became Foreign Secretary, he had managed the double life that many MPs indulge in – a formal sagging out-of-time marriage in the constituency and a girlfriend in London. I'd signed his mortgage application for a flat in Pimlico just around the corner from my house.

The moment he became Foreign Secretary his life no longer belonged to him. Bodyguards, a driver, his private office of three high flying FCO officials, his diary secretary, the staff at Chevening (the fabulous Kent Jacobean official residence where Robin loved to stay), all had to look after him, drive him and assure the security of his new partner, Gaynor. She was pleasant but shy.

I noted in my diary:

The establishment – what Cobbett called 'the thing' – is out to get Robin because he is (a) a successful foreign secretary, (b) he is running a Foreign Office which is not dividing the Labour Party down the middle as was the case under previous Labour administrations, (c) doesn't suffer fools gladly or bother too much with all the diplomatic niceties. In exchange, Britain has a good relationship with America, has opened all sorts of doors to partnership in Europe, and is doing innovative policy which pleases both the country and the party. There has been an absolutely filthy campaign against him, but he will weather this bit of pressure just as I expect Clinton will survive in America.

Very quickly it became clear that collegiality between Cook and his ministers was rare to non-existent. His assistant ministers never really felt at home with him. Doug – 'Douggie' – Henderson, the cheerful marathon-running Scottish trade-union official, had been made Minister for Europe. He knew little about Europe, could not speak or read a European language, and was ignored by Cook and Tony Blair despite political skills honed in domestic politics. Two university lecturers turned MPs, Derek Fatchett from Leeds and Tony Lloyd from Manchester, were other ministers. They were earnest, friendly colleagues but did not bother the FCO officialdom overmuch.

We all had a meeting in February 1998, and I noted that:

Robin is in extremely cheerful mood as if all his crises are now past and he is in a positive sunny upland where there are challenges to be overcome but no problems to drag you down.

The meeting was dominated by Whitehall turf-fighting. The row, predictably, was over the newly created Department for International Development. Clare Short has gone bonkers because on Tuesday Robin announced that the dependent territories would have a new status, there would be a special ministry for them (I think he meant Minister, with the job going to Liz Symons, the FCO junior minister in the House of Lords) and they could all have British passports. These a dozen or so left-over islands from the heyday of British imperialism like Bermuda, the Cayman Islands, Gibraltar, or the Virgin Islands. Most had converted themselves into lucrative tax havens and paid their own way from various financial arrangements that would be illegal in mainland Britain.

Part of the problem is the chalk and cheese nature of Clare and Liz Symonds (a former member of the TUC General Council, now an FCO minister in the Lords). They are both intelligent, forceful, achieving women but have such different backgrounds, style and routes in politics that they were destined to be permanently at war once they found themselves working in the same field. The Permanent Under-Secretary, John Kerr, intervenes to say that since DfID has been removed from the Foreign Office it has now £2 billion annually to spend. In contrast, the Foreign Office, once its obligatory subscriptions to international organisations are taken into account has only £50 million to spend on projects dear to its heart.

As always with Robin chairing, the meeting meandered all over the place with no proper discussion or sticking to an agenda. Half of it was taken up with a purely logistical discussion on a visit by foreign ministers from the Party of European Socialists in the context of the UK's presidency of the EU. Could Robin offer them dinner at 1 Carlton Gardens, the Foreign Secretary's London residence?

The PUS John Kerr said he saw no impropriety so the tick from the Permanent Under Secretary was there, but I intervened to say I didn't think it was a good idea after all the sensitivities on government hospitality to use a government building and in particular, a private residence, for such an event even if it would be the PES that would pick up the bill. Robin got a little cross at this, saying, 'I don't see why I can't invite people to my residence if I want to,' but Doug Henderson and Derek Fatchett came in on my side. We don't need any negative publicity after the recent weeks' stories.

One factor that emerges is that Blair is simply not interested in rolling out the red carpet for the European socialist leaders. He was willing to let them use 10 Downing Street for a meeting, but not willing to give up time for a dinner the night before. This coolness to Europe that comes out in the form of these signals from Number 10 is extremely short-sighted.

1998 was the moment when it became clearer that there were limits on New Labour reformism. The budget might have been delivered by Ken Clarke. Two issues I had been campaigning on – to encourage worker participation in firms by allocating shares to employees and support for married couples with families – didn't feature. I was bitterly disappointed. To have spent so much in opposition consoling myself that when we were elected these kinds of measures would get through, only to discover that they wouldn't, was galling.

On the international stage meanwhile, Labour was striking a different tone to the inactive Tories. We loved Blair's success in Northern Ireland and the Good Friday Agreement which ended the 30 years civil war type conflict in Northern Ireland. Those who wanted more international engagement liked Blair's willingness to use military force in Sierra Leone, and supported overflights in Iraq to stop Saddam Hussein murdering Kurdish Iraqis. Blair was also facing down Slobodan Milosevic after the appeasement line of the Tory FCO over Sarajevo and Srebrenica. One of the very real reasons why Blair went to war with Iraq was because of the popularity of his military actions.

Closer to home Europe never went away. Far from giving up their anti-European obsessions the City elite and Tory-party money men were making it clear that they expected to see the Conservative Party turn hard right against Europe. In May I had a glimpse of the new force field of Tory anti-Europeanism funded by very rich men as I noted in my diary.

In the evening I went to a dinner organised by Carla Powell, the woman whose salon, thanks to her marriage to Charles Powell, Margaret Thatcher's great assistant, has been the most famous in Conservative circles for years.

The event is to launch a book by a man called Rodney Leach on Europe who works at the same bank as Charles Powell. We turn up at a posh hotel in Knightsbridge and bit by bit a coven of Europhobes assembles. There is Paul Johnson with his watery eyes and his once flame-red hair now turning white. He is off the drink and in deep national disgrace because a former girlfriend of his revealed all in the *Daily Express* about his proclivity for spanking activities in bed.

Then there is William Rees-Mogg looking more gaunt and white-haired than ever but still passionate in his hatred of all things European. Michael Howard appears with his model wife and then Bill Cash. I spotted Norman Stone who had come back from Ankara for the evening with his Garrick Club bow tie, looking irrepressibly vulgar. He seemed to be less bloated so a diet of Turkish Delight can be doing him no harm.

There was one of the Saatchi brothers who was close to the Conservative Party. Then the divine apparition came in. It was Margaret Thatcher coming through a side entrance in a fluorescent light blue dress walking very slowly and sedately like an ageing goddess amongst her fawning *serviteurs*. The whole event was becoming more and more surreal.

Roger Liddle turned up with his wife Caroline Thompson who is now a big cheese at the BBC World Service. She giggles to me that I was responsible for taking her out on strike when she worked at local radio in the 1970s and I beg her to keep my militant past buried. Roger says that Cabinet Ministers were told they couldn't attend the event – a high mass of the anti-Europeans to show they were still around despite the election of a pro-European prime minister.

Charles Powell is acting like a major-domo, ushering everybody into dinner. To my horror I find it is a sit-down hotel meal. Then an introductory speech from Charles Powell and up stands the author, Rodney Leach, who is introduced as some kind of polymath because he is a great bridge player as well as being a banker and has written his book.

He makes a rather tedious speech attacking Europe for its social policies, its federal inclinations and all the usual rant of the Europhobes. I mutter under my breath getting noisier all the time and I see blacker and blacker looks aimed at me. The publisher of the book says I am behaving disgracefully, and Mrs Leach is very angry.

I realise I have gone a bit too far and am creating a scene. Polly Toynebee says, "I think we should walk out. This is absolutely disgraceful." I decide not to and instead try to cool everything down by apologising profusely, buying a copy of his book and giving £17 to the publisher and making sure Leach signed it and then after the speech is over going round and getting other people like Norman Stone and Andrew Neil to sign it as well.

Bill Cash sits down for a good chat but too much wine was taken by then and I just smiled benignly at everybody. I had talks with Andrew Neil and Norman Stone, both of whom are effusive in their greetings and I suppose there is just a solidarity between those of us who like to be outspoken and cause a row irrespective of our politics.

Mrs Thatcher sat regally at her table with an upright back, looking neither left nor right but fixing her eyes somewhere to hold her head erect.

I left with a lot of other people and got a taxi home having drunk and eaten too much and again made a scene which no doubt will be spoken of loudly in the salons of Tory Europhobia.

At the time I thought I was describing the end of Euroscepticism. I was wrong. It was only just getting under way. The banker, Rodney Leach, paid for and was first chairman of Open Europe, the most successful and professional of the anti-European think tanks in London. Its daily website attacks on Europe, avoiding crude language and usually based on facts (if carefully selected) was effective. Its many staff, including an office in Berlin, fanned out into world of seminars and conferences and appearances on television and radio tirelessly to promote the anti-European cause. Rodney Leach was rewarded by David Cameron with a peerage and thus made a legislator. From this platform he continued to preach against Europe. It was a message to other bankers in the City who crave honours, above all becoming a Lord.

Malcolm Pearson, also a Lord prominent in the insurance sector in the City, moved from the Conservative Party to UKIP and was briefly the UKIP party leader. 'Global Britain,' the think tank he founded with two other peers opposed to Europe, was one of the myriad of anti-European foundations, think-tanks, even political parties that have been financed from within the City to crusade against the EU. 'Global Britain' was later adopted by the Tories as their description of the nation after we turned our back on Europe.

Over the years they have changed names, leaders and sponsors. Business for Sterling, New Europe, the Referendum Party, No, Open Europe, Global Britain, United Kingdom Independence Party and Business for Britain. All were dedicated to the simple proposition that the European Union is inimical to British interests. Some sought electoral success, others worked through the Conservative Party. Stuart Wheeler, for example, became UKIP's main financial supporter. He was persuaded to make his major donations to the Conservative Party in 2001 when William Hague was the party leader who sought to win the 2001 election on the claim that the pro-European Tony Blair's re-election meant the end of Britain. He was rewarded for his work against Europe when Boris Johnson made him a peer.

# 1999

The year started with Robin Cook. His former wife, who he'd brutally dumped on the tarmac of Heathrow Airport in the summer of 1997 after his London relationship with his secretary Gaynor was revealed, got her own back. Did the *News of the World* keep a 24/7 watch on his Pimlico flat? Did someone chatter or sell the story? We will never know.

Henry Kissinger wrote of the 'aphrodisiac of power.' We only learnt long after the affair of Edwina Currie's passionate relationship with John Major, and of her anger when he did not, as Prime Minister, offer his lover a senior ministerial job. She got her revenge and Margaret Cook got hers with a tell-all extract in the supposedly serious *Sunday Times.* It was published in January 1999 during the recess.

She accused him of non-stop womanising, but this amounted to six affairs over thirty years. It would have hardly been noticed by François Mitterrand or Jacques Chirac who was known all over Paris as '*Monsieur dix minutes, douche comprise.*' And let us pass over Prime Minister Boris Johnson who 'Everyone knows is a sex addict' as top Tory Sasha Swire wrote in in her diaries describing her friend's rise to Downing Street. Margaret said Robin was a drunk who consumed too much

Scotch in some months of depression in the 1980s. I had never seen Robin the worse for drink and even during late nights in the Commons he ate and drank sparingly.

Robin's aide, David Mathieson, asked me to call Robin in the Foreign Secretary's official residence, Chevening. The official residences of top ministers are closer to mausoleums than real homes, with furniture from posh 1950s railway hotels. I called the number and Robin answered himself. I asked him how he felt, and he said it was pretty grim in Chevening. I tried to cheer him by saying that six affairs are hardly going to condemn him as a womanising fornicator, the drink accusations were improbable and nobody would believe it while the crucial difference with other scandals was that there was no hint of financial impropriety. I burbled away and Robin said I was succeeding in cheering him up. He also struck me as a cat who walked alone with few intimate friends.

The newspaper coverage may have demoralised him but no one in politics noticed. Tony Blair has just been visiting Washington to meet Bill Clinton and stiffen him up to take action in Kosovo. On the day of the scheduled meeting with Clinton the news broke that the Republican majority in the House of Representatives had voted to impeach Clinton over his relationship with a White House intern, Monica Lewinsky. Blair was due to do a White House press conference with Clinton and was asked if he wanted to call it off given the only story was the impeachment. Instead he went out and told the American and world media that Clinton was his friend and he valued their relationship and he would continue to support and work with the beleaguered US president.

Simon McDonald, later the head of the Foreign Office and a peer, but then a rising diplomat covering politics at the British Embassy in Washington, described to me how a senior Senator came up to him and said: 'Simon, this is a town of trades. Your prime minister has just given the biggest help to a US president by a visiting politician ever seen. You can ask for anything now and the White House will have to give it to Britain. That's the rule here in Washington.'

Simon said he rushed back to the embassy to report the conversation and ask what big concession the UK should request from the White House in exchange for Blair's public support of Clinton. Memos went backwards and forwards between the UK embassy on Massachusetts Avenue and Downing Street and the FCO. A high-level committee was set up to discuss and decide what it was Britain should ask for. It held meetings. More papers were written. In the end Whitehall decided it didn't want to ask anything of Clinton. When in doubt the Foreign Office writes a paper, which is edited and re-written, refined and polished, and then carefully tucked away in a file. Nothing happens.

Peter Mandelson being forced to stand down left the other big beasts of Labour and the government cheered up. There was a spring in the steps of Gordon Brown, Robin Cook and John Prescott at seeing Mandy brought down more than a peg or two. On the other hand, Mark Seddon, the young and sparky editor of *Tribune*, asked me to contact Peter Mandelson to see if he would write for the hard-left weekly. I teased Peter about the suggestion and offered to write his columns for him if he chose to turn left within the party.

At a dinner at St Antony's College, Oxford Anne Clywd, the Welsh MP, an ex MEP, former *Guardian* journalist and a powerful campaigner for human rights, especially for the Kurdish people which led her to take a strong line against Saddam Hussein, told me that at the weekly meetings of a small committee of Labour MPs elected by fellow back-benchers, she, Chris Mullin and Jean Corston had all told Blair he could not bring back Mandelson to the cabinet. 'I think Blair understood this, though he refused to take any notice of what we said about ending cooperation with the Liberal Democrats and made quite clear he was going to pursue that agenda.'

I liked Anne and Chris and Jean and felt more at ease with these old Labour friends dating back to the 1970s than with the new generation of loyalist managerial MPs Blair promoted often from the North East like Alan Milburn or Steve Byers. There was no personal disagreement and relations were friendly. Alan liked to dismiss me as 'Euro-freak' and Steve Byers at dinner in the Members' Dining Room said the *New Statesman* would become more readable if I stopped writing for it. They were right on both counts but this supercilious and superior tone grated on many Labour MPs who would never enjoy the swift promotion of their fellow MPs upon whom Blair's radiance shone.

Labour MPs were getting twitchy about the council elections in May. I was also worried about the European Parliament elections at the same time. Jack Straw had changed the rules to a clumsy form of regional proportional representation. The regions were far too big for any MEP candidate or team of candidates to connect to voters. Five years before in 1994

Labour triumphed in the European election and Labour MEPs constituted more than ten per cent of the entire European Parliament. Now I could sense the return of racism and xenophobia, represented by the anti-Semitic British National Party and this new beast, the United Kingdom Independence Party with its fluent, forceful MEP called Nigel Farage. William Hague took every opportunity to denounce the EU as an alien presence in Britain.

I expressed my fears about the summer elections to Dennis Skinner.

'You're dead right to be fearful, Denis. We are going to be fucking slaughtered,' he said.

I told him about my idea that we should lift the regressive BBC licence fee off pensioners, and he said 'I've already said that to Gordon Brown. In fact, I told Tony we need a good budget for the working class. Do you know what he said to me? "Yah, yah, Dennis. A budget for our core voters, you're quite right."'

'I said to him, "No, Tony, we want a budget for the working class."'

'"Yah, something for our core vote."'

'And do you know the bugger just can't say the words "working class!"'

The 1999 election news for Labour was not encouraging. We lost thirty-two seats in the European Parliament election. Both Labour and the pro-EU LibDems saw their vote share go down to the profit of the increasingly anti-European Tories under William Hague. UKIP also increased its vote and tripled its number of MEPs. This admittedly was just two more MEPs to join Nigel Farage. But it should have been a warning. Labour lost control of thirty-five major councils and 1,239 councillors including friends in Rotherham lost their own council seats. Sheffield now had a Lib-Dem council.

> **Lesson 30**. *With the UK out of Europe winning seats in the European Parliament doesn't matter. Labour never took the EP elections seriously. This was a mistake. Every election counts and should be fought to win. That increases morale and weakens the Tories. Labour over-focuses on the Commons and under resources all other elections.*

Worse for Blair was what happened in London. Labour had promised to give Londoners back some democratic control of their city with a directly elected Mayor. The star politician for London Labour Party activists remained Ken Livingstone who Blair and the ruling New Labour elite distrusted and disliked as much as Margaret Thatcher had.

Ken was an MP by then, producing unreadable economic bulletins written for him by academics, being endlessly provocative and cruelly witty about the government. He and I were invited to debate Europe by the executive committee of the left-controlled Fire Brigades Union. They assumed I would be the pro-European and Livingstone would make the Tony Benn anti-EU case. In fact, Ken outdid me in Europhilia describing Britain as 'a pimple in the armpit of Europe' and urging the swiftest possible adoption of the Euro and passage to a fully federal Europe running affairs in Britain.

He decided to run for Mayor of London. Blair was horrified and pushed Glenda Jackson and Frank Dobson to put themselves up as candidates. Tony of course had supported One Member One Vote, OMOV, as the authentic democratic way of ensuring small left groups lost all power in constituencies or on deciding policy. That had been the demand of the Labour right for twenty years as the way of dealing with the Bennites, Jon Lansman and Ken Livingstone. Now to their dismay they found that due to OMOV the votes cast by Labour Party members in London would endorse their nightmare London Mayor, Ken Livingstone.

They hurriedly cooked up an electoral college to fix the vote for Dobson. Ken announced he would stand as an independent and easily beat Frank to be elected Mayor of London. He was expelled from Labour but was a success as Mayor introducing the congestion charge, copying the free bikes idea of Paris and liberating Trafalgar Square from its snarling polluting traffic by creating a vibrant, colourful event and people-packed pedestrian zone between the National Gallery and Nelson's column.

In Scotland too, the new force in the Scottish Parliament in Holyrood, Edinburgh were tartan nationalists. Labour's efforts to make the governance of Britain more democratic was not being rewarded with votes in the ballot box. The defeats for Labour in 1999 in local elections, in the European Parliament, and for the Mayor of London should have been a warning. How does a party of the left not just win power but stay attractive both to party members and activists but also the wider voting public? The memory of the eighteen Tory years before May

1997 was still overwhelming but the enthusiasm for Labour was wearing off.

I picked up on this in November at the monthly meeting of the Rotherham Labour Party. The secretary, a veteran of decades of loyal Labour service in one of the more deprived wards, said the Labour Party there was completely dead. 'No one comes to any meetings. We appointed an assistant secretary, but I haven't seen him six months. The chairman never talks to me. Most of our members are in their eighties. The new ones want to join the Labour Party but don't want to do any work for it.'

But my mind was elsewhere. Blair had now appointed his fourth Europe minister in two years. None had made a mark. How could we be serious about Europe with this endless turnover of ministers? The tea room was full of chat about Robin being replaced as Foreign Secretary by Peter Mandelson. I went to Italy with Tony for a Third Way conference with Bill Clinton, Lionel Jospin and Gerhard Schröder. The left – or rather the non-conservatives – were everywhere in office but what were we achieving?

## Part 2:
## THE 21$^{ST}$ CENTURY

# 2000s

## 2000

The year began with an interesting New Year's Day exchange about politics and the historical roots of the difference between Labour and Liberals. It was between Jonathan Powell, Tony Blair's chief of staff, and Ralf Dahrendorf, a German politico-sociologist. Ralf had ended up as a fixture on the London intellectual and academic scene as head of the London School of Economics and of St Anthony's College, Oxford's security and foreign policy graduate college. He was a peer, a former European Commissioner and a regular pontificator on European political issues in the broadsheets.

The debate happened in Davos, Switzerland. We were all there at an annual family New Year outing to take part in the British-Swiss parliamentary ski races. Both Swiss and British MPs brought their children along. We paid our own way. The pleasure of skiing hard, good political talks with Swiss ministers and MPs and getting to know Tory MPs made it a great week. Plus the bonus of real quality time with my four children who I patiently taught to ski.

I encouraged Jonathan Powell, his journalist wife, Sarah

Helm, an old friend, and their two girls to come out. Jonathan had done part of his gap year in Davos and loved all mountains anywhere in the world. I invited everyone to dinner and sat back to listen. I noted in my diary:

> Jonathan cross-questions Dahrendorf all the time about what Blair is achieving and Ralf obviously doesn't think very much. At the end of the dinner Jonathan looks across at him and says it surely makes sense to define the 20th century as the Tory century because the progressive forces – that is the Liberals and the Labour Party – had split at the beginning of the century. This is the Andrew Adonis thesis, which lies at the heart of a lot of the historical underpinning of the Third Way.

> 'No, that is complete nonsense,' Dahrendorf insisted. 'The Labour Party, like other social democratic and socialist parties, was set up to respond to the clear material needs, which the Liberal parties were denying existed. It was formed in opposition to the fact that the Liberal parties were allied with the Conservatives. The parties of the left at the beginning of the century represented real material interests. It wasn't an artificial split. In any case, it hasn't been a Conservative century. The welfare state has been introduced and a lot of things that the parties of the left called for have been achieved.'

> Dahrendorf's rigorous dismissal of a core element of the No 10 historical analysis dismayed Jonathan but he

has no real answer to the uncompromising analysis of the famous German professor.

Dahrendorf asked him about the chances of a coalition of Labour and Liberal Democrats. Jonathan was dismissive about the account that had just been published based on Paddy Ashdown's diary that two cabinet posts had been offered to LibDem MPs. 'I was there. I was at all those meetings. Tony made no such pledge. Paddy simply over-read the signals and allusions that Tony was making but there was absolutely no commitment given. Paddy's diaries are completely wrong.'

Dahrendorf asked if a coalition with the LibDems could be possible in the future. 'Maybe after the next election or the election after that, when we have a majority of just one,' Jonathan replied. I said the difficulty with that idea was that forty or fifty Labour MPs would be voting against the government, since in the North the LibDems were now the real enemy and had replaced the Conservatives. Dahrendorf nodded vigorously and I caught a flicker of dismay in Jonathan's eyes as if part of some huge strategy seemed to be put into question by the reality of local politics.

Dahrendorf said he didn't really understand what Blair was up to. 'Gordon Brown is interesting. He is a real intellectual. But they all seem to look to America. It's a very American-influenced government.'

We argued whether not to have held a referendum on Euro entry in October 1997 was a key missed moment. 'You need a referendum because it will set you free. At the moment the UK Government is completely cramped on its Europe policy. Until you win the referendum and restore parliamentary control over the decision-making process you will not be able to move freely on Europe,' Dahrendorf declared.

I told him that I could not agree that given the strength of sterling and the mood of the country we would have won a Euro referendum and even if we had, it would have been at a terrible divisive cost. The good Lord Dahrendorf, a former European Commissioner and for whom Europe underpinned the transformation of Germany into a functioning democracy, was not impressed.

So in January 2020 the status of left parties; electoral alliances; referendums to solve the question of Europe. Even twenty years ago the arguments were stale. The fact that Labour is still having them is an even bigger problem.

Back home it was the usual who's up and who's down on politics. Ken Purchase was a warm working-class Labour MP, a Wolverhampton toolmaker, one of those skilled trained metalworkers smarter than most university-trained politicians. He had a real feel for Labour values. Robin Cook had chosen him as his parliamentary private secretary to maintain a strong link with Labour industrial working-class Midlands network and Ken served him loyally and well.

We hit it off, despite different backgrounds, as I could talk to him about his beloved Wolverhampton Wanderers and drop names like Billy Wright, Derek Dougan, Stan Cullis and Bill McGarry, legendary Wolves managers. We shared the same detestation of the racist poison the Wolverhampton Tory MP Enoch Powell had poured into English politics.

Robin Cook, or rather the Foreign Office, got into trouble over the so-called 'Sandline' affair when a private mercenary organisation called Sandline was involved in helping to restore the democratically elected government in Sierra Leone after it was overthrown in a violent coup, whose leaders enforced discipline by cutting off the arms of the young children of their opponents. The British High Commission had sent compromising cables back to London about its involvement with Sandline to restore democracy. Private initiatives by British diplomats and their ex-army now-mercenary friends came straight out of a John Le Carré novel. The cables were leaked, and the Tories tried to create a story about improper and secretive activities going on under Robin Cook's nose.

He knew nothing, nor did his junior minister, Tony Lloyd about these. I called Tony on a Sunday morning after seeing pictures in the *Sunday Times* of a Sandline helicopter on a Royal Navy frigate. I told Tony to prepare for a row in the Commons the next day. Poor Tony got a very poor brief from officials and made a hash of his explanation in the Commons. The story exploded into a major row. Robin was furious as the heat turned on him for not knowing what was going on in his department. An emergency meeting was called of ministers, including Liz Symonds and all top FCO officials.

I suggested a quick statement-cum-apology in the House and the promise of a full inquiry – the usual government manner of burying a problem. Liz Symonds, who had been head of the First Division Association, the trade union of senior, civil servants, and who still in a sense represented the mandarins, protested. 'I don't know, Robin, if Denis's idea will work. We don't want to push a stick into this hornets' nest and start making it worse.'

Ken Purchase heaved his bulky form up in his seat and putting on an exaggerated Black Country accent said, 'Sorry, Liz but you sound just like one of them Nalgo officials when I was chairman of Wolverhampton Social Services Committee telling me I couldn't hold an investigation into paedophilia.'

Poor Liz crumpled under Ken Purchase's brutal assault. He meant it kindly and Robin also accepted that trying to brush the gaffe away would make matters far worse. It was why ministers have to be elected politicians, not unelected peers or mandarins.

**Lesson 31.** *The politics of government are best handled by elected politicians not unelected peers or outsiders brought is because they had made a name in business. Having a sixth sense that something would blow up into a political and media problem comes with elected political experience. Blair, Brown and David Cameron had a weakness for appointing ministers from the business sector and giving them instant peerages. It was never successful.*

As the new millennium got under way Ken was in a bad mood. 'I am fed up with being Robin's PPS. I don't see any point in my going on. It's useless talking to Robin. He is incapable of working with a team. He now seems to have fallen in love with Caroline Flint as he gets excited at everything she says. I am simply wasting my time. Robin is finished. He won't survive the next election. Oh, I know he has to stay in the Cabinet. He needs the money. But he will do whatever Blair tells him.'

Poor Ken. I noted in my diary,

He is the salt of the old Midlands industrial working class. Aged 60, he must have felt that the driving force of socialist energy that Robin appears to represent would have helped to make this a transformational government. Instead it is a principally transactional government, managing brilliantly, achieving significant progress in areas like the Northern Ireland and the House of Lords, but on core issues that matter to Ken and his world values – good jobs, public services, health, making his community seem fairer – not much is really moving.

# 2001

The year I became a minister. Though winning a second term and then the horror of the Islamist suicide attacks on New York were the overwhelming events. Both changed politics and Labour in ways not yet properly worked through. Labour had held power after second elections in 1950, 1966 and 1974 but all those second-term Labour governments quickly became unhappy and ended in defeat. Even with the divisions over Iraq, Labour remained coherent and pushed forward with progressive reforms including a massive increase in health care spending. Labour then did what it had never done before – win a third term.

I liked becoming a Minister. In fact I had been more often in Downing Street or working on European affairs for Blair than any of his ministers for Europe.

William Hague had turned out to be a completely ineffective leader of the opposition. He was at times the wittiest speaker in the House of Commons but against the rather serious and faux earnest style of Tony Blair, Hague's Oxford union banter with its light, polite delivery and jokes failed to land a punch.

So he decided his best line of attack was to make the Tories the anti-European party in contrast with the pro-European Blair. William Hague called for referendums on the two very minor EU treaties of Amsterdam and Nice, and encouraged senior Tories to indulge in populist anti-European diatribes. David Heathcoat-Amory, a senior Tory MP, wrote a book saying the Treaty of Amsterdam meant the abolition of Britain. This was laughable but set the tone for the later extravagant language of the Brexit debate which carries on to this day. Hague was cheered on by the off-shore owned press like the *Daily Telegraph* and *Daily Mail* and the Murdoch papers.

We edged towards the general election. I published a list of sixty seats where Labour voters could vote tactically to keep a Tory out, with the implication being they should consider voting LibDem. Of course, this provoked a huge stir as it is *verboten* ever to advise tactical voting in Labour and certainly not any votes for the hated Liberal Democrats. There were moans and some snapped comments in the tea room but Sally Morgan, Blair's political secretary, phoned up from Number 10 to say Tony Blair approved of the article, as well he might. In the past Labour had refused to accept the obvious: that there is rarely a majority of votes in Britain for Labour. In 1945 (after a war) and 1966 (after a Tory cock-up) Labour had won but could not win a majority in parliament in subsequent elections. If we wanted to win a good second term after the success of 1997 and in order to hold power under first past the post, then we need as many Tory votes as possible to be siphoned off to the LibDems.

**Lesson 32.** *The debates about electoral reform are eternal. While we wait for enough support to develop to move to a new voting system, at the very least Labour should support what the French call 'republican voting'. That means voting for the best candidate to beat the Tory rightist. If Labour stands a chance of winning, vote Labour. But if that is not the case always better a LibDem, or Green, or independent than another Tory MP.*

Electoral reform was no longer on the agenda but tactical voting should never be off it. I hoped maybe one of the LibDems might come out with a list of seats where LibDem voters could vote Labour to deny a Tory MP a seat. No such luck. The LibDems were never capable of thinking outside their own little box.

I was getting fed up with waiting to be a minister. Four years of working intimately with a sequence of foreign office ministers left me in no doubt I could do the job as well as any of them. I discussed this with Robin Cook as we waited for a meeting to start leaning over the great balustrade looking down the giant FCO staircase.

'I think you should be on the front bench, Denis. I know your name has been considered. I'll certainly have a word about it with Tony. But have you spoken to Anji?'

Anji Hunter was Blair's gatekeeper, a super smart political operator and a warm woman, though I hardly knew her. 'No, but I have good contacts with Jonathan Powell and I will raise it with him,' I replied.

'Call Anji. She's more powerful than Jonathan. You should be on the front bench.'

In the end I did not call Anji partly out of pride, though in politics if you don't ask you don't get. While many were friendly, the courtiers around Blair exuded the sense that there was coterie of gate-keepers who controlled access to the great man and decided so much behind his back. Perhaps it is inevitable but the courts around the Labour leaders I encountered were as much a problem as a protection for the man at the top. Of course as an MP I could see Tony in the Commons. Courteous as he always was, inevitably he was forever rushing from Despatch Box to his office behind the Speaker's chair or rushing for his car to fly somewhere or return to Downing Street his head buried in his red box.

I also enjoyed political networking in Europe. I'd worked hard to help get Robin Cook elected as president of the Party of European Socialists. It was a grand title especially with so many sister parties in government including in France and Germany.

But the Foreign Office was never going to be helpful to a Labour foreign secretary even if he was head of the Federation of the majority of governing parties in Europe. There was no support for Robin. There was no Secretariat. There was no one to work on translation. There was one woman at the Labour Party in charge of all its international relations, and diligent as she was, she spoke few foreign languages.

I kept working hard in the Commons always looking for an opportunity to attack or mock Hague and the Tories. It wasn't hard as they still looked as if they were entitled to be sitting on our benches and running England. It was fun having Brian Wilson, one of the great left journalists of our generation who had set up the *West Highland Free Press*, briefly at the Foreign Office as a minister.

Brian and I had dinner in the Members' Dining Room where anyone sits with anyone. John Battle, the delightful do-gooding cerebral Leeds MP joined us with Kate Hoey, an Ulster unionist. Poor Kate who was already typecast as Labour's most fanatical right-wing anti-European must have seen my face and said, 'I'll have dinner with you, Denis, providing we don't talk about Europe.'

'Fine by me, Kate,' I replied, 'as long as we don't talk about foxhunting.' She was as in favour fox-hunting as she was hostile to Europe and proclaimed support for fox-hunting was the number one topic in her inner-London constituency.

Brian told us a delicious story about an exchange with Margaret Thatcher when both flew out to celebrate the tenth anniversary of the victory over Saddam Hussein after his invasion of Kuwait. 'I'm just sitting down comfortably in first class when suddenly I hear a voice which says "Hello, I am Margaret Thatcher and I hope you enjoyed the celebrations."

'I said yes, and she says, "You know, we should have finished the job ten years ago." I said I agreed with her and added that's what I thought at the time.

'Mrs T continued, "Of course, I was out of office at the time when the decision was taken not to finish off Saddam Hussein."

'And then she looked over her shoulder where John Major was a seat or two behind us and said in voice everybody could hear, "It's so very difficult when the country is led by weak men," she boomed, fixing her gaze on Major. "There is nothing worse than a weak leader. I was very fond of George Bush. A dear man. But weak, terribly weak."'

Back home Blair launched the general election, which thanks to Hague's incompetence as a leader was unlosable. He told us at a weekly meeting of the Parliamentary Labour Party (PLP): 'If we are able to establish on our own merit that we can win this election – not because people don't like the Tories – if we can get elected on our own merits, we can change our governing philosophy. This election, if we win it and the people choose us, because they like the way we have governed the country, we can lay a foundation for progressive politics.

'That is the biggest prize of all: outward looking and racially tolerant. We are fighting for a value system. We've now got a Labour party completely different from the one that was there when I entered Parliament.

'We understand the need for a balance between enterprise and fairness but I want to win a bigger battle. I want to win a battle to change the values which govern our country. What kind of people do we want to be under a Labour government? I want a Labour government that ushers in 21st century progressive politics.'

It was 'the vision thing' as George Bush Senior said. His inability to articulate one helped Clinton to bring him down. Journalists are a cynical lot and resist the vision thing, finding it glib and unconvincing. But I don't see how politics can be done without vision. We have to know where we're going to and why. We need a clarity of ideas and principles that can be readily communicated to the public so that they know them too. If not, governance is just management. And even then, management has principles.

Just before the election was announced I was told to go on BBC Radio 4 Today programme to make the case for tactical voting. Perhaps it worked. The LibDem vote rose to 4.8 million votes and fifty-two MPs. Labour lost just five seats, down to 413 and Hague's Tories were stuck in the doldrums. Between them Labour and the LibDems won 15.5 million votes nearly twice as many as the Conservatives. If this voting alliance could have been sustained the Tories would be out of power for a long time. Tony Blair and Charlie Kennedy were like an older and kid brother. When the much more posh Nick Clegg came along, his natural sibling was David Cameron, both sharing a similar background of wealth and privilege.

On the Monday after the election I get a call from Blair inviting me to join the government as a Foreign Office minister. It was the lowest rank, Parliamentary Under Secretary, but that didn't matter as I was now a minister, with staff, a car and driver, and that most prized possession of anyone in the Commons, a red box. John Kerr, the FCO's Permanent Under Secretary, a chain-smoking brilliant diplomat, an Oxford educated Scot, deeply cynical and deeply pro-European called me up. He is already cheerful as his arch-enemy Robin Cook has gone. Two clever, cocky Scots who were always convinced they could never be wrong were not made for each other.

'Look, Denis, you speak Spanish, so you had better do Latin America. You know Hong Kong and have worked in Japan so you can have the Far East and Australia. But you'll have to have one tricky area – the Middle East or the West Balkans'

I went straight for the West Balkans as this was one of Europe's problem areas. The Middle East nations and peoples – Israel, Palestine, Syria, Iraq, Lebanon, the Gulf kingdom and emirates – were a nightmare of hates and bad politics. I could see nothing that a junior FCO minister might do that would be of any use at all.

Jack Straw, the new Foreign Secretary, who I didn't really know and had never come across much in all my years working on political campaigns, was warm and welcoming. I knew his Eurosceptic reputation, but I found a very hard-working, courteous, friendly man – a seasoned, expert Parliamentarian, a few years older than I. He had none of the intellectual all-round political vision of Robin Cook but then none of Robin's Lone Ranger failings and quirks.

Robin became Leader of the House. Addressing the PLP, he promised reforms of how Parliament worked and a radical legislative programme. He was cheered to every corner of Committee Room 14. Afterwards, he told me his dismissal from the Foreign Office came as a shock even though Keith Vaz had warned me two months ago Straw would become Foreign Secretary and Robin Leader of the House.

'I didn't have any inkling at all it was going to happen. Nor did Jack. His Special Branch people were already in place at the DETR (the Department of the Environment, Transport and the Regions which Straw was initially told he would run). So there was no bad faith. I don't know what the reason was or even who decided. I think it was Tony, Alistair (Campbell) and Anji (Hunter) late on Thursday night or Friday morning.

'It was the sheer brutality of it. I spent Friday in a state of complete shock. By Saturday it had turned to bitterness and I was almost ready to give it all up and go back to the back benches. But I have seen too many people in this place become so bitter when they give up the chance of doing anything as a matter of protest. I had a very icy call with Tony. I told him that it was no way to run a government to abruptly on the spur of the moment make decisions and announcements like this.'

I was sad for Robin, but politics does not spend any time on commiseration. For one politician to move up, another has to move down. It is age-old law and won't change.

I plunged into my new role, taking every opportunity to travel to the parts of the world I was nominally responsible for at the FCO. My Spanish helped in Bogota and Caracas. My support for taking on Milosevic helped in Pristina and Sarajevo. My forays once or twice a year to Hong Kong meant I was at home in that extraordinary place.

I went to Australia for the second time in my life and loved it – who doesn't? We flew back home from Perth via Singapore on 11<sup>th</sup> September. As we disembarked at Changi Airport there was complete chaos. Business professionals were screaming down their mobiles. Two giant TV screens up in the long hallway showed some skyscraper on fire. Then a small image in the corner of the screen, a plane, banked and flew straight into another identical skyscraper.

I recognized the twin towers of the World Trade Centre in Manhattan. What had happened? No one knew. The first-class lounge was full of passengers trying to talk to New York, many in tears as phones thousands of miles away refused to answer.

Thus the 21st century begun. As an observer-participant in some big moments of history – the Portuguese carnation revolution in 1974, or the moment of Polish Solidarnosc in 1980, or the end of apartheid and Sovietism ten years later, and even the historic Labour win of 1997 – it was always a thrill to be present as an activist and witness. But this was something else. The world from my Singapore vantage point had changed, changed utterly. Unlike Yeats I knew a terribly ugly evil was being born.

# 2002

On the way back from an away day at Chevening all the FCO ministers including myself were told to avoid central London as there were anti-capitalist demonstrations. I just wanted to join in. Why was it impossible under Labour to say aloud that capitalism, the brand espoused by Thatcher and Reagan, by the City and Wall Street, still did so much damage? It needed reform, reform, reform. Gordon and his team seemed to have been captured by the classical Manchester liberals of the Treasury who despised Keynes and wouldn't let a radical idea loose in Whitehall.

**Lesson 33.** *Her Majesty's Treasury is the beating heart of the British conservative state. It attracts the best and the brightest from Eton and Oxbridge though now and then it does a little demotic and let's in a state-educated clever clog. It runs Britain for its own meritocratic class and their interests. Occasionally, at moments when the need for new thinking is unstoppable as after 1945 the Treasury thinks afresh. Most of the time and certainly during the Blair-Brown government it made ministers conform to Treasury orthodoxy. Making the Treasury work for all of Britain is Labour's biggest challenge.*

I put a lot of effort into the local elections in Rotherham. It seemed only fair as the support of Labour friends and comrades meant I was enjoying one of the most privileged and satisfying periods of work in my life. But the Labour Party was changing. My Rotherham Central seat contained most of the town's 9,000 strong Kashmiri population. The vocabulary of immigration in Britain is simplistic to the point of caricature. While we are conscious of the difference between Scots and Welsh, between someone from Yorkshire and someone from Devon, or can recognise a London, Birmingham or Geordie accent, immigrants were lumped together as 'Asian' or with the ugly derogatory term 'Paki'. Later the clunky describer BAME became modish.

Most of so-called Pakistani immigrants came from Kashmir which has its own identity and where people speak Mirpuri, a distinct language, even if they can read Urdu.

Naturally enough some of the younger Kashmiri men gravitated to politics and sought election as councillors. They ran as Labour because Labour controlled Rotherham council, awarded taxi and mini-cab driver licences, decided on planning permission to make money from building, enlarging or renting out houses and allowed Baptist chapels to be converted to mosques.

I liked them and having already dedicated part of my political energy to combatting racism, especially in the media, many of their causes were my own. But I found it hard to handle the treatment of women. The wife of Rotherham's Kashmiri peer, Lord Nazir Ahmed, could not read or write and signed her name with a X. She had been brought over to marry Nazir as a teenager. Surely, she might have been allowed to learn spoken and written English?

Another energetic young Kashmiri councillor would invite me in for a cup of tea. We would sit in the large living room with chairs around all the wall and he would call out 'Tea!' A panel would open in the wall and a hand would hold out my cup of tea. Mahroof was in his thirties, well educated and already spotted by the Labour Party and other government bodies as an up-and-coming future leader sent off to America and on other trips to broaden his horizons. I liked him but could not quite handle the invisible wife at home who never came out to join in anything Labour was doing.

This is where identity and tradition crash into hard fought

values of human rights and equal opportunity. I have always found it bizarre that good men in the Labour party would willingly go to the wall for the rights of the oppressed around the world, but look away as women are systematically shunted aside in our own communities. Even raising the issue made me uncomfortable. And yet, that hand reaching through a partition to pass me a cuppa felt even more uncomfortable.

There were disturbing reports from Leeds University researchers of higher levels of disability in some of the children arising from these cousin marriages. Once, discussing this with Jack Straw and senior FCO officials in the Foreign Office, I suggested that one way to speed up community integration was to ban cousin marriage, as is the norm in twenty-four America states and some countries. A very senior FCO official replied: 'Yes, banning cousin marriages might help with our Pakistani community but you don't think it might prove a problem for the royal family?' I gave up even thinking about the idea.

In the local elections, Labour did well. In my constituency, it was Kashmiri councillors who were elected. The older, white activists shrugged their shoulders but were uneasy as control of the party was slipping into the hands of men and women whose values and language and views on gays or secularism or Jews or women were not those of traditional Labour. But the LibDems lost control of Sheffield and for many defeating the LibDems gave more pleasure than defeating Tories. Personally, I had no problems with LibDems winning seats as they did in Liverpool. The main opponent of progress and social justice was the Conservative Party. If LibDems won Tory seats, that was fine by me.

Everyone could sense the drift to war in Iraq. I sat in on the debate in the Commons on the famous dossier justifying a strong line against Saddam. I heard William Hague tell MPs that it was clear Saddam Hussein had weapons of mass destruction. I wasn't clear this was the case but assumed Hague, as a former party leader and cabinet minister, had access to secret state information and knew more than I did. This was reinforced by other conversations from people outside the government. In Stockholm, at a lunch soon after I became Europe Minister in the autumn, the head of the Swedish intelligence agency assured everyone that Saddam had such weapons. I thought that if neutral, cautious Sweden, which trades into every corner of the world, thought that then maybe Saddam did.

Regardless of whether Saddam had these weapons or not, the UK's embrace of Washington's panting desire for a full-scale invasion to replace the Iraqi government damaged Labour's standing in Europe. The hope of creating a pan-European reformist network of progressive governments, which seemed so high at the beginning of the century, took another blow when the French socialist prime minister, Lionel Jospin, was beaten in the presidential election in May by Jean-Marie Le Pen, the leader of the racist Europhobe *Front National*.

I was tipped off by a political insider friend in Paris that the result of the first round of the two-round presidential election would see Jospin eliminated. I called Jonathan Powell to tell Tony. Both were utterly shocked. Le Pen was an anti-Semite, a racist and a crude populist – such as we had not thought possible to emerge to challenge the centre-right president, Jacques Chirac. It was the emergence of the new populist, identity-based, Brussels-denigrating, xenophobe politics in Europe. Soon enough it arrived chez nous.

I would spend the next decade or so representing Blair and Labour in Europe working with sister parties and like-minded comrades, speaking and writing where- and whenever. But finding the holy grail of a common centre-left programme proved elusive.

Labour couldn't do much as we had no money to spend on any international travel or networking. Such as I did was at the edge of what parliamentary expenses permitted, but at least I wasn't fiddling like so many other MP friends, who boasted openly about buying and selling houses in the rising London property market, using their MPs' allowances or putting endless family members on the parliamentary payroll. These actions are simply illegal in most democracies but in the House of Commons are permitted as a way of padding out salaries.

Labour had a golden opportunity in the anger over Tory sleaze and dubious political party financing under John Major to clean up all the rackets and get democracy to pay for democracy, as was the norm in most countries – except of course in the United States. In democracy after democracy, parties – right as much as left – had given up crawling after big money funding but instead agree that a grant from the government – completely transparent and with every penny accounted for – was a better way of paying for democracy. There was much that Labour did after 1997 which any Labour Party member could take pride in. But the refusal to end the practice of big money paying for politics was a considerable failure. The one miserable little bill we got passed barely moved the dial except to stipulate that donations should be published, as if that made any difference.

Now that I was a minister I was invited to more and more events where politicians gather with everything paid for by the rich. On a summer weekend it was down to some Rothschild manor where Bill Clinton turned up and did a Third Way star turn. His combination of laser-like intellectual insight and folksy storytelling was compelling, and I could see how he'd risen to the presidency of the United States. But I lived in Europe. Britain could not escape its geography. Top left intellectuals and party officials were also invited from France, Italy, Sweden and Germany although Tony Blair made clear he had no interest in working with or through the existing structures for democratic left party work, like the Socialist International or the Party of European Socialists.

I shared his frustration at the talking-shop nature of these outfits, but progressive politics is not going to arise from a gathering in luxurious surroundings of a self-selecting group of individuals paid to spend a weekend together by a multi-billionaire whose hobby is politics.

And then there were the Royals. One MP's perk – if that is the right term – was to get tickets for Labour party members to attend the Buckingham Palace Garden Parties if they so desired. It is an utterly boring event unless you like cucumber sandwich with the crusts cut off, or little cakes with too much sugary pink icing. This year my agent, Anna Chester, the best person any Labour MP could wish for, was there with another friend, Dominic Shellard, a gay professor of English at Sheffield University who was also a Labour councillor in Rotherham.

They told of a wonderful exchange between Prince Edward, the Queen's youngest son. The Prince asked a man, 'So where do you come from?'

'From Sheffield."

'Oh, that's in the north isn't it? What's it like?'

As the person the Royal was talking to did not know what to say, Edward went on. 'And what does your wife do?' he said indicating the woman beside the man.

'She's a teacher.'

'In a private school?'

For Anna and Dominic it was all they needed to hear to confirm everything they'd already thought about the royals.

On a plane to Mexico for a ministerial visit I bumped into an old Oxford acquaintance, Gyles Brandreth, who had turned himself into a one-man campaign to cheer up the nation. He had been a Tory MP 1992-1997 and remained a very witty speaker. We gossiped on the plane over a drink and I said I had seen the Queen the previous week and she looked very good for her age with excellent legs.

I forgot that dear old Gyles would dig up and sell his late granny to get a story in the press. Nonetheless I was alarmed to read in the *Daily Telegraph* his account of our conversation and my views on the shapeliness of Her Majesty's legs. My heart shrunk. Talking out of school about the Queen was the worst possible crime for an FCO minister. I went into the Foreign Office and saw officials turning their faces from me in horror at what I had done.

I knew the Queen's private secretary as a friend and neighbour with a house in France close to where I often stayed. I called him in a panic. 'Robin, Robin', I stuttered but he interrupted me. 'Don't say anything, Denis. Her Majesty says this is the nicest thing ever said about her by one of her ministers.' Phew.

The year ended badly. Our natural partners in Europe – Germany and France – as well as all our sister parties and governments with the left in charge or in coalition were adamantly opposed to any action to deal with Saddam. But Blair was equally adamant Britain had to follow the lead of George W. Bush, Dick Cheney and John Bolton.

The arguments are over now. Iraq was a disaster.


# 2003

Just six years into the Labour government and things weren't going well. No one in 1997 could have imagined we would be sucked into our own version of the Vietnam war. But that's hindsight. At the time, it didn't seem so problematic.

Saddam seemed like another Slobodan Milosevic. These were the kind of monsters Labour had used military force to intervene against on humanitarian grounds and depose. Everyone would have preferred a UN resolution as cover to take action. But equally all but the most obdurate knew that a UN resolution was not possible as China and Russia would impose their veto. Both countries under their respective authoritarian leaderships saw the United States as a foe to be challenged. Neither would join in concerted international pressure to face down a Saddam, a Slobodan, or any genocidal mass-murdering despot, sponsor of terrorism or practitioner of torture.

Then there was the problem of proving a negative. How could one demonstrate beyond doubt that Saddam Hussein did not have weapons of mass destruction? He had used them in the form of chemical gas bombs to murder 5,000 Iraqi Kurds in Halabja in 1988. A further 10,000 were injured.

Italy, Spain, Portugal and the democracies in East Europe were with Blair and Bush. But public opinion wasn't. The politics of it were miserable. I had castigated the weakness of the Major government and ministers like the Foreign Secretary, Malcolm Rifkind, for sitting on the side-lines and refusing to take action to stop mass murder and terror in the Balkans or in Rwanda. Liberal intellectuals like Michael Ignatieff, the Canadian professor and Channel 4 TV presenter, developed the concept of The Responsibility to Protect based on the French ideas of *Le Droit d'Ingérence* (the Right to Intervene later called the Right to Protect R2P in UN jargon) developed by the French socialist minister, Bernard Kouchner, an intellectual and doctor who was one of the founders of *Médécins sans Frontières*.

That right to intervene under international law to stop a greater evil was invoked by Blair in Kosovo, Sierre Leone and Indonesia. Simple to say but often a judgment call. What's the greater evil and on what basis is that judgement reached? These are the troublesome questions that Iraq raised with only imperfect answers possible. In the end the judgement of history, whose scales always oscillate, condemned both the non-intervention of John Major in the middle 1990s and the intervention of Blair a few years later. Success in geo-politics has many parents. Failure is blamed on whoever is in power.

Curiously, at the time the vote on Iraq seemed less than dramatic. I attended nearly every Commons debate or vote on Iraq including the big one in March 2003. 412 MPs, including myself and most of the existing cabinet, and future prime ministers like David Cameron, Theresa May, and Boris Johnson voted to intervene against Saddam. About a quarter of Labour's tally of MPs voted against. They ranged from sour Europe-hating right-wingers like Kate Hoey to the lifelong endlessly polite and cheerful left-winger Jeremy Corbyn. There was no rancour in the Chamber and division lobbies.

Jack Straw had invited his wife, Alice, and their two student-aged children to his room where we all drank red wine after the vote. It was not a celebration. Had the vote gone the other way, both Straw and Tony Blair would have resigned. We did not know then how badly Iraq would turn out. The drink was more one of relief that the government was still there.

**Lesson 34.** *Try not to do war. If a Labour government must do one it has to have majority support, rid the world of some evil, and above all win. All wars are bad for Labour. One that a Labour government loses is a disaster.*

I had suggested we copy the French and hold an annual gathering of all British ambassadors in a conference at the Foreign Office, a kind of giant away-day. It worked well. Blair told a sweet story about what our diplomats have to do. He described arriving for some overseas trip after an overnight flight. He was in jeans and a t-shirt with all his clothes in a suitcase in the hold. To his horror he saw through the window as the plane taxied, a red carpet, a military band and a full government reception party waiting for him. Someone called down to one of the local British diplomats about Blair's size in the receiving line.

The young man was ordered on to the plane.

'Good morning, Prime Minister. What can I do for you.?

'You can start by taking your clothes off,' Blair recounted. 'He didn't blink and said, "Righty oh," in as jaunty a way as could be imagined,' Blair said, as the ambassadors purred with contentment at having a prime minister who appreciated the crazy thing diplomats do in the service of their country.

Blair argued for a close relationship with both America and Europe. On Europe he told the ambassadors, 'For fifty years we hesitated over Europe. We have never known how to profit from our membership.' And on America, 'We are close to the United States not because they are powerful but because many of their values are our values.'

It remains unclear to me which values are uniquely shared between a British centre-left government and the USA that are not also shared with our European allies. One of our smartest diplomats, John Holmes, who had been head of the Downing Street foreign policy secretariat and was now ambassador to France was blunt. He told Blair to his face that the perception everywhere in Europe was that Britain was too close to the United States – i.e. Bush's poodle – and 'could not the Prime Minister make it clearer at times that Britain divided sharply from the US on a number of key issues?'

Blair looked up at his former private secretary and laughed. 'I see you're getting quite close to the French, John,' he said. But he then fumbled and hesitated and used all his little 'I mean', 'you know', and 'well, well, well' verbal ticks as he didn't really have an answer.

Without exception my Muslim political friends were hostile to the war in Iraq. How dare we contemplate bombing a Muslim country? I asked them if they had objected to bombing a Christian city like Belgrade to stop the massacre of Muslims in Kosovo and Bosnia? They fell silent. I wasn't making debating points. This was never a politics I had imagined being involved in. I had little respect for some of the leaders of the Stop the War coalition who excused the behaviour of some of the foulest regimes on earth as long as the leaders of those countries denounced western democracy.

The LibDem leader Charlie Kennedy was putting himself at the head of the anti-war marches. Fair enough. But there had been no one keener than his predecessor, Paddy Ashdown, in calling for heavy military intervention by the West in the Balkans and in other instances. The LibDem foreign affairs spokesman, Menzies 'Ming' Campbell, son-in-law of a general who had parachuted at the head of his men into Arnhem, was also robust on the use of force to uphold democracy.

The war with Iraq would go on to break the Labour government, destroy Blair's reputation and put a dent in the R2P doctrine. And perhaps that was a good thing. When you declare war, maybe there should be a blowback powerful enough to bring down the mighty.

The facts on the ground changed my opinion about the

war. To quote John Maynard Keynes, when the facts change, I change my mind. I decided that Iraq, along with nearly every northern (I prefer that term to western to include Russia) military intervention from Kabul in 1979 to Kurdistan in Iraq in 2003 and Syria after 2011, had ended in disaster for the both the interveners and the local habitants. We had liberated the Kosovans from the brutality, ethnic cleansing and murders of its colonial Serb masters, and had stopped the Indonesian army from running amok. But I never would have argued for an armed intervention against the apartheid regime and its racist cruelties in South Africa. Nor against the evil anti-Semitic religious dictatorship in Iran.

I later wrote my *mea culpa* in *Le Monde* and in the *Independent*. What I could not believe was the stupidity of David Cameron, Nick Clegg and William Hague in making exactly the same error in Libya and Syria as Blair had in Iraq. Churchill did not do the Dardanelles twice. Nor did Macmillan repeat Eden's folly at Suez.

Then back to Europe. I went to the Treasury and had a long talk with Gordon Brown. I noted in my diary:

The first thing that struck me is how much he had let his body go. His stomach was bursting at his rather grubby white shirt buttons and his face was heavy with jowls and drooping flesh like a jockey who had been told to carry all sorts of extra weight. His hands were now back to their nail bitten state. We were in a funny little ante-chamber to his office with some easy chairs. He sat on a sofa in front of a coffee table covered with papers marked with yellow post-its.

'I am pro-European, Denis,' he said. 'The political case for Europe has been met. I think the economic tests have been passed. But is the country ready for Europe yet? Does the country feel that European values are our values? Do they see Europe still as being too corporatist and capitalist and not really embracing British values?'

I reeled back mentally. Was Gordon seriously saying Nordic Europe, or German social democratic Europe, or socially progressive statist France were too capitalist compared to Britain, which had destroyed manufacturing and mutually owned economic enterprise to worship at the shrine of finance capitalism which, he, Gordon, had not challenged?

To be fair he urged me to make the case for Europe so that Britain would see its values as being in line with those of Europe.

'It's not the economic case we have to make really, it's the political case. People will vote Yes in a referendum on economic grounds but then they will vote No on political grounds because they don't trust Europe and they don't see Europe as being in line with British values. That's what we have to change,' Brown said.

Those were powerful arguments and I said to him they needed to be advanced. Of course, I did not want to say that you can't persuade the British to like

Europe if people like the Chancellor, especially a good and popular one like Brown, never made the case for Europe. I am not allowed to be impertinent. 'Well, I am thinking of making a speech on Europe. I am not sure yet but maybe I need to say something,' he grunted.

Of course, the speech was never made. The next moment with Brown was in a meeting in the cabinet room with Blair to discuss ideas emerging from the convention on the next EU Treaty. There was some early talk of electing the President of the European Commission. Brown was adamantly opposed. 'He will simply become a prisoner of vested interests in the European Parliament. We cannot allow this to happen. If the president of the Commission is elected, he will no longer be independent. If that happens, I insist that we demand that the work of the Commission to do with competition policy, state aids and fiscal oversight is handed straight over to independent agencies. It will be impossible to work with an elected president of the Commission in these areas,' Gordon insisted. I noted,

Blair looked at him with amazement and eyes glanced left and right across the table as officials listened to this drivel. In the end Blair lowered his glasses a bit on his nose and looked at Gordon and said, 'Well, I really don't think we are going to be able to re-open the question of some form of election for the President of the Commission, Gordon. That's already been agreed. I really don't think we are going to be able to go back on that.'

While I was enjoying parleying with Brown and Blair in the cabinet room, Labour Party membership was shrinking – down twenty per cent in Rotherham. For all that, Labour did OK in the municipal elections in May. Blair was in command at Parliamentary Labour meetings. Iraq had not yet turned into the gruesome spectacle of a religious civil war it was soon to become. The European Union has been enlarged to take in eight new members. The 1945 Yalta division of Europe had been healed.

The Conservatives were in no better shape than when led by William Hague. Winding up for the Government in a Europe debate I described the new Tory leader Michael Howard as 'unwelcome in Europe, unwanted in America and unelectable in Britain' which got a great cheer from our benches. Labour won the vote by 491 as the anti-European Tories just slunk away. Jack Straw patted me on the thigh and said it was the biggest ever majority for the Labour government since 1997.

Blair got a standing ovation at the Labour Party conference in September. His decline into unpopularity over Iraq was not immediate. The autumn was taken up with the tragedy of Dr David Kelly, a government scientist, who had unwisely spoken off-the-record to a BBC freelance reporter called Andrew Gilligan, later close to Boris Johnson. There was an almighty fuss with the Director General of the BBC having to resign, a committee of inquiry be set up, and in due course, Alistair Campbell left Downing Street.

Blair was defended by the veteran left-wing MP Dennis Skinner at the routine PLP meeting on Monday at 6 p.m. Skinner told Labour MPs: 'Kelly should have been sacked.

We can now see that what he did would have got anybody in local government dismissed out of hand. Let's be honest. Spinning is a good thing. We have to get over our arguments. All great politicians have had spin doctors – Thatcher, Churchill, Gladstone. I reckon spinning started with Jesus Christ. He had twelve spinners working for him.'

I was stunned as Dr Kelly seemed a decent man even if the journalist who made him famous had just been over-keen to get his story. For Skinner to gloat over the establishment's treatment of a scientist whistle-blower was wrong. Nonetheless Skinner got his laugh and cheers, and Blair was off the hook at least as far as that Monday night gathering of Labour MPs was concerned. The Skinner-Blair relationships was one of the more curious all through the Labour government. Dennis was a legend of the militant left. But he wanted a Labour government more than anything else. Blair had delivered that. So, Dennis Skinner became Tony Blair's biggest champion in the tea room and the Monday evening meetings of Labour MPs.

I got into my own trouble a bit later on. I made what I thought was a banal speech to my constituency in which I urged British Muslims to turn away from the growing force and magnetic appeal of Islamist ideology and its hate of the west and of Jews, and its support for violent action. I was inspired by the sad case of a young man from nearly Sheffield who had been groomed by Islamists to go out and kill Jews in Israel. He killed himself but it was an early sign of a new evil that would grow.

I had not seen or heard the slightest evidence of support from the 9,000 strong Muslim, mainly Kashmiri community in Rotherham about any extremism or support for violence. My speech was not aimed at them but when it went out on press agencies all hell let loose. London-based Islamist activists denounced me as a racist. The BBC's World at One devoted most of a programme to make various attacks on me. The *Observer* carried a whole page attack on me by the former students' union leader, Trevor Phillips, who was never short of quotes to get himself headlines.

Back in the Commons MPs quietly said, well done. I met Britain's most famous soldier, General Sir Mike Jackson, at a Foreign Press Award reception and he said: 'Well done, Minister. It's about time someone spoke out on the issue.' I didn't see myself as speaking out but just worried at the rise of Islamist ideology and its insidious grooming of so many young British minds.

General Jackson added, 'We've got plenty of them in the Army, some damn fine chaps serving in Iraq. But we need to get their leaders to speak out against terrorism. Prince Charles is very keen on all of this. I was with him yesterday going through the changes in the Army and he was banging on about the need to get more Blacks and Muslims and I said to him: 'Look here, Sir, we are doing our best, we've got some officers now in the Household Division and a lot more coming along.' He asked me why there couldn't be a regiment of Sikhs a bit like there is a regiment of Gurkhas. Completely batty. What on earth am I meant to do? I told him that the Gurkhas were all recruited in Nepal but how on earth am I going to go up to Wolverhampton to recruit a regiment of Sikhs?'

# 2004

The worst year of my life. My first daughter, Clare, born in 1979, was killed in a stupid sky-diving accident in Australia. I got the news at the March spring Labour conference in Manchester. I had gone there from a giant march of solidarity in Madrid for the 1000 victims of an Islamist bomb that exploded at Madrid's main railway station.

I gave a speech about Europe to the plenary on a Sunday and as I came off the platform I checked voice-mail to hear the broken voice of Carol Barnes, Clare's mother, saying, 'I have some terrible news about Clare.'

There is only one kind of terrible news about a twenty-five-year old. She had been killed in a sky-diving accident near Melbourne, Australia. Carol and I had separated in a friendly enough way after I began working in Geneva, not long after Clare's birth. But I came home most weekends to take part in political activity and always saw Clare. She came to stay with me, and became a big sister to my three daughters and son and was utterly part of the family. She stayed with my mother in Glasgow, came on holidays in France and Italy and on walks up Mont Blanc with me. Now she was dead.

She wasn't made for conventional life and loved to travel. She met up with a charismatic man whose passion was sky-diving so it became hers. They had split up but still lived in a communal house. She had little money and her kit was made from different parachutes and harnesses.

I poured myself into my ministerial car in Manchester and headed south. Jack Straw was first on my mobile to tell me to get out to Australia and the Foreign Office would lay on all support out there. Then Cherie followed by Tony came on and both found good words as I went down the M6.

I had to tell Clare's grandmother now approaching 90 and not in great shape. And her half-sisters and brother. Every thought of every sort went through my mind. Children should not die before their parents. Carol and I were numb on the BA flight out.

In Melbourne we went to see the field into which she plunged and scattered arms full of white flowers over the dry, dead grass. We went to the mortuary where I held the tiny frozen hand of my dead daughter for the last time. The funeral and cremation were done well by two gay Anglican priests and the warmth of Australia and Australians helped in our grief. We brought her ashes home and I have never been back to Australia.

When a tragedy like this happens I doubt if there is a better place to be working than as an MP in the House of Commons. MPs reach out with a giant collective embrace as one of their number is wounded. The work expands to fill the day. Many MPs have also lost children and part of our life is to reach and empathise, as well as one can, to constituents who face sudden loss.

My MP friends knew how to keep talking about politics, as did my officials in the Foreign Office, and Jack Straw whose kindness I shall never forget. I went up and down to my constituency and again everyone in Rotherham enveloped me in South Yorkshire affection. Letters of condolence came in from the German chancellor, Gerhard Schöder. Other prime ministers on the centre-left of European politics who had become friends sent letters as well as the network of foreign ministers headed by Dominique de Villepin, the flamboyant and endlessly book-writing Foreign Minister of France.

But something left me. Politics never stops for death of any sort. I went to work but I paid less and less attention. An MP had to fill in endless forms to claim all sorts of moneys to do the job and I just filled in the forms and got the money without paying any attention to what I was claiming or why.

There were ministerial problems to sort out. The biggest was the management of the enlargement of the European Union. London and other cities in Britain, indeed all the capital cities of Europe, were awash with energetic young men and women from Poland or Slovakia or Lithuania doing every job under the sun with more energy, drive and often better skills than the local natives. The East Europeans in the EU could travel to West Europe as tourists after the end of communist control of their countries after 1990. It was the least the West could so. To demand entry visas applied for in advance of a trip to London from fellow Europeans was unthinkable. Ryanair and Easyjet were flying eight times a day to Polish and East European cities with the planes packed in both directions.

Once in London or Berlin or Paris, these young East Europeans could, if they chose to, disappear into the informal cash-in-hand employment market. I had had work done in my house, some solid book shelves put up by a young Polish carpenter. Other friends hired young East European women as mother's helps. Britain in particular demanded no proof of identity from anyone in the country. Unlike other European democracies we did not an identity card system. Unlike other European democracies we did have free health care. Anyone could register with a GP or turn up at hospital. Millions of non-Brits from Ireland, Pakistan or India had already taken advantage of the uniquely British approach of requiring no proof of ID or a record of insurance contributions to access the NHS, education or any social welfare benefits.

The eight new EU member states could be subject to a seven-year transition period before their citizens enjoyed the full rights of all citizens of an EU member state to travel, live, study, work or even retire freely without a visa or special permit in another EU member states. Some countries like France and Germany applied that seven-year transition period. Germany rendered it pointless by passing in 2004 an 'Immigration Law' that granted to employers pretty much the right to hire anyone they wanted from the new EU member states. France was Number One tourist destination for the Francophile Poles and other East Europeans, and French farmers, the restaurants, hotels and cafés and French tourist sites all relied on East European workers even if technically France was applying a seven-year transition.

In Whitehall there was as struggle as to whether Britain should apply the seven-year transition or just accept the reality that hundreds of thousands of Poles and other East European were here, their friends would come, they ensured that thousands of small British firms remained profitable without relocating production to cheaper low-pay areas like Turkey, North Africa or Asia. The new European arrivals would rent homes from British landlords, pay tax and National Insurance, do their shopping, eat out and drink in British supermarkets, restaurants and pubs as had white, Catholic immigrants. Rather like the Irish in the 20th century, they would fit in well with the local population.

Jack Straw was hostile, as were many MPs friends who were already picking up Powellite xenophobia encouraged by Tory leaders like Michael Howard, as well as the nationalist populists of UKIP and the BNP. I argued inside government this was a moment to reform the workings of the labour market so that more British workers could be trained for jobs that skilled East European craftworkers snapped up, that workplace inspections and union rights should be strengthened, that the NHS should train more young Brits to be doctors and nurses, and that identity cards should become routine. I was pissing in the wind as no one in the neoliberal Treasury wanted any restraint or social responsibility requirement to be placed upon Thatcherised Britain.

The whole world seemed to be on the move. Travel across frontiers was just a matter of paying some money. Everyone could see on the internet the attractiveness of the western way of life. Since the 1980s Britain had stopped training and turned to imported workers to make up the gap. During the height of the 1980s unemployment, British workers went as illegal immigrants to find work in Germany giving rise to the '*Auf Wiedersehen,* Pet' TV comedy series.

The European Parliament election in June reflected this mood shift. The Tories led by a now rabidly anti-immigrant Michael Howard overtook Labour but actually lost MEP seats which went to UKIP. Labour got only a million more votes than

UKIP and the new anti-immigrant xenophobe party was firmly established thanks to a clumsy proportional representation system for electing MEPs that Jack Straw had devised when Home Secretary.

Selling Europe was proving impossible. I expected nothing from the Murdoch papers, the *Daily Telegraph, Express* or *Daily Mail,* but was disappointed that many of the *Guardian's* core correspondents were hostile to Europe. The paper published endless inaccurate attacks on the new constitutional Treaty including one from the general secretaries of two powerful unions, the TGWU and AEEU.

> **Lesson 35.** *Labour cannot rely on any newspaper to be fair and accurate in its political coverage. It needs its own channels of communication to party members and potential voters. Not many Labor voters read the Telegraph or Mail but the constant attacks on Labour in the Guardian demoralize progressives.*

In the late 1980s the Thatcher government had spent £25 million in public information campaigns to promote the European Single Market. Boris Johnson spent ten times that amount to promote Brexit Britain in 2020-21. My budget as Europe minister to explain the EU to Britain had just been cut to £150,000 as no one in Gordon Brown's Treasury had any interest in the EU which was just seen as an irritation and source of problems.

I met and had a long talk with Joe Biden who came to a European conference as Chair of the US Senate's Foreign

Affairs Committee. He told me how he began life defending Black Panthers in Delaware and I told him about my radical youth organising NUJ strikes. He said he wanted America and Europe to come together but it was going to genuinely difficult with Bush.

'Condi Rice will be the new Secretary of State. But she will take all her orders directly form Cheney. They will be worse than this administration. Colin Powell has lost all influence with the president. He never gets to talk to him and Bush just isn't interested in listening to him anymore.'

He added that Powell could have had a restraining hand on the administration's rush to military action in 2002 and 2003 but that the 4-star general, the first African-American to command the US military, was too much of a loyal soldier to challenge the elected president.

I found Biden the easiest US politician I'd ever talked to. We were both basically 1968 generation political activists who had been elected – him much earlier than me – and were still active trying to make sense of the fast-changing world.

The Labour Party conference was an anti-climax. Blair made the most pedestrian speech of his leadership. Jack Straw defended Iraq, and a resolution opposing the war and calling for troops to come home was defeated 8-1. But many constituency parties had not bothered to send a delegate and MPs were thin on the ground. The party wasn't over but it had lost its fizz.

# 2005

Once again like a smelly overflowing sewer, the noxious Enoch-Powellite politics of immigration was put back into our political life.

In a full-page advertisement in the *Sunday Telegraph* in January Michael Howard printed a personal letter announcing that race and immigration would be his main topic in the weeks running up to the election. Naturally the *Daily Mail* and *Sun* played up Howard's racist dog whistle appeal.

Labour ministers and MPs were terrified of telling the truth and accusing Howard of being a racist even though that was exactly what he was up to. The BBC, other TV channels and most of the press refused to call out Howard's opening the door to putting xenophobia and closet racism back into our political life.

This loss of Labour self-confidence was everywhere. I attended Cabinet committees on Europe but Jack Straw and other ministers were now increasingly nervous defending the EU and the policy of freedom of movement, which were the norm between Britain and the Republic of Ireland even if Ireland exported over many years all its unemployed and for twenty-five years had sheltered terrorists who thought nothing of murdering innocent British men, women and children.

The answer, I argued, was to adopt a very tough policy of internal labour market management to control immigration. If we produced enough skilled workers or filled all the vacancies for doctors and nurses in the NHS with young men and women who'd worked hard to get good science A-levels in order to go to medical school but were denied places because the doctors liked to maintain a closed shop, we would not need to invite in a single immigrant worker to the NHS. The same was true for skilled workers in construction or IT or many other trades and sectors of the economy. But the apprenticeship system was destroyed under Margaret Thatcher and made still weaker under John Major. As a result, we have the worst trained workforce in the EU and the lowest productivity. It is much easier to import workers from anywhere in Europe to do these jobs.

Employment agencies also imported large numbers of unskilled workers from Europe. Tony and Gordon resisted the EU Agency Employment Directive which at least tried to control one aspect of this wage-cutting abuse which pocket-lining bosses liked. The trade unions had been virtually expelled from most private sector workplaces and there was hardly any workplace inspection so employers did what they liked.

I had a drink with an old friend David Goodhart who had been the labour editor of the *Financial Times* and then gone to launch the magazine *Prospect*. He was an engaging wealthy Old Etonian and son of my parliamentary ski race comrade, Sir Philip Goodhart, who had been on the hard right of the Tory Party in the Commons. David was a fine journalist and under his editorship *Prospect* was very well written and full of refreshingly contrarian arguments in contrast to the predictable *New Statesman* features under its then editor who became famous after printing an overtly anti-Semitic front cover.

David was now bored with Labour. He wrote an article in *Prospect* which argued that Britain had distinct ethnic groups and that only so many who were not part of the settled community could be admitted to a nation before the balance got upset. I noted at the time: 'This is the most awful right-wing rot and is the concept that underpins all divisive politics based on ethnicity for more than a century. This ethnic or race based political sociology is meat and potatoes to the *Daily Mail* and the *Daily Telegraph* and the *Sun*'. Sadly, I had to acknowledge that a fine mind was crossing the road to walk with the right.

The mood in politics was changing. Robert Preston, a gifted journalist, wrote a biography on Gordon Brown which was just a long attack on Tony Blair. I noted in my diary that

It reads as if it was dictated by Ed Balls. The tone is so contemptuous of Blair that it is barely journalism so much as a long whine by the Chancellor and/or perhaps one of his associates. I don't doubt that Brown has very serious complaints about Blair but equally Blair must ask why Brown has failed to support him on so many key policies. All nasty stuff.

The smears were growing thick and fast. Dominic Cummings, one of the more unpleasant hard-right Europhobe gossip merchants, wrote a blog in which he said the tabloids 'have got a sex story involving one of the senior ministers involved in unconventional positions.' This was a pure smear that never materialised as a news story but Cummings specialised in this kind of fake news innuendo which demeaned politics and public life.

Slowly the fun was going out of being in politics. The Labour government faced no real opposition from a second-rate

Tory politician like Michael Howard, let alone a fifth-rate one like Iain Duncan Smith. But a sense of purpose was missing from Labour's ranks.

The EU constitution or constitutional treaty, to give it its proper name, was turning into a nightmare after the decision in France and the Netherlands to hold a referendum on it. About the same time, our expected election meant it was a hot political topic. The text of the treaty was certainly not as important as the extension of powers of Europe during the Thatcher era, but we were also lumbered with the decision to hold a referendum on it in the UK.

I wrote at the time, 'I am pretty certain what the result would be (of any UK referendum on the EU constitutional treaty) though we will first wait on the Dutch and French results.' Those two countries voted down the proposed Treaty which let Tony Blair off the hook. It would have been better to hold the UK referendum in 2005. It would have been lost but perhaps cured British politics of the idea that plebiscites were the best way to deal with complex international economic and political relations.

Tony Blair held meetings for ministers to spread the election message. 'We've lost progressive voters because they feel on Iraq and other issues we simply haven't been left enough and we've lost switchers – the undecided voters – back to the Tories. The question of Iraq is not the rights and wrongs of what happened there but voters feel that we care more about what is happening abroad than what is happening in my town. There is insecurity that requires reassurance. People do feel insecure. Things have got better for most but people remain insecure about their pensions, about their communities, about old values disintegrating around them.'

This was Tony: the permanent, middle-class, Middle-England man. He understood intuitively the problems and the prejudices of so many people who wanted to find a politics that could let them vote Labour safe in the knowledge that a Labour government would seek to both progressive while respecting the attachments of British people whose families had lived quietly for generations minding their own business.

In the end the best thing Labour had going for the party in the 2005 election was the record of the Tories since 1997. Under William Hague, they had turned into a nasty nationalist party holding Europe in contempt. Iain Duncan Smith was impossible to take seriously. Michael Howard had pandered to the worst prejudices of everyone whether it was on locking up as many women and non-violent prisoners as possible, his contempt for trade unions or his overt dog-whistle pandering to anti-immigrant racism.

In a debate on Europe, John Redwood said the UK should threaten to withdraw from the EU to make Brussels conform to our wishes. Another Tory anti-European David Heathcoat-Amory had said that if Britain voted 'No' to the constitutional treaty 'we would have the world at our feet and we could dictate to Europe.'

I had lunch with my nominal pair, Nick Soames, at the Turf Club, one of those exclusive London clubs for the aristocracy. Pairing had become irrelevant given the huge Labour majority after 1997. But Nick was terrific company with no self-restraint of any sort. It was impossible to have a conversation with him without his referring to 'my grandfather' – Winston Churchill. People treated Nick as a high Tory Falstaff keen on his food and drink and his hunting. There was quite a lot of that in him, but he had a sharp knowledge of geo-politics, upheld his grandfather's and father's pro-European enthusiasm and remained a one-nation Tory. I always told him if I was not going to vote so he might take an evening off if his whips allowed it.

He came to lunch in a bright-orange overcoat, a trilby hat and a handmade suit with the sleeves turned up at the end – an odd upper-class affectation. I told him John Redwood was bringing out another book in preparation for a leadership bid after the election. 'Deadwood, you mean,' Soames snorted and snorted again at the idea of 'little Liam Fox' running for the Tory leadership.

George W Bush had just paid a visit to Britain where he had spoken very warmly about European integration as had all US presidents since the 1950s. Another snort from Soames. 'Oh, I know, those silly cunts like Bernard Jenkins are always flittering over to Washington to try and crank up the Pentagon but it won't work. I certainly won't campaign against the (EU) constitution.' When I had come into the Commons eleven years ago and Nick asked me to be his pair, he was enjoying life as Minister for the Armed Forces where, as a former cavalry officer, he was in seventh heaven. Now he was approaching sixty and twiddling his thumbs on the backbenches.

'Actually, Denis, I hate politics as the moment. The only reason I am doing all of this is because I love the Commons, I absolutely adore the Commons.' I knew what he meant. I was enjoying being in government but found Labour politics intellectually empty and without interest or passion. We had become mere administrators. But the Commons remains an awesome place. Of course, for Nick, being an MP was his birth right as a Churchill but I still got a tingle-toe feeling every time I walked through the Members' cloakroom.

The lunch with Nick was a moment of amusement and fun and a rare glass of wine at midday – he drank Coca Cola – in what was becoming a less and less interesting time in the Foreign Office. The endless briefing by the Brown camp against Blair's team of ministers especially Alan Milburn, whom Gordon saw as some kind of rival to his right to take over as prime minister, was tiresome and demoralising.

Jack Straw remained friendly, and a decent man, as well as a super professional political animal. He was always good to work with but his latent English national protestant suspicion of continental entanglements was rising to the surface. Europe was no longer a political project of interest to Brown, Straw and most ministers who remained staunchly mono-lingual with no experience of working or living in Europe.

The general election flattered to deceive. Labour won 355 MPs, but with a popular vote share of 35.2%, the smallest of any majority government in UK electoral history. Michael Howard now had 198 Tory MP as the first past the post electoral system favoured the incumbent Labour Party as long as it was led by Blair with his unique bond to British voters.

The Liberal Democrats did well with sixty-two MPs. Their leader Charlie Kennedy was an attractive politician though his fondness for Scotland's national drink meant getting close to his face in a crowded division lobby risked being knocked over by whisky fumes. But clearly Britain was not reverting to being the Tory nation it was in the 1950s and 1980s. Yet so tribal was Labour, and especially the team around Gordon Brown, the chances of any cross-party alliance to keep a progressive reformist pro-European government in power seemed impossible. And as Labour gave up on Europe they really didn't need a pro-European of conviction as Europe Minister. I knew my red box time was up.

Blair's conversation firing me was gentle and friendly.

'Hi, Denis. How's it going?'

I congratulated him on his third election win.

'Yeah, that's great, but I'm afraid I've got bad news for you, Denis. I'm going to have to let you go.' I didn't protest or whine. There was no point. I had had a great eight years at the Foreign Office. The Labour government, indeed all EU governments were running out of steam on how to make Europe come back to life.

He softened the blow by saying, 'Please come in and see me in Downing Street, Denis, because there's still stuff I'd like you to do for me in Europe and we can have a talk.'

'Thanks, Tony. It's been a rough couple of years for me and I've been very loyal and supportive and I really just need to go away and absorb this.'

'Well, good luck then,' he said, and that was it. My life as a minister was over. Douglas Alexander, an aide to Gordon Brown, was made Minister of Europe. I liked Douglas. He knew almost by heart every speech John F Kennedy or Robert Kennedy ever made and had a complete collection of the West Wing movies. If ever there was a Kennedy quote in a Gordon Brown speech, and there were many, Douglas would have written it in.

He sent a friendly hand-written note saying he had no idea he would replace me and had warm word about my work which I appreciated. From a No 10 insider I learnt that I was caught in a pincer movement between Gordon Brown and Jack Straw. Gordon wanted a high-level Minister of State job for his young protégé and Jack, who could sense the going of Blair and the arrival of Brown, wanted to stay in the cabinet so did whatever Brown wanted. So Douglas was named to Straw's team.

**Lesson 36.** *If you are lucky enough to be made a minister savour every moment. It won't last. And don't whine when the time in office ends. You are still an MP and that beats working for a living.*

I was well treated. I was named to the Privy Council, the highest rank an MP can get. It serves little purpose except you get to be called 'The Right Honourable.' No extra pay, no getting ahead in any queue. When I went to be sworn in, I found all the rigama-role dating back to Tudor times hilarious. You actually kneel in front of the Queen, slobbering over her gloved hand. You swear an oath to protect her from all possible enemies especially the French and the Vatican. I was sworn to the Privy Council with the Tory MP Patrick McLoughlin. A lady-in-waiting chatted to us to put us at our ease before the audience. She told a story of having dinner with the Queen the week before. Pope John Paul had died, and his replacement was a German cardinal who took the name of Pope Benedict. The lady-in-waiting described how a flunky came rushing into the meal to bring the news.

'Ma'am, ma'am, they've elected a new Pope. It's some very old German and he'll only be a stopgap.'

The Queen looked up. 'Thank you, but Cardinal Ratzinger is a year younger than me and if you don't mind, I'd rather not hear about stopgaps while I'm having dinner.'

I was named as a UK delegate to the Council of Europe and put on the NATO parliamentary assembly. The Labour Party still considered me its representative on the Party of European Socialists and the invitations never stopped to speak anywhere and everywhere on Europe with as many trips as when I was a minister, though no longer with the same luxurious privileges.

Not for the first time I found being an MP a fulfilling job. I was gone as a minister but political life would go on.

## 2006

Unlike the first full years after the election wins in 1997 and 2001, the mood was not great. The Parliamentary Labour Party celebrated its 100th anniversary with a little debate in the House of Commons. At the end everyone started to sing the Red Flag. Tony Blair joined in with gusto and seemed to know all the words, which was more than I did. The irony of the most non-socialist, at times almost conservative leader of the Labour Party ever in its history, belting out the words of this socialist hymn was too delicious. Yet bit by bit Labour MPs were dividing internally with growing opposition to what the Labour prime minister wanted to see on the statute book.

Labour was uneasily coming to terms with the fact that its third term in office was far removed from the 'Bliss was it in that dawn to be alive, and to be young was very heaven' of ten years ago. Politics was now a slog. Iraq had turned into a disaster and all the Blair haters were out in full force. He foolishly went too far with proposals aimed at tackling terrorism in Britain. The Islamist tube and bus bombing in London in 2005 were a shock. I was horrified but the British elite had spent too much time sucking up to Islamism rather than tackle its ideology and extremism.

Now as so often in British history, there was a great awakening. Instead of working to drain the sources of Islamist hate by withdrawing from Afghanistan and detaching Britain from its alliance with the hard-right faction in the USA grouped around Vice President Dick Cheney and US Ambassador to the UN John Bolton, the new Labour government proposed a major assault on civil liberties: a ninety-day detention without being charged. The Commons rose in revolt and Blair was defeated by a coalition of Tories, Liberal Democrats and forty-nine Labour MPs. I remained loyal but it was the end of Blairism.

The TB-GB war was now out in the open. Blair's chief European civil servant described to me how in from his tiny office next to the cabinet room where Blair worked, and which was full up with a sofa and his desk, the sound of Gordon shouting at Tony and 'crockery being thrown at the wall' could regularly be heard. This was not about ideology. Brown's Treasury had continued the right-wing pro-profit economic model developed since the 1980s by Margaret Thatcher and John Major. The pound was hugely overvalued which made holiday-makers feel good and kept inflation under control but at the cost of pricing UK exports out of markets, especially for those goods made in industrial areas such as Rotherham where the steel industry was hanging on by its fingernails.

Brown and his aides briefed us endlessly against any of the next generation ministers Blair appeared to be promoting as his successor. Alan Milburn, Steven Byers, Patricia Hewitt, James Purnell or David Blunkett were all trashed, or ugly stories about them somehow found their way into the papers. In truth, the younger ambassadors of New Labour grouped around Peter Mandelson from the 1990s onwards were all technocrats. None had much cut-through politics. They could do the Despatch Box or the Today programme but when I went back home to Rotherham and had a curry with Labour comrades no one ever mentioned any of the men Blair hoped would knock Brown off his perch.

Göran Persson, the shrewd social democratic prime minister in Sweden, once said to me that a democratic left party 'should behave like a government when out of power and like an opposition when in office.' But Labour didn't have the political maturity or political education to operate like that. It was just personality, personality, personality.

The former ambassador in Washington, Sir Christopher Meyer, a flamboyant Tory, who like me enjoyed wearing red socks, published his memoirs. He described Jack Straw, Geoff Hoon and John Prescott as 'pygmies' but called Peter Mandelson and myself 'Maasai' ministers able to exercise ministerial authority instantly and well. Flattering, but I was no longer a minister.

I reverted to what I like best – campaigning for progressive causes I thought important. One issue was the enormous sex trade in Britain. Women, often still teenagers, were brought into Britain to be sex slaves in massage parlours, or via mobile phones for British men, who thought that as long as they paid they could penetrate women as often and however they wanted. Prostituted women, often drug dependent or very poor, were controlled by male bosses. I was no puritan or moralist but reckoned if this was just normal work or 'sex work' then surely the men who paid for such services would not worry about being made accountable.

I began working with left feminists and MPs like Vera Baird, Harriet Harman, Fiona Mactaggart and Gavin Shuker, as well as the Tory MP Anthony Steen on the need to make men legally accountable for buying the bodies of trafficked women. It was uphill work as the police – many of whose officers got free blow jobs in exchange for turning a blind eye to what was going on – were not interested in naming and shaming the men who made this sex trade so lucrative. The Crown Prosecution Service and the Director of Public Prosecutions appointed by the Labour government also took little interest. It was so much easier to arrest and charge some poor woman living in the direst poverty, often bringing up children alone, who had not paid her BBC licence fee or overclaimed a housing or some other benefit.

The Crown Prosecution Service was fixated on filling up our already overcrowded prisons with men and women who were not guilty of violent crimes. It was an open secret that many top Tories like Michael Gove or David Cameron had snorted cocaine, as had loads of journalists in Westminster or the City world of fund managers and corporate lawyers. Nothing was ever done to these public schoolboys, but if the police could lay their hands on some discharged soldier who agreed to deliver the white powder to the decadent rich then he – the delivery man – would face a prison sentence. The purchaser and consumer of the drug came from the same class and educational background as the CPS prosecutors and judges, and would be protected.

I set up an all-party Committee on Inquiry into Anti-Semitism as I now had the freedom to investigate the rising tide of Jew-hate in Britain and across Europe. I had written my first ever political pamphlet nearly 30 years ago about race hate. At the time, I'd described the hates the worshippers of Enoch Powell had generated as having the same lineage as pre-1939 or indeed pre-1914 anti-Semitism. Now the beast was back and it was infecting the left as much as the right.

I was pleased at a positive vote for ID card legislation after the idea of identity cards was endorsed in the Labour manifesto approved in the general election. I could see no way we could control free movement of people from Europe if we had no way of knowing who was in the country. I had lived in Switzerland and France, two countries where ID cards were the norm and where democratic activity and dissent were stronger than in Britain. And yet the Tories, LibDems and many friends on the left described the idea of having ID cards as introducing the Gestapo overnight.

What I didn't know was that having passed the law early in 2006 it would be fully four years before ID cards were issued. I never got an explanation for the delay. The Home Office, by far the most incompetent department in Whitehall, and with ever-changing Home Secretaries who never got a grip, was in charge of ID cards. Was the four-year delay just routine for the Home Office? Or was there some political sabotage by civil servants more closely aligned to Tory or LibDem thinking, or even the *Guardian's* hostility to letting us know who lived in the country?

The year was full of open rows about when Blair should go and how fast Brown should take over. Alan Milburn moaned about Brown, and Andrew Smith moaned about Blair. For backbench MPs it was utterly demoralising to see the party rotting visibly from its head down. The Brown camp briefed non-stop on the need for Blair to go as soon as possible.

The Tories had a new young and attractive leader in David Cameron who at times bested Blair at the Despatch box, which hadn't happened under Willian Hague, Iain Duncan Smith or Michael Howard. When Blair went to a third world summit in Sudan, Cameron asked if he had visited Khartoum 'to see if he could find Gordon's body?' The Commons exploded in laughter as much from Labour as Tory benches. A Prime Minister thus mocked is not in a good position.

Blair also got into trouble with a police investigation into loans made to the Labour Party by rich men, some of whom became peers. Jack Dromey was Treasurer of the Labour Party, a position bestowed on him as a senior union official. He said he had not been informed about loans that had come into the party to fund the 2005 election from rich donors. They only wanted one thing – a peerage or knighthood or some access to Blair and ministers. Again and again I pleaded for public financing of democracy to stop this rotting, infectious corruption of crawling to the rich to pay for politics. But the government had run out of reforming energy and vision.

> **Lesson 37.** *Labour needs to grasp the nettle of democracy paying for democracy. It has to be a long slow campaign to change public opinion and win a majority to modernise party financing along standards and norms in most democracies.*

I went back to Rotherham to find my constituency party, and all my friends who made Labour work there, now openly angry over government decisions. The technocratic apolitical ministers Blair preferred seemed to be taking all their ideas from management consultancies or business financed think tanks and had lost touch with the progressive and reformist traditions of the democratic left.

My agent Anna Chester, one of the warmest, most serious and best-intentioned women I have ever met in politics, sent me a text reading 'Labour have today changed their emblem from a rose to a condom as it more accurately reflects the Government's political stance. A condom allows for inflation, halts production, destroys the next generation, protects a bunch of pricks, and gives you a sense of security while actually being fucked.'

Anna never used coarse language and her joke reflected just how far Labour rank-and-file members and the hard-slogging local activists, who are the backbone of democratic party politics, were losing faith and hope as they watched Gordon Brown obsess about ousting Blair.

I went to see Tony in his Downing Street study in September and told him that I, as a life-long Labour Party guy, was very sad it was happening like this to the maximum profit of all of Labour's enemies in politics and the media.

'Yes, it's not been good for the party,' Tony replied sadly. 'I had Gordon in here yesterday and I just said to him: "If it carries on like this it's the party that will be destroyed and we'll lose the next election." He just doesn't seem to get it. He knows I am going next year but the way it's been done this week has not been good or helpful.'

That Blair understatement was more than true. From September 2007 to December 2019, the Labour Party just lost its way, its belief in itself, and at a crucial moment in British history, could offer no leadership to the British people.

At the Labour Party conference in September, I told a *Tribune* group meeting that the Deputy Leader should work to renew the party and not seek to be deputy prime minister with his or her time taken up with cabinet business. We need to get to politics more than administration and management of the state, I pleaded. But I was wasting my breath. Friends like Alan Johnson, Peter Hain, Jack Straw and Harriet Harman were already promoting themselves as the successor to John Prescott who was standing down as Deputy Leader of the Labour Party. This was as much about keeping a seat at the cabinet table as being No 2 in the Labour Party. Under Gordon Brown it would be a one-tenor opera. There would be no Team Gordon.

Maybe it's impossible to renew or recharge a party after ten years in government. I admired Gordon's manifold abilities but knew in my bones he was not going to win the next election. So did many Labour MPs, despite formal surface loyalties. Labour had achieved much since 1997 – Sure Start for poorer children, thousands of uniformed police support officers patrolling streets, a massive increase in the NHS budget, most social housing renewed, gay rights, the expulsion of most hereditary peers from Parliament. But now that élan and energy had gone and a dull, protean managerialism had taken over.

## 2007

A decade of power. The longest Labour has managed in our 100-year history. But no celebration. The bitching against Blair and Brown, between Blairites and Brownies continued unabated. Tony goes. Gordon comes. But Labour was not a happy party. Maybe it's in our DNA. The left is there to do opposition. Not power, not government.

The mood in the tea room was morose. Everyone knew Blair was going and Brown was his only possible replacement. But everyone knew – even if few wanted to discuss it openly – that Brown was not a winner.

I seemed to be writing once a week in some newspaper or other with regular columns in *Newsweek* and *Le Monde,* and was endlessly on the BBC and other TV and radio outlets. I travelled whenever I could to European capitals to get close contacts with sister parties in Europe, claiming back the expenses from Parliament, which turned a blind eye to MPs travelling anywhere in the UK, so I reckoned that a few Eurostars to Paris or Brussels or Easyjets to Madrid or Warsaw wouldn't break the parliamentary bank.

I invited Harriet Harman to speak at a Rotherham curry night. She was going to run as Deputy Leader. Her opponent was to be Jon Cruddas. I liked Jon but could never quite understand his political project. It seemed to be based on undergraduate sociology. It sounded left and I'm sure was sincerely meant to be left. But I couldn't work out a storyline, a project, specific laws or reforms despite the fluency of his speaking.

Harriet worked the Rotherham activists brilliantly mainly by telling stories at my expense. But our friendship as well as mine with her husband, Jack Dromey, was now three decades strong and there were few in the Labour Party I liked or admired so much.

Her views on Gordon were clear: 'People don't understand how very insecure he is. That's why he works so hard. He wants to cover everything. He is completely exhausting to work with. He's always phoning up, phoning up, phoning up four, five, six times a day to check some minor point.'

Charles Clarke insisted to everyone who would listen that Brown would not succeed as prime minister. I told him I shared his misgivings, but it was pointless trying to organise a pre-emptive move against him.

'He is going to be Prime Minister, Charles, and you and I and all of us just have to accept that,' I told him early in March, adding, 'If after nine or twelve months he is absolutely useless then we shall have to get together and tell him to go.'

'That will be impossible, Denis. Once he is installed it will be impossible to dislodge him,' Clarke replied. He was right.

Brown produced his last budget as Chancellor. He announced an income tax cut and promised a 'British century.' He was now putting 'Britain' or 'British' into every speech.

Yvette Cooper, David Miliband and I discussed the budget in the tea room. David asked Yvette, who had written economics columns for the *Independent*, 'Is it really a tax-cut? What does cutting the ten per cent bottom rate mean in terms of who will win and who will lose?'

Yvette looked up blankly. 'Didn't you discuss all this in the cabinet before the budget?' she asked.

'Yes, but Gordon rattles off the figures so quickly no one could understand them. As usual.'

Yvette and I looked at each other. David Miliband was seen as the heir to Blair, the rising young intellectual policy shaper in the next generation of Labour. He was the only possible challenger to Brown. But he did not seem to know or understand what was in the budget that had just been announced.

Everyone liked and admired David Miliband. But was he really a politician? Friends in No 10 said he had to have his arm twisted to go and run for a safe Labour seat in the North East. He had instant promotion as a minister and then into the cabinet. Unlike the normal jealousy of any court favourite given fast promotion, David, I judged, did not have an enemy in politics. But then he had never had to fight a political fight, stick out his neck, wait through boring years of opposition and unelectable leaders to finally get a crack at power. Had he decided he would run against Brown it would have been an almighty row. Miliband would have been required to show if he had the inner toughness and arrogant ruthlessness to lead the Labour party.

In April we talked on a train heading north to our constituencies. David said he would write an article in the *Observer* confirming he would not stand for Leader. I urged him to wait. If the local council elections were bad (and they were) MPs would come back to the Commons uncertain that Brown would be the man to save their seats. That would set off a chain series of chemical political reactions.

But David shook his head. I asked him who he talked to in the cabinet. Jacqui Smith, a likeable but lightweight minister. Alistair Darling, which was a way of talking to Gordon Brown, John Reid, the ex-communist Scot who moved like many ex-CPers hard to the right and had denounced the Home Office (which he headed) as 'unfit for purpose.'

I noted 'what I have long thought; that David isn't at the heart of any effective team, still less a cabal. He is a proud, confident intellectual and is full of ideas. But politics requires a chopping savagery and an ability to create networks and teams of sustained supporters.'

Brown, by contrast, was back in his back-slapping mode and came up as friendly as could be during a division. 'What are you doing, Denis?' I told him I had just been in France where it was likely that the energetic rightist, Nicolas Sarkozy, would win the presidency in May. I said I would like to come and talk to him about what was happening in Europe. But I could not understand his reply though admittedly it was in a crowded buzzing division lobby. It was a succession of grunts. When he wanted to bury himself in his Scottish accent Gordon was completely unintelligible.

And just as we were adjusting to having the first Scottish

Labour prime minister since Ramsay MacDonald, the news came through that Labour had lost Scotland. In the spring elections to the Scottish Parliament, the Scottish Nationalists had beaten Labour. In the 1980s and 1990s Gordon Brown had been the first man of Scottish politics. Now Alex Salmond was to be the First Minister, in effect, the Prime Minister of Scotland.

Labour had won 56 of the 72 seats in Scotland in 1997 and the same number in 2001. They lost seats in 2005 but were still seen as the dominant party in Scotland. Not anymore. In many ways New Labour had been born in Scotland with one of the most extraordinarily talented generation of politicians emerging from a national region: John Smith, Robin Cook, Donald Dewar, John Reid, Helen Liddell, the lawyer-politician Derry Irvine, Alistair Darling, Brian Wilson. Even Blair had been educated in Edinburgh and his press genius, Alistair Campbell, played the bagpipes claiming some Scottish heritage.

A new generation of younger Scots like Douglas Alexander and Pat McFadden were clearly cabinet members in waiting. But even as Brown and his clan of New Labour Scots moved south to conquer state power in London, they left no one behind to mind the political shop and ensure their base was protected. It was one of the biggest misjudgements in Labour history. Brown installed obedient and second rank politicians to run Scotland after the death of Donald Dewar who was as stellar a politician and of the same generation and Glasgow University background as John Smith.

**Lesson 38.** *Labour has to be present everywhere in the UK and ensure a strong presence in the new parliaments* *created under 21ˢᵗ century devolution. If all good talent feels the only satisfying politics is in Westminster then the doors open to nationalist and other parties that do keep a strong presence away from Westminster. Labour's overwhelming dominance by talented Scottish MPs after 1990 perhaps meant it did not pay enough attention to English discontents. In Germany, the centre-right party in Bavaria, a very distinct region with own identity and history and dialect with some resemblance to Scotland, was organised separately from the Christian Democrats elsewhere in Germany. Is there a case for a separate Labour Party for Scotland and to force Labour to think harder about being a party of England as well as the UK as a whole?*

In theory, Scotland had powers to run an independent tax and economic policy and could shape its own destiny. But when Labour controlled the Scottish government Brown ensured that there was no deviation from his policies as Chancellor which were designed to attract the middle-class Thatcher voters of England. As a result, the SNP added attractive social and public sector policies and insisted that control from London and the priority given to English needs should be replaced by a distinctly Scotland-first politics.

Brown had no answer to the SNP challenge and none of the intellectually diffident Scottish Labour MPs dared challenge him. Labour had only ever been able to form a majority government thanks to its Scottish MPs. The win for the SNP was a severe warning that Brown was losing support even in his own backyard.

The big question after Brown took over in mid-summer was whether to hold a quick election and secure an independent mandate for Brown rather than rely on the 2005 election victory Blair had won. The arguments and press speculation went back and forth for the rest of the year.

I went to every Labour MP I could find at the Labour Party conference to ask a simple Yes-No question to holding an early election. The vote was 2 to 1 against. I passed on the news to Gordon's people. I certainly felt that the rising tide of xenophobia and the sense of drift after a decade of Labour made a fourth election victory doubtful.

Labour's loss in Scotland had put a question mark over an early election. Steven Byers told me he thought Brown's fatal weakness was his caution, his unwillingness to take decisions. 'Gordon hates taking a decision,' Steve said. 'He should have shut down the election story much earlier. But all the people who brief him can never tell him he's wrong.'

# 2008

Gordon's first full twelve months as PM. A year of two halves. The first six months just about everyone and even the No 10 cat said he was useless and had to go. By the end of the year, he was the man who 'saved the world' as the American Nobel laureate economist, Paul Krugman, put it. Gordon had showered praise and honour on Alan Greenspan, the dominant world banker of the previous 20 years, whose passion for deregulation and encouraging greed led to the giant financial crash of 2008-9 doing lasting damage to people's incomes, retirement plans and savings.

Brown had put up a plaque to Greenspan in the Treasury and given him an honorary knighthood as early as 2002. Greenspan took his eye off the many money-making schemes that allowed the Bernie Madoffs and other wolves of Wall Street to get rich, and in due course these Ponzi or pyramid schemes collapsed, setting off a worldwide financial crash and recession.

In Britain, Brown ensured the crash did not turn into a long depression as after 1929. It was a crisis made for Gordon who moved decisively to place British banks under state control and to nationalise some of the most corrupt banks. He played a leading role in European and global fire-fighting in response to the Wall Street-Greenspan crash. It was the last time a British prime minister was a commanding world figure.

This was all high global politics and economics which the denizens of Davos or the clever clogs at the *Economist* understood. Did it make any difference to the average Labour Party member? Indeed, would headlines about high finance impress voters in Bootle or Barnsley, who were going to have to make their mind up on what Labour was as we entered the second decade of a Labour government for the first time in its history?

I was doing my own in-the-clouds politics working hard on European and international issues. The new EU Treaty of Lisbon was being shaped. It created two new posts. The first was President of the EU Council of Ministers, a kind of super chairperson job for someone to convene meetings and chair all the meetings of presidents, chancellors and prime ministers in the EU.

The second post was the EU foreign policy supremo. It seemed to me that Tony Blair was more than equipped to do either job. I wrote up the idea in *Newsweek* and other English and French papers.

But everywhere I hit resistance, big opposition to Tony having a leading role in Europe. It was not so much the military intervention in Iraq but what was seen as blind obeisance to George W Bush, whose bombastic 'Mission Accomplished' slogan on a US aircraft carrier seemed an insult to the soldiers who had been killed, were still being killed or were yet to be killed in Iraq and Afghanistan. The idea of a 'war' on terror made no sense. Americans snatching men off the streets, torturing them and then dumping them in a concentration camp in Guantanamo Bay seemed odious, and a practice linked with totalitarian regimes, not the United States.

I also doubted if Tony would want to be the EU's High Representative for Foreign policy. Each EU foreign minister or his or her president or prime minister thought foreign policy should be an expression of national politics and outlook on the world, not an issue to be decided by majority vote on the basis of lowest common denominator policy papers written by Brussels officials.

The sad fact was that too many countries had joined the euro to take advantage of its low-interest rate without the slightest intention of reforming their economies; clientelism and cronyism could be found in varying degrees from Germany to Greece, damaging the new currency's operation in its first decade.

I remained committed to making Europe work since the alternative of a return to the kind of nationalism advanced by UKIP, the BNP, Rupert Murdoch or editors of the *Telegraph* and *Daily Mail* seemed far more dangerous. The Federation of Poles of Great Britain published a dossier of fifty hate headlines denigrating Poles – 'Polish killer', 'Polish rapist', 'Polish fraudster' – published by the *Daily Mail,* in a campaign of xenophobic hate against Europeans working in Britain not seen since the paper in the 1930s published openly anti-Semitic headlines and stories against German Jews escaping from nationalist Germany to Britain. The xenophobic hate of the *Sun* and *Daily Mail* and dog whistle racism on immigration from Tory MPs was now feeding into election results as BNP councillors were elected for the first time in Rotherham in May elections.

At the Labour Party spring conference in Birmingham there was no enthusiasm in a half-empty hall decorated with two large Union Jack flags like some boring Tory regional event. David Miliband asked me to help write the closing bit of his speech in the Commons on new EU Lisbon Treaty. I gave him some jokes about William Hague which he laughed at but didn't use.

I noted in my dairy: 'In the end David isn't a naturally combative speaker. He is a professor or head of a policy think-tank explaining earnestly to a seminar what is going on and trying to highlight some of the contradictions in order to tease out some clearer thinking. But a brute force politician he isn't.'

It was at the Labour spring conference in 2004 that I learnt of the death in a skydiving accident in Australia of my daughter,

Clare. Now her half-brother, James, called up to say that their mother, Carol Barnes, whose life I had shared before moving to work in Geneva, had been felled by a stroke and was unlikely to recover consciousness.

Carol was a young sixty four, as full as ever of life and fun and jokes, and up for sharing a bottle of her favourite Sauvignon Blanc. I'd stayed with her in Brighton when Labour or the TUC held conferences there and she was always welcome at the Commons for a drink or a meal. Carol was a brilliant broadcast journalist presenting the World at One and then News at Ten. She was also an NUJ activist and firmly on the left. We had great fun together but when I had to leave London to work it was hard to sustain our relationship, though we did our best especially with our daughter, Clare. We both moved on but remained very good friends seeing each other on my regular trips to London and even more often when I became an MP.

The days passed fast as I held her hand in hospital with no response. Although her lungs and heart pumped away there was nothing else there. With her son it was decided to turn off the life support. Her funeral was attended by endless stars of ITN, Channel 4 News and LBC, led by her and my friend, Jon Snow, a great LBC, ITN and Channel 4 news presenter. We remembered and honoured a friend and fine journalist. Her death coming after Clare's left me bereft and unable to pay detailed attention to the endless form filling that MPs are required to do.

Then straight back to politics where Nick Clegg was calling for an In-Out referendum on EU membership. This was his response to William Hague and David Cameron calling for one on the Lisbon Treaty. It was useless trying to tell Nick, as it had been with Charlie Kennedy or Paddy Ashdown, that holding a plebiscite on EU membership would be a disaster if it went the wrong way and no help if there was a narrow Yes.

**Lesson 39.** *Lyndon Johnson said some policies and politics were like peeing down your leg. 'It sure as hell feels warm to begin with.' Labour became obsessed after 1995 with announcing referendums in place of taking clear policy decisions. They sounded good to begin with but ended up producing very damaging outcomes for Labour (and the UK) in the short, medium and long term. Plebiscites were also a LibDem obsession. Labour should have left plebiscites in the history books.*

My perpetual quest for trying to figure out what made for successful Labour politics came to life in a debate with Ed Miliband at a routine meeting of Yorkshire Labour MPs. I asked how a democratic left government stays in power after it had held office for a decade or more – as was now the case with Labour. I cited Sweden and one of two other European countries as successful examples of it. Ed asked me to write a paper. I wrote to him posing the question: 'Supposing a party that still has good policies can't connect with the public because its leadership is rejected?'

I got an instant email in reply saying the problem wasn't Gordon, and Ed was very sure that with better presentation and better ideas Gordon could come through very strongly. 'Oh, God. If only I could believe that,' I wrote in my diary.

John Monks, the wisest trade union leader of his and

subsequent generations, was now running the European Trade Union Congress from Brussels. From this detached viewpoint he argued, 'The basic problem is that with Gordon we don't know, no one knows, what his line is. With Tony you knew what he stood for and what he would accept and what was out of order. You just don't have that from Gordon at all. He avoids taking decisions and that's fatal.' Senior Labour MPs like Steve Byers and Gerald Kaufman told me Brown had to go, as did Barry Gardiner and Fiona Mactaggart. Easy to say. But how?

The Gordon question could neither be answered nor would it go away.

Gordon however remained a politician to his fingertips. In October he brought back Peter Mandelson from the European Commission to be minister for Trade and Industry. The return of the Number One Blairite, Peter Mandelson, to sit alongside Brown, pleased the business world who attended event like the Davos World Economic Forum but did little to reduce the rising anti-Gordon vapours which were coming from more and more Labour MPs.

I went to America to campaign for Barack Obama and his win was a good omen for the continuing vitality of progressive politics. Back home Blair's chief aide, Anji Hunter, was clear that the Tories would win the next election. I agreed with her. Meanwhile the constituency Christmas Party was a jolly affair. At the last surgery before Christmas, a woman came in to complain that the town centre Woolworths was closing down. She said a Labour government should nationalise it. Might that do the trick? Taking more town-centre chain stores and all of Woolies into the wonders of public ownership?

# 2009

It was now clear Labour was over and done with. Gordon Brown was just not up the job of being prime minister. He went with the flow of all the big western democracies in stepping in to stop banks from closing their doors after the crash of 2008. He liked to blame that on bad behaviour by dubious banks, finance houses and mortgage lenders in the southern states of the USA. But Gordon had claimed to be the master of economic strategy so why hadn't he taken precautions? The financialisation of the economy and the blind worship of the finance houses of the City had gathered pace ever since Brown became Chancellor in 1997.

George W Bush had gone to be replaced by America's first black president, Barack Obama. I dutifully shook Obama's hand when he came to address MPs and state dignitaries in Westminster Hall. The pleasure of seeing an articulate, ideas-passionate African-American in the White House, in comparison to a mainly pale, male, stale Labour political class, was no compensation for the sense that Labour had lost its way.

Politics was getting ugly. Key aides of Brown including his personal press officer, Damian McBride, his former press aide, Charlie Whelan and another Brown fixer, Derek Draper, were caught exchanging emails about how to smear Conservative frontbenchers. Labour was losing by-elections.

Worse, it was unleashing a nasty new scapegoating of foreign workers in Britain. Brown had started the process when he said he would create 'British jobs for British workers' which unfortunately for him was one of the slogans used by the racist, anti-Semitic leader of the British National Party. Britain's economy had always depended on workers from outside the United Kingdom, from the Irish to those who arrived in the Windrush boats from the West Indies in the 1950s. Rotherham was home to 9,000 Kashmiris. Now, Labour MPs like John Mann were tabling Commons motions attacking foreign workers.

The only beneficiaries of this descent into the gutter were the political descendants of Enoch Powell now in the BNP, UKIP and parts of the increasingly xenophobic anti-European wing of the Tory Party. David Cameron was breaking all links between the Conservatives and their fellow centre-right parties in Europe organised in the European People's Party group. This was the first political Brexit, though the word had not then been coined.

The answer of voters was clear. Labour's attempt to court the xenophobic vote failed. In the European Parliament election in June, Labour came third below UKIP. And in Yorkshire the British National Party had an MEP elected. In a live TV debate with Nigel Farage, I teased the UKIP leader when he started attacking all MPs over expenses' claims. I asked him how much he had claimed in expenses as an MEP. Part of Farage's communication style was to not dodge or swerve round questions but give the impression of replying with a straight answer.

'Well, I think if you put it all together over the last ten years, I've probably had £2 million out of the European Parliament.' Bingo I thought to myself as £2mn was way above any of the claims MPs had made for reimbursement for their expenses which had become the political topic of the year. Farage's money did not matter to voters. They sensed Nigel was fast and loose with money but liked his style and the way he articulated the growing xenophobia in Britain which all parties were trying to tap into.

A thief who had got through a security barrier of a firm charged with preparing a list of MPs expenses for publication sold his disk to the *Daily Telegraph* for £300,000. What had been common discussion in the tea room with MPs exchanging tips on how to maximise allowances now became public knowledge. We, or Parliament, had only ourselves to blame. Suddenly the public saw MPs putting down subscriptions to pornographic TV channels, buying and selling properties in London to make speculative gains on the ever-rising house prices in the capital, husband and wife MPs claiming two sets of allowances when they shared one home and rented out the other, new kitchens installed, or giant TV sets, plus the costs of gardening and home maintenance all paid for by the taxpayer.

MPs like the Home Secretary Jacqui Smith were forced to resign. Brown had no idea what to do. Labour had made merry with ministers in the John Major government as sleaze merchants with the fingers permanently in the public till. Tory MPs were exposed as fiddlers on a massive scale as were LibDem MPs. But it was happening on Labour's watch and there were still many more Labour MPs than those of other parties. Blair had been accused of accepting money for the Labour Party in exchange for peerages.

I carried on with all my political work but was happy to escape to Europe for meeting of the Party of European Socialists (PES) where I represented Labour on its executive committee. The Party of European Socialists approached David Miliband to offer him the post of EU foreign minister (High Representative in the jargon). This was a new position created by the EU Lisbon Treaty. David held a meeting with the European socialists' president I had set up. He refused the offer and told me afterwards, 'We have to stay here, Denis, and save the Labour Party.' I shrugged and said inwardly, 'Good luck on that.' I was pretty certain David would no longer be Foreign Secretary after next year. The European foreign leadership post seemed tailor-made for him but it was his decision and I did not have the energy to argue it out with him.

I wasn't too worried about my own expenses. A few years previously, the *Guardian* had reported on my use of a garage attached to my Rotherham home which I converted into an office. My predecessor had had a small one-room office up a flight to narrow stairs which people had difficulty in accessing it. I reckoned that if my office was next to my home it meant I could work evenings and weekends without having to leave my house.

My staff had the run of the house and garden to prepare food, watch TV in comfort, and everyone in Rotherham was well aware of the arrangement as reporters, trade unionists, councillors, local business leaders came to see me in my house where parking was easy. Naturally I charged the running costs of the office, a converted garage, as my MP's salary would not cover that these expenses, but I always made clear to party activists if they wanted me to open a small office somewhere in the constituency that was also fine by me.

Now the right-wing tabloids and the local paper reprinted the *Guardian* story which had been sent to the paper by local political opponents and run in the paper without first checking the facts with me. It made no impression when first published but now in the context of the unfolding MPs' scandal it seemed as if I was as bad as others.

In the Commons, there was just a general misery and a sense that on this, as on so many other issues, Gordon Brown was lost and unable to find a solution. In June the former chief whip, Hilary Armstrong, liked and respected in equal measure sat down beside me in the Commons and said Labour would get fewer than 100 seats if Gordon Brown stayed. We were joined by Dennis Skinner.

'You know all those people overseas, Denis. Can't you get Brown a job somewhere?'

I asked Dennis what he meant.

'You know, the World Bank or the IMF.'

I told him that the top positions in both organisations had been recently filled.

'Yeah, but that doesn't matter. He can go in as No 2 on the understanding he'll take over shortly.'

Dennis Skinner, the loyalists' loyalist, and the left-wing's left-winger was as desperate as we all were.

At the Monday evening meetings of the Parliamentary Labour Party there was open revolt.

Hazel Blears was forced out of the cabinet after Brown had described one of her expenses' arrangements as 'unacceptable.' But his associates like Ed Balls or the Chancellor and long-time Brown loyalist, Alistair Darling, were revealed to have claimed for properties in a manner that was clearly improper. But they did not suffer Brown's accusatory criticism, and everyone felt the singling out of Hazel Blears, a popular and energetic Salford MP and minister, was unfair.

At the next PLP meeting the south London MP, Siobhan McDonagh, whose sister, Margaret, had been the Labour Party's general secretary, told Brown to his face that he was 'delusional' if he thought he could lead Labour to victory at the next election.

Tom Harris, who had been Labour's communications director in Scotland, told Gordon, 'You are unable to lead us to victory.' He was followed by Charles Clarke, who as a former Home and Education secretary, as well as a long stint as Neil Kinnock's Chief of Staff as the pair of them sought to rebuild Labour in the 1980s, was blunt:

'There is no sense of direction of purpose any more in Gordon's premiership. Gordon is responsible for a style of politics based on dishonesty and bullying. And Gordon bears the responsibility for this which is why David Cameron wants him to stay on as prime minister. Either we should have a secret ballot, or we should move straight to a leadership election. Gordon, you should have the courage to resign.'

Malcolm Wicks, one of Britain's most respected experts on family policy and an MP since 1992, told his fellow MPs and their leader about his father who had been a Labour councillor serving in County Hall for thirty years. 'I joined the party in the mid-sixties. Many in in this room have similar family involvement. Labour, at its best, has always put principle and party above personality.'

Malcolm softened his voice so you had to concentrate on his words. 'But, Gordon, if in the weeks and months to come

– not now – it is clear that we are heading for an appalling election defeat, will you continue to put our party first.'

Gordon was saved by Neil Kinnock who made a bellowing speech shouting it was the death wish of any political party to get rid of its leader.

But the dam had been broken. Labour MPs talked of little else in the tea room. Party activists also knew we were heading for defeat with Brown.

In the autumn Charles Clarke convened meetings attended by 40-50 Labour MPs to see what could be done to remove Brown. But in politics you can't beat someone with no one. Charles might have seen himself in No 10 but few others did. The plain fact was that Blair and Brown had so utterly dominated Labour for the last 20 years that the party had not allowed anyone next generation leadership to develop. We were stuck with Gordon.

**Lesson 40.** *Labour should have possible replacement leaders in waiting. But this requires a more collegial leadership approach instead on the fixation of just one man which has been the Labour style this century.*

# 2010-2021 What Next?

## 2010

The first Sunday of 2010 I was writing in my attic study when Geoff Hoon phoned up to announce a New Year putsch against Gordon Brown. He says he was proposing to send a letter to all Labour MPs asking for a secret ballot on Brown's future. Hoon wanted to know if I would support the initiative.

Of course I agreed that Brown would cost many of our MP friends their seats. I went on to ask Geoff if we could seriously envisage going into an election contest for a party leader taking up several weeks and only make Labour even more unpopular as divisions within parties always cut their popularity with voters.

And there remained the perpetual political truth: You can't beat someone with no one. There were ambitious figures in Labour's ranks but none with the reach or connection to the party – let alone the public – to take on Brown.

The next day in a deserted holiday Commons I bumped into Ann Coffey, a no-nonsense Scot who was a north-west MP and had been Alastair Darling's loyal PPS for years. She just saw the problem in terms of men without testicular courage. She denounced both Brown and members of the Cabinet in equal measure. 'They moan all the time but are never prepared to move. Why should anyone bother to follow any of them when they are just cowards. Of course Gordon is a complete disaster, but nobody is going to get rid of him now.'

I went off to Davos to race against Swiss MPs in the annual UK-Switzerland parliamentary ski week. I had just finished an exhausting, steep, deep powder off-piste run when my mobile rang. It was Charles Clarke to announce Geoff Hoon and Patricia Hewitt were launching their putsch in an hour.

It was pointless. Brown unleashed a barrage of MPs like Diane Abbbot, Ed Balls and Martin Salter to express undying devotion to their dear leader and to trash, in unpleasant personal terms, Hoon and Hewitt who were leaving the Commons in any case.

As with Kinnock after 1987, or Corbyn in 2019, there was no mechanism to remove a leader who was heading for defeat. In wars generals who cannot win battles are replaced. Why not party leaders who are going to cost fellow MPs their jobs?

Ex-ministers like John Prescott and Chris Mullin, or the former Labour Party general secretary, Peter Watt, were producing memoirs or diaries which shone a bad light on the Labour government. They were gobbled up by the *Daily Mail* or Rupert Murdoch editors, who paid out large sums to print pages. At the risk of stating the obvious, it only helped the Tories.

Labour was descending into the proverbial ferrets in a sack. Everyone was now at odds with everyone else. However, the ditch-Brown-movement just fizzled out and we made our way through a cold winter towards the coming election with few believing we could win it. David Cameron came over as an attractive liberal Tory, keen, so it seemed, on ridding the Conservatives of their homophobia and keen on putting women and BAME MPs on his front bench. Yes, he was rich and had had a gilded Eton, Oxford, safe Tory seat sort of life but that was no different from Tory prime ministers and cabinet members over many decades.

I criticised in the Commons and in the press, Cameron's decision to enter into an alliance in European politics with right-wing nationalist Poles some of whom, as MEPs in the European Parliament, had made anti-Semitic remarks or denied Holocaust atrocities carried out by Poles in the Second World War. But there was no real traction in that. The plain fact was that Britain, as a whole, had now fallen out of love with Europe.

Curiously, the mood in the constituency remained friendly and positive. On the doorstep there was the usual truculence about immigrants. Fifteen years ago, it was about Pakistani, or rather Kashmiri arrivals. I was told again and again about the privileges they had, the free cookers or fridges, or how planning permission was granted for house extensions that would not be granted to Yorkshire – i.e. white – people. I always asked for details, the name and address of anyone abusing the system and when confronted with being asked to provide evidence to back their urban myth prejudices, people just crumpled.

Now the anti-immigration prejudice had moved on to Europeans. They were visible enough in Rotherham. The local Catholic churches were full of devoutly Catholic Poles. Cheap cars with Polish or Lithuanian number plates were seen on streets. An East European food shop opened and Tesco had shelves for Polish food. Anyone who had bought a council home was able to rent it out at a profit. For the many, however, who had never found decent paid work after the great de-industrialisation of the 1980s and their children, who discovered the neoliberal policy makers in the Treasury had ended all the decent apprenticeship schemes, life was not what it was cracked up to be.

Canvassing on a council estate I knocked on the door of a man with a clearly Hungarian name. It was opened by an unshaven fat man in his early 30s.

I asked him to vote Labour in the election.

'Labour? You want me to vote Labour! You've let them all in, haven't you? You can't hear English spoken no more in town centre. They should never have been let in. No. I'll never vote Labour again since you let in all them Europeans.'

The iron rule in canvassing or Voter ID, as it was now called, is to spend no time in argument but just find out fast if the person will vote Labour so he or she can be reminded to do so on election day. Still, I was fascinated by this man's Hungarian name and asked him if indeed he was Hungarian.

'Aye, yes, my Dad came over here from Hungary' he said waving his arm behind his back over an event – the 1956 Hungarian uprising crushed by Soviet tanks – that happened before he was born.

'So, are you saying your Dad should not have been let in as a European immigrant?' I asked.

'Aye, bloody right he should have never been let in.'

You can't argue with that.

Having voted for Identity Cards in the 2005 election, the

Home Office, with its usual incompetence and lethargy, was finally issuing them. In March I got one which for a few months allowed me to travel around Europe without a passport just like anyone from Ireland, Spain or Germany could.

But a succession of less-than-stellar Home Secretaries since 2005 did nothing to give officials a kick in the backside and get the ID cards out to reassure British people that finally we would know who had come into the country and where they were. Only a few thousand cards were issued in the spring of 2010. Had that process started in 2006 or 2007 we would have had 10 million or more issued. The absurd fears promoted by Tories, libertarians and the press that ID cards meant the Gestapo arriving in Britain to demand "Papers!" would have been shown to be hollow. Instead the ID card fiasco showed how ill-prepared Labour ministers were to handle the arrival of new European workers.

The election was not quite the rout that many feared. David Cameron could only form a government in coalition with Nick Clegg. I thought Nick was taking a huge risk. He would be seen as Cameron's poodle and anger in the country would turn against LibDems implementing Tory policies. As indeed it did.

After the election came the election of a new leader. Both David and Ed Miliband asked for my support. I was quizzed by Jim Naughtie on *Today* and said while David had the reputation of being a high-grade policy intellectual, his brother, Ed, was 'the nicest guy in Labour, indeed the nicest guy in politics.' I tried to be as kind as I could about Ed even if I wasn't voting for him and stammered on, 'the nicest guy in ...' when Jim put me out my misery and said 'in the world.'

I was blunt with David Miliband. I told him that from all my experience working with and writing about centre-left parties in Europe and the world 'the plain fact is that once a social democratic or Labour party has done two or three terms in office, more than ten years in power and then loses an election it is almost a law of political gravity that they do not come back at the next election. 'So, if you become leader and you have my support, it's going to be a ten-year haul to renew the party, think of different policies and find new people who can reconnect to voters.'

David looked glum. 'Well, thanks very much, Denis.'

'Sorry, but that's what going to happen. Cameron and Clegg are reasonably popular, not stupid, and it's going to take us at least ten years and two elections to get back – if then.'

**Lesson 41**. *Never assume after a period in government it is easy to win back power. It is usually a two or even three election project. Tiggerish ex-ministers should be quietly retired to Select Committees and new faces brought on, not the tired out ex-ministers voters have rejected.*

I was busy enough with all my European work on the Council of Europe and representing Labour on the Party of European Socialists. My book on anti-Semitism continued to sell and I got invites from America and Europe to speak on anti-Semitism.

Like many MPs I had been casual and stupid with claiming money using parliamentary expenses. I wasn't in the big league of fiddlers who speculated in the London property market using the allowance to have a base in London. Nor was I employing children and other family members as so many did. There were no exotic giant TV screens, or subscriptions to porn channels, or getting new kitchens installed paid for by the expenses system.

But the BNP with whom I had been in almost permanent warfare since I denounced their racism and anti-Semitism managed to get their revenge. One of their members in London was senior retired Metropolitan Police Detective. The institutional racism of the Met was well known and the BNP had a network of police officer supporters.

I had been cleared in one inquiry by Sir Thomas Legg into mortgage payments. I replied regularly to the Commons bureaucratic, a former Home Office official who was moved from the Home Office by his superiors because he was not well regarded and found a sinecure as the parliamentary commissioner. He handled complaints against MPs at a time when the job entailed very little work.

Now he was submerged by complaints about fiddling, thieving MPs in the press. In my case no one complained or accused me of anything except the BNP's retired police officer. He presented the charge sheet as if seeking the Crown Prosecution Service's authorisation to charge me in court.

It was a Kafkaesque experience. That I was imperfect I knew. I repaid thousands of pounds even though they had been expended with full knowledge and authority of the House of Commons Fees Office – the finance office that handled MPs allowances. Yet each time the BNP asked the parliamentary bureaucracy to take up their case against me I received a letter from the commissioner. I faithfully replied. I assumed he would ask me to see him to be interviewed to explain each and every one of my expense claims.

No such request came. The BNP complaint just stayed on file with no invitation to me to come and answer any charges.

Then early in September came the bombshell. The commissioner announced he was referring me to the police. This was approved by the chair of the Parliamentary committee that dealt with the issue. He was Kevin Barron, my neighbouring Rotherham MP who I considered a friend.

I asked him why the BNP case was taking so long and why the commissioner never interviewed me. 'I don't know, Denis. We have no control over him.'

For the Labour Party the reference to the police of a senior ex-minister and privy councillor was a shock. Everyone expressed solidarity and many Tories, like the former Tory chief whip and party grandee James Arbuthnot, now a peer, came up to me in front of other MPs and said clearly, 'We know you, Denis. We know you are not a crook.'

It didn't matter. The decision of Barron and the parliamentary commissioner to refer me to the police was a death sentence. I was suspended from the party whip with the usual negative publicity that that entailed.

But I refused to surrender to the BNP. I knew I had been stupid. I had done what others had. I had lived in world at the BBC and Fleet Street where padding or fiddling expenses was the norm in the 1970s. I was aware of trade union practices involving expenses which were less than honest. In the FCO the system of so-called ambassador's *'frais'* (the word for expenses in French) was widely seen as a perk of the job which in reality was a supplement to the nominal FCO income.

I did not see myself as a criminal. Peter Mandelson advised me to get a good lawyer. I turned to Bindman's, the legendary Gray's Inn Road left-wing solicitors who had helped me to get money from the *News of the World* when my phone was hacked.

But I was wounded. I kept up my work as an MP even if I had to give up my role at the Council of Europe which was open only to MPs nominated by their parties.

The future was full of fear. I still today have no idea why the BNP had such influence in the parliamentary system or why I was never asked to explain face-to-face and directly the accusations they made against me.


# 2011

Cameron's and Clegg's sharp turn to the right quickly led to a deterioration of public services in Rotherham and reduced steel output in South Yorkshire. Then, when Clegg and the LibDems supported the tripling of student fees, I was delighted to see my son leading fellow sixth formers in protest against this Tory-LibDem attack on students.

I seemed to be as much in demand as ever to appear on TV and radio and write comment pieces for papers. My book on anti-Semitism, including the details of BNP Jew-hate which led the BNP to submit its complaint, was selling well. The Jewish community in Britain continued to invite me to their dinners and functions. I was doing political work in Europe and ambassadors in Madrid or Paris offered me a dinner and bed for the night in exchange for political intelligence.

In May I was the only English speaker at a great gathering of the French Socialists in Paris to commemorate the 30th anniversary of the election of François Mitterrand in May 1981. Everyone assumed that the boss of the International Monetary Federation, Dominque Strauss-Kahn, known as DSK, would return to France from Washington to be the socialist candidate against Nicolas Sarkozy.

Strauss-Kahn was a brilliant economist and wonderful explainer of current political problems, always proposing policies that made sense and would win votes. But he had an appetite for women, probably only matched in Britain by Boris Johnson. I sat at the lunch beside the secretary of the Socialist Party, Jean-Christophe Cambadélis. I asked if DSK had the Socialist Party nomination sewn up.

Jean-Christophe was categorical, laying out not just the calendar to secure the nomination but how DSK would go on to win the presidency.

'*Mais, Dominique et les femmes*?' I asked thinking the endless womanising stories about the great left seducer would cost him votes.

'Come on, Denis. This isn't England. We know that if your politicians sleep with women who aren't their wives, it's the end of their careers. This is France. We're different.' Boris Johnson proved him wrong. DSK proved him wrong. A week or so later DSK was caught in a Manhattan hotel with a woman. Every detail was leaked to the French media as if pre-cooked. That was the end of him.

Again and again, MPs back home and politicians I met abroad asked about my case. I explained what was at stake was a few thousand pounds all of which had been expended on networking in Europe, had been receipted, and in any event the money was repaid.

Colleagues in the Commons wished me well. I could see in their eyes however they knew the ancient English need for scapegoats and for public sacrifices to be made 'to encourage the others,' as Voltaire put it.

The Tory journalist, Daniel Johnson, made clear that the chances of any MP getting a fair trial given the massive hostile reporting on the expenses scandal was very low. I knew that already. I left dealing with the Metropolitan Police to my solicitor. I told Kevin Barron, who had authorised the forwarding of the BNP complaint to the cops, that so far it had cost me £30,000 in lawyers' fees. 'Oh dear, that wasn't meant to happen, Denis,' he said.

Oh dear, indeed.

I spoke to the Clerk to the House of Commons, the most senior Commons official and asked why I had not been interviewed or allowed to put my case to the Commons functionary in charge of investigating accusations against an MP. 'I'm sorry, Denis. We can't do anything with him.'

I couldn't quite put a finger on why the two Eds – Miliband and Balls – were not cutting it. One of Miliband's first decisions as Leader was to axe the long parliamentary Labour tradition of electing some members of the shadow cabinet. Of course, this had been divisive and allowed weeks of tea room manoeuvring by MPs hoping to win support.

MPs, for good or ill, did know the qualities of their colleagues better than most. The shadow cabinet elections in previous decades were the way the future leaders of the Labour emerged.

For that all, MPs like Tony Blair and Gordon Brown or Robin Cook, or in an earlier era, Harold Wilson or Barbara Castle and Tony Benn were elected early on in their parliamentary career to the shadow cabinet by their fellow MPs. The leader decided who got which position, but all MPs were involved in this act of collective choice of the leadership of the party.

Now Ed decided to abolish these elections and copy the Tory practice of the party Leader selecting who would serve in the shadow cabinet and who would have which jobs. He went further and parachuted two brand new MPs – Chuka Umanna and Rachel Reeves – straight into the shadow cabinet.

I liked both and had campaigned for Rachel when she was selected as the candidate to succeed John Battle, one of Labour's best MPs of his generation, when he stood down in Leeds. Chuka was smooth, dapper, always in a freshly laundered and ironed white shirt with a tight little tie knot and elegant suit. He had done something in the City and now represented Streatham where I was currently living when in London. Both were fluent on television and spoke well in the Chamber. But they struck me as so young, with very little political hinterland other than working to win their selections. There was no policy or political profile to their name and neither had any kind of political base.

I didn't doubt their ability but worried that instant promotion so fast would not help their careers. Their innate abilities would surely win promotion in due course. There was much muttering in the tea room about Ed M's favourites while many other talented MPs with proven experience and abilities were left off the front bench.

> **Lesson 42**. *The **FührerPrinzip** – all power to one man, ie the leader – doesn't fit Labour as a parliamentary opposition. Electing 12 members of the Shadow Cabinet allows MP who know better than anyone which of their number can perform in the Commons, or on TV and radio. It is imperfect but creating a court of favourites all chosen by the Leader means a front bench with too many duds.*

Ed Miliband also made a point of attacking some of the policies of previous Labour government. This pleased many on the left and in some union circles, for whom finding any words of support of Labour's record 1997-2010 was like swallowing live vipers. It sounded odd from a man who had been Gordon Brown's closest aide since 1997 and an MP rapidly propelled into the cabinet by Brown after his election as an MP in 2005.

Miliband had to confront the rise of so-called 'Blue' Labour promoted by a family friend, the academic Maurice Glasman, who Ed put in the Lords in 2011. Glasman was an engaging, enthusiastic college lecturer. He had a vision and wanted to recreate an imagined labour community of mainly white working-class men. Had he spent time with white working-class men outside of London he would have discovered that many of their passions and priorities were very far removed from the NW1 traditions of liberal multi-cultural and lifestyle tolerance which any modern progressive party espoused.

White van men were not interested in Ed Miliband's much proclaimed green agenda, derived from his work in promoting the Paris conference on climate change when he was environment secretary. They disliked all duties paid on petrol and diesel, loathed bicycle lanes and hated seeing lorries driven by Europeans on British roads while upholding the age-old right of any group of Englishmen to go wild on summer holidays to Zante or Ibiza or go on sex tours to Bratislava or Riga.

David Cameron attacked as an alien concept the idea of 'multi-culturalism' early in his premiership. It was a dog-whistle to the xenophobic Nigel Farage or Iain Duncan Smith right. Ed was put under pressure by 'Blue' Labour to copy UKIP and Tory calls for new controls on Europeans coming into Britain. I argued in articles and Fabian speeches for a new approach to managing immigration by changing labour market operations. Mono-culturalism was more pernicious than multi-culturalism, I argued.

For the UK unilaterally to tell Europeans they could not come to Britain was just a disguised way of saying Britain should leave Europe. Ed was not remotely interested in such politics. Key advisors like Stewart Wood, an Oxford don in the Lords, and his press officer, Tom Baldwin, also rejected a turn to anti-Europeanism and a promotion of English nationalism, which some former ministers like John Denham were now advocating.

In truth, being leader of a party in its first period of opposition was mission impossible. Clement Attlee had been useless between 1951 and 1955 and William Hague had been unable to make any impression after 1997.

I enjoyed organising a conference in Rotherham under the

heading '1931-1951-1981' which examined why Labour, when it went into opposition, got stuck there. A team of top Labour historians headed by Andrew Gamble came to discuss with politicians like Gerald Kaufman who began his long political career as assistant general secretary of the Fabian Society in 1951 and David Owen who was at the heart of the Labour split in 1981. They all agreed Labour had to change when it went into opposition. Easy to say but not so easy to put into practice as Ed Miliband was finding out.

I wrote a short book, *Why Kosovo Still Matters*, arguing that Europe's failure to stabilise the Western Balkans nations and states that had come into being after the defeat of Slobodan Milosevic's Greater Serbia project in 1999, was a signal failure. Britain could have played a role under Cameron and Hague, but their anti-European hostility meant that day-by-day Britain was losing influence in Europe. The book had a handsome endorsement from Christopher Hitchens who died soon after. He was one of my closest friends since Oxford days and we thought as one on so many political questions. I wished I could write even a sentence as well as Hitch could write entire articles or books.

His reading was stupendous, and he never forgot anything he read. He was far better than Google or Wikipedia on the history of the European and US left in the 20th century. I loved every moment spent in his company, sober but mainly blotto. His brother Peter called me from Christopher's death bed in Houston to give me his farewell. A light in my life went out with his death, even if he'd ignored all my warnings that a daily intake of a bottle of Scotch and forty cigarettes was unlikely to guarantee long life.

In politics you need outside intellects to bounce ideas off. Christopher was in the Trotskyist International Socialists when young and took pleasure in the toppling of a falangist mass-killer like Saddam Hussein towards the end of his life. I thought Trot politics juvenile and came to realise that the destructive forces unleashed by the Iraq intervention and now the interventions in Libya and Syria were, on balance, worse than the rule of the tyrants in those countries.

I also learnt from talking to him on politics, as I did from friends like Calum McDonald, Scarlett MccGwire, Colin MacCabe and my brother Martin, a doctor now serving on the NHS Executive Board. Anyone in politics must be under permanent intellectual challenge or else politics is pointless.

The politics of being in opposition resumed. I marched with Ken Livingstone and Sadiq Khan in a big protest organised by the TUC against austerity. For Ken and me marching through London was what we had done for decades. Sadiq was born the year I joined Labour. I'd helped him a bit as he had an office opposite mine in the Commons in 2005. I liked him loads. He was going to be big in Labour, but would he be brave enough to stand for something different or just set his sails to the prevailing fashionable winds of the left?

I organised a room at the Commons for Jude Law and Tom Stoppard where exiled actors from the last dictatorship in Europe, Belarus, performed with our local stars. Despite the best efforts of the BNP to end my career as an MP, I was still enjoying every minute.

Rotherham politics were looking up as Labour won every seat in the municipal election after steady door knocking at weekends. There was satisfaction in seeing UKIP candidates being defeated despite a fawning interview-profile of Nigel Farage in the *New Statesman*.

In the Commons the Parliamentary Commissioner let off the LibDem cabinet minister, David Laws, after it was revealed he had paid a boyfriend £50,000 in some dubious form of rental arrangement, by any standards an abuse of public money. Labour MPs had a go and the Barnsley MP, Eric Illsley, who had served a short prison sentence over some mortgage payment issue, called up spitting in fury at the double standards. But the plain fact was that the fiddles of the new Tory-LibDem government members were mainly excused while the civil servant deciding everyone's fate threw the book at Labour MPs.

## 2012

The muttering about Ed Miliband got worse and worse. Maurice Glasman blasted him in a *New Statesman* saying that Miliband had no strategy, narrative or story. This was pounced on as a huge internal Labour attack on Ed. I doubted if there was a single person in Rotherham who had ever heard of Maurice Glasman, but the plain fact is that Ed put him into the House of Lords, so his judgement again came into question.

At an early New Year dinner I hosted there were moans from the *Guardian's* political correspondent, Nick Watt, and from one of my best political friends, the ex-Labour MP for the Western Isles, Calum MacDonald, who'd lost an ugly homophobic campaign waged by the SNP even though he wasn't gay, just unmarried.

Nick said that Ed Miliband was going to be in real trouble. 'He has had a year of honeymoon grace but now the media will turn on him as they did over Kinnock and Foot, or in their different ways, William Hague and Iain Duncan Smith,' Watt predicted. Calum was also contemptuous of the current political leadership. The situation in Scotland was absolutely dire. There wasn't a Labour person of any weight or strength. More worrying in the tea room, and in casual conversation with any Labour MP, including the PLP chair, Tony Lloyd, was the sense that Ed's probation had come to an end and he was now on notice.

The Fabian Society started each year with a conference, a keynote event for Labour. In 2012, the North-East Labour MP and shadow minister, Helen Goodman, ranted about all the foreign immigrants who had come in during the last period of the Labour Government. I couldn't believe my ears. The same week there had been a good study by the prestigious Migration Advisory Group Committee, a government-sponsored outfit, which showed that the rise in unemployment especially amongst young people was due to the economic slowdown and could not be blamed on foreigners.

I told the conference that in the 1970s we heard complaints from Labour supporters and from the poorer elements of the white working class that too many Indians, Pakistanis and Afro-Caribbeans were being allowed in and were taking their jobs and their homes and their benefits. Now once again the same rubbish was being said about East European immigrants, who actually paid taxes and social security and are far less of a drag on the economy than many British citizens. In the 1970s it was the right that promoted such Powellite anti-immigrant feeling. Now it was being endorsed by a shadow minister.

Depicting Cameron and Clegg as monsters with the Sir Galahads of Labour coming to the rescue was unconvincing. In the Commons I asked Cameron if it made sense to keep sending troops to Afghanistan 'to be target practice for the Taliban.' I believed we should cut our losses and bring the soldiers home. I reminded the prime minister of a speech I'd made earlier in the Commons when I said the problem was that the generals who commanded British forces in Afghanistan rotated every six months. They arrived and spent two months working in a new plan, followed by two months of executing it, followed by two months preparing a report to explain why it didn't work. Still they were promoted for failure. Failing upwards leaves a sour taste but when the cost is measured in lives, it's not acceptable.

Cameron sneered at me. 'They say the first sign of madness is an MP quoting himself in the Chamber.' Other MPs were surprised as I had not attacked Cameron and many, I knew, agreed with my analysis.

The next day in Portcullis House, with its large open forum of coffee bars, tables and seats where MPs, researchers and journalists all mingle and gossip freely, I was standing when suddenly there was a tap on my shoulder. I turned. It was the Prime Minister. 'I was a bit rough with you yesterday, Denis. I'm sorry. I actually think much the same and I shouldn't have had a go.'

I just mumbled thanks for his courtesy and off Cameron went. I doubt very much if Gordon Brown or even the endlessly polite Tony Blair would have done the same to any Tory MP who had criticized them in the Chamber. Cameron went up in my esteem. Part of it was the effortless self-confidence that comes from bottomless wealth, Eton and Oxford, and a gilded road to high office. Nonetheless, Cameron was not Michael Howard or Iain Duncan Smith and seemed to be several stages removed from the ugly nationalism and right-wing ideology that was growing within the Conservative Party.Moreover the Cameron-Clegg style was not producing negative responses from the public. Their honeymoon continued. Ed's was now definitely over.

The Vice Chancellor of Sheffield University invited me to be a visiting professor running a project on the EU and nearly every week I found myself in some European city or town speaking on the UK and Europe.

I worked on local issues including a major scandal about dodgy breast implants involving a clinic in Rotherham which exploited so many women by inserting these leaky plastic products into women's breasts. The Speaker continued to call me regularly to speak. I took a lead in organizing a Commons debate on the so-called Magnitsky laws. This campaign arose after I had met a remarkable American, Bill Browder. His grandfather, Earl Browder, had been general secretary of the American Communist Party in the 1930s and during the Second World War. Earl Browder had been a fully committed Stalinist, trained by the Communist International. He ran for president of the US in 1944 but, when the Cold War got going after 1945, fell foul of both Stalin and the McCarthyite anti-communist witch hunts in America.

His grandson, Bill, had returned to Russia after the end of Sovietism in 1990 and become a major player in the new wild west capitalism that took off. But Bill refused to pay off the Putin network of ex-KGB agents who were the real power in Russia in the 21st century. His life was threatened and he moved to London and became a British citizen, still making money in Russia. The Putin kleptocrats wanted a share. Bill refused and sent in a lawyer, Sergei Magnitksky, to investigate. Magnitsky was arrested and in effect put to death as a warning to others not to challenge the Putin network.

Bill poured his energy and money into exposing the killing. He began campaigning for what he called Magnitsky laws which would deny to Russian officials and Putin agents the right to own property or live or open accounts in the West. It was a cleverly targeted move. What the Russian elite wanted above all was to use the ill-gotten new wealth to own houses in Mayfair, have their children educated at Eton and be accepted as legitimate.

Working with Chris Bryant and Tory MPs like Dominic Raab, we got a unanimous motion passed in the Commons. It called on the Government to introduce Magnitsky legislation in the UK similar to a law the US Congress had passed. William Hague as Foreign Secretary treated the Commons resolution with contempt. We later discovered the massive donations from Russian oligarchs to the Tory Party, so the Tory high command did not want to upset Putin. The Russian embassy in London put out a statement accusing me of being 'rude and provocative.' I took it as one of the finest compliments paid during my parliamentary career.

In France, an old friend, François Hollande, won the presidency. The Socialist Party had appeared down and out after the socialist prime minister, Lionel Jospin, was beaten by the extreme right-wing racist, Jean Marie Le Pen, and eliminated from the presidential election in 2002. Hollande kept plugging away at sensible, modernizing left politics and it paid off though he was not a successful or transformational president.

More and more I was coming to realise that Labour's problem was not peculiar to its identity as a British party. Across Europe, the big 20th century parties of the democratic left, the Social Democrats in Germany, the socialists in France, Italy and Spain as well as Labour in Britain were losing support. They offered 20th century responses to 21st century problems. And they faced an onslaught from party activists who wanted a more aggressive left-wing approach. This led to breakaway group who formed separate parties in France, Germany, Spain and Greece. In addition, party discipline kept breaking down. François Hollande despite having put the socialists back in the saddle of power with ministerial posts and new progressive policies faced non-stop internal party attacks that sapped his authority and the possibility of the French socialists staying in power for more than five years. There were comparisons with Labour but the party had become inward-looking since Blair left and no one was interested in learning from sister parties a few miles away across the Channel.

All this time, the Metropolitan police investigation, with a

Detective Chief Inspector, a Detective Inspector and a Detective Serjeant were trawling through all my finances, bank account, credit cards and the thousands of forms and invoices and receipts I had submitted as an MP. My solicitor dealt with all the interaction with the police. I had never been interviewed about the BNP complaint by the parliamentary commissioner so did not know exactly which one of the accusations on the BNP's charge sheet the anti-European press enjoyed publishing was the main charge.

In 1992 when in Geneva I had set up a small outfit called the European Policy Institute. It published reports, a bulletin and organized seminars. I should have closed it down when I became an MP but Robin Cook, as shadow foreign secretary, asked me to do a report and organize a conference on Labour's future policy on the EU. So it dribbled on.

**Lesson 43**. *Upon entering Parliament it is better if a new MP just divests him- or herself of any links with previous employment or organisations. They can come back to haunt you.*

MPs had the right to go anywhere in the UK on parliamentary expenses. In theory such trips, first class train tickets or planes and hotels were meant to be 'wholly and exclusively' about parliamentary business. But mostly this travel was for party political purposes: a political meeting or a visit to a constituency to talk to a local party. It was accepted as a fiddle and no one in the Commons administration bothered to control the expenses.

Given much of my parliamentary work was related to Europe I thought it was reasonable to apply the same criteria to reclaiming money – about £12,000 over five years spent travelling to meet fellow politicians in Europe, buy local newspapers and political weeklies or political current affairs books in French, German or Spanish. My mistake, and stupidity, was to use the European Policy Institute to claim back the money. No one challenged how the money had been spent. Unlike so many other MPs I was not lining my own pocket. But it was clearly false accounting, just as the expense forms my fellow BBC and Fleet Street journalists when I began my BBC and newspaper career, were fraudulent false accounting. As were many MPs' expense claims.

Together with my lawyer I went to the Lewisham police station to be interviewed by the police. It is a formulaic occasion but unlike the parliamentary commissioner the police really wanted to find out what had happened and the reasons I had acted the way I did.

I was overjoyed in July when I got a letter from the Metropolitan Police, also speaking for the Crown Prosecution Service, saying that they were closing the case and there would be no prosecution. Being cleared was a huge relief and I was clapped back in to my first meeting of the Parliamentary Labour Party and warmly congratulated by Ed Miliband. My local Labour party in Rotherham also held a celebration party. The nightmare was over.

There were two local political problems to deal with. Cameron had proposed a reduction in the number of MPs from 650 to 600. The new constituency boundaries were published and the three Rotherham seats were reduced to just two. I faced going into a selection battle with my neighbouring Labour MP, Kevin Barron who was chair of the Parliamentary Standards and Privileges Committee, which had authorized sending the BNP complaint to the police in 2010. Another local MP, John Mann, told me I would have no problem. 'You are Rotherham, Denis. Kevin will be made Lord Barron and sent off to the Lords.'

I fell out badly with Barron when the northern correspondent of *The Times*, Andrew Norfolk, who, after some brilliant investigative journalism, exposed the practice of Rotherham's Kashmiri taxi drivers seducing adolescent young women and school-age girls and having sex with them or even pimping them to sleep with other men. It was disgusting, utterly horrifying. The practice of Asian taxi drivers abusing these girls was happening from Oxford to Newcastle and in due course all over the country. Many men were rightly sent to prison. It unleashed a wave of racist hate politics against Muslims that has still not abated. These men had committed the crimes. To add insult to injury, their colleagues and friends must have known what was going on but said nothing.

I still do not know why not a single victim, nor the police and social workers who knew what was going on, had not come to me. I could have raised it in the Commons. As soon as I did know, I immediately raised it in the Commons and demanded a full statement from the Home Secretary. In Rotherham Town Hall, in front of councillors at a routine political meeting between the town's MPs and Labour councillors, Kevin Barron rounded on me and denounced the reporting in *The Times* as damaging Rotherham. My NUJ instincts rose up and I said we could not sweep this under the carpet, Andrew Norfolk and *The Times* had rendered a great public service, and Rotherham had to clean up this poison.

So relations between Kevin and myself were not in a good place. And then I learnt the parliamentary commissioner had refused to accept the decision of the Metropolitan Police and the CPS. He was going to re-open the BNP complaint and was clearly determined to remove me from Parliament.

I had no idea where to turn. I asked former chairs of the Parliamentary Standards Committee what to do. They all said, say nothing. So I said nothing. The parliamentary commissioner had never interviewed me prior to sending the file to the police. Now after the Met's twenty-month-long and very thorough investigation it seemed unfair for one man to bring back to life the BNP accusations because he was not satisfied with the police's work.

That the CPS and the Met had investigated and cleared me meant nothing to the bureaucrats of the Commons. I knew the BNP would win and in due course the Standards Committee did the BNP's dirty work and removed me from the Commons.

I had only myself to blame for the mistake I had made. It was a sad end to eighteen years as a Labour MP. But it was not the end of politics nor my commitment to the values Labour stood for. On my last day in the Commons, David Davis, a Tory foe over eighteen years on the question of Europe came over and in front of other MPs gave me a very public hug. Other MPs, Tory and Labour, said sadly, 'Good luck. It is so unfair. There but for the grace of God. It could have been any of us, Denis.'

On the Andrew Marr programme on the Sunday after I left

the Commons the then-shadow Home Secretary, Yvette Cooper, was asked if the police should re-open my case. She was caught off guard and said maybe Yes. Charlie Falconer, a top QC, a peer and former Minister of Justice was aghast. In his view, Yvette's statement was an encouragement to turn my leaving the Commons into something far worse. Now the police and the CPS did a reverse ferret and announced they would prosecute me. I never found out who in the CPS took the decision. I later met in court one of the Met detectives, who had cleared me in July. I asked what new evidence there was and why the U-turn. She turned away embarrassed.

I had been critical of the CPS's failure on dealing with sex crimes and had said so to the face of the Director of Public Prosecutions at a meeting in the Commons. The CPS, though, is a law unto itself and never has to account for its decisions.

I had made enemies in my career: other Labour colleagues, the BNP, the CPS. And I had been stupid. You can't make those kind of enemies and leave yourself stupidly vulnerable. In the end I had only my stupidity to blame.

The main winner though was the BNP. Congratulations to everyone who cooperated to ensure that.

## 2013

I was skiing in St Moritz in January 2013 with a friend the ex-*Guardian* foreign correspondent, Martin Walker. We watched David Cameron's speech announcing a Brexit referendum. I said to Martin: 'We're fucked. Any plebiscite will be on immigration and all the anti-immigrant hates and fears going back to the Enoch Powell era of the 1970s will now have an outlet.'

I wasn't being clairvoyant. Nearly every referendum in the 21st century on the continent with Europe or the EU on the ballot paper has resulted in a 'NO' vote. In Sweden, France, the Netherlands, Ireland and the Netherlands again, referendums asking for endorsement of a decision taken by European national governments, as well as the institutions in Brussels resulted in rejection. The term 'Brexit', which I'd begun using the year before, subconsciously segueing from Grexit (Greece leaving the Euro currency or indeed the EU itself), was now in wide circulation.

I could not believe the risk David Cameron was taking. When voters opted for Brexit, as I knew they would, his career would be over. If in the 18th century Lord North entered history as the man who lost America, in the 21st century David Cameron would go down as the man who lost Europe.

**Lesson 44.** *Labour never had a policy on Brexit. Ed Miliband and his entourage just preferred to avoid the word or keep fingers crossed. Anti-European Labour MPs like Gisella Stuart and Kate Hoey were not challenged over their lies, and denigration of Europe. Labour needs to have policies on big political questions not just hope they will embarrass or trip up the Tories or other rival parties*

While no longer an MP after the BNP's victory I had a new political cause which kept me firmly in the heart of politics. It was clear Brexit would now become a burn-up political cause for the rest of the decade if not longer.

So when I packed in as an MP I was happy to be relieved of the innumerable chores an MP has to do or the even more innumerable bores an MP had to spend so many hours with. I missed some of the theatre of the Commons and the company of friends but not the same old conversations, the same tired jokes, the same obsession with who's up and who's down and what was in the newspapers which dominates most of an MP's waking hours.

I was welcomed into a monthly gathering of ex-Labour MPs who met for a drink in a Kennington pub to gossip and report on the mood of the party in different parts on Britain. I continued to take part in Commons sporting events. Not a single MP saw me as a crook and all knew the BNP had got first the parliamentary bureaucracy and then the CPS to do their dirty work.

Parliament in any event had lost its bite. The Cameron-Clegg austerity government seemed in control. They lost mid-term seats in local elections in May to both Labour and significantly to UKIP. Cameron's offer to hold a Brexit referendum instead of taking on the UKIP lies and demagogy was not helping the Tories. Nationalist populism is an appetite that grows with feeding and so w UKIP and the BNP were growing, not mainstream parties, as anti-European populism took off.

I was only focused on my appearance in court. The CPS and the Metropolitan Police had already cleared me last summer but now the pleasure of landing a biggish fish from the MPs' expenses scandal was too good to forego.

I consulted every judge and QC I knew. To a man and woman they said: 'Denis, don't even dream of a fair trial or finding a jury anywhere in Britain that will not be utterly biased against an MP after all the publicity since 2010. You don't stand a chance and the DPP and CPS team know that perfectly well.'

So I resigned myself to going to prison. My QC friends who knew the judge said he would send me to prison. The judge had insisted on taking my case at the Old Bailey instead of a crown court where such cases involving small amounts of money are normally heard. On the day before Christmas Eve 2013 he sent me inside. My books were confiscated on orders from Chris Grayling, then the minister in charge of prisons and not a nice man. As I left the dock, I turned to the press bench, shrugged my shoulders, and said: '*Quelle surprise.*'

This raised my stock in Belmarsh where prison warders asked me: 'Did you really talk back to the judge in French?' I was flattered that Britain's most notorious high security prison reserved for terrorists or men like the Soho nail bomb murderer (whom I would later meet) and other serious gunmen and violent criminals would be where I would spend Christmas.

I can recommend a short stay in prison to anyone. You lose weight, sleep long hours and well, stop drinking alcohol, meet endlessly interesting people, watch day-time television and all the old movies and musicals, and have no interruptions for long, consecutive writing. I only spent seven weeks in Belmarsh and then Brixton and was soon out and about. Someone had to be the scapegoat for the far worse, and in money terms, much more serious fiddling that went on in the Commons. I could look at members of the cabinet and some of the most prominent MPs as they appeared on television. I had glanced at their expenses and they were rotten to the core.

But the parliamentary establishment and the DPP could not send all of them to prison. Finding someone to make an example of is a time-honoured tradition and if it had to be me, so be it. I had the most peaceful few weeks of my life.

# 2014

I came out of Brixton prison where I spent the first weeks of the New Year fitter, healthier, weighing less than I had ever managed in eighteen years as an MP. I was earning more money than as an MP. People both in London and on the continent laughed at the idea I was a serious criminal.

They were fascinated by my experience. The first words Tony Blair said to me after he called up to invite me for coffee at his Grosvenor Square office were: 'What's it like?' I realised that I was almost unique as an MP or anyone in my circles in having been inside Belmarsh as a prisoner.

In fact, it was clear that prisons were one area of public service which no one really understood. You could have ministers, or MPs, or civil servants, or journalists who had been soldiers, parents, patients, car drivers, teachers, local councillors, lawyers, doctors, architects with real-time lived experience of so many sectors where public policy decisions were taken. But none of them had the faintest idea of what it was like to be inside one of Her Majesty's Prisons. However, other than Rory Stewart, briefly a Tory prisons minister, no one was interested in what I had learnt in Belmarsh and Brixton.

Now all that was behind me and I could pick up political life again.

Thankfully there was a new cause almost made to measure for my political energies and life-long engagement. That cause was Europe. For the next years I poured my energy and such abilities as I had into fighting against the isolationism and xenophobia of the BNP, UKIP and the growing anti-European prejudice rising in the nation.

Ed Miliband was a natural pro-European but he was being pulled and pushed in too many directions. He was a loyal Gordon Brown aide and his closest aid (beside Ed Balls) in the Treasury where a residual dislike and suspicion of European cooperation, other than on an intergovernmental basis, had been the norm since the days of Thatcher. Yet he also sought to distance himself from the achievements in government of Blair and Brown. His trashing of Brown's economic policy felt wrong, even if it won some cheers among the left of the Labour Party. Now that Labour was in opposition and had no responsibility for government, any and every left proposal was coming back into play in constituency parties and comment pieces in the *Guardian* and *New Statesman*. If Labour before 2010 had made so many mistakes, why on earth had Ed stayed part of the team and accepted a promotion to be an MP and then minister from the Blair-Brown New Labour generation?

**Lesson 45:** *A new Labour leader should not trash his or her predecessor's record. It demoralises all MPs and party*

*members who supported the earlier leader or measures*
*without generating any new support. By all means come up*
*with new policy or positions that reverse decisions taken*
*by a defeated Labour government or leader. Labour's love*
*of dumping on what previous Labour governments and*
*prime ministers have done is debating-society politics, not*
*establishing Labour as a serious party of power.*

It wasn't his fault but now in the fourth year of Ed's leadership the party had lost the dynamism and sense of purpose it had developed from 1990 onwards. My foreboding that it was going to take much longer to get the Labour Party once again match fit and able to connect to voters just grew and grew.

After 1979 Labour in opposition always did well in European Parliament elections. They were a protest vote on a low turn-out. In May 2014 the Tories lost seven MEPs and Labour gained seven but the big winner was UKIP which scored the most votes and had more MEPs than Labour. Cameron had pandered to the anti-Europeans in the Tory Party since becoming leader in 2005. Instead of taking on the xenophobic prejudices of UKIP he tried to incorporate some of them. On this issue the metropolitan Liberal Cameron was not convincing. So voters opted for UKIP instead.

There was no considered reaction to UKIP overtaking Labour and the Tories in the 2014 elections to the European Parliament. Nor had there been any reaction to the SNP becoming the biggest party in Holyrood, the Edinburgh Parliament, and forming the Scottish government.

Professor Matthew Goodwin was so carried away with UKIP

success in the European Parliament election he wrote endless columns proclaiming that UKIP would win four or five seats in the 2015 General election.

This seemed to me to be nonsense and UKIP failed to gain a seat in national elections. Nigel Farage was the useful idiot of much deeper forces both in England. These same dark forces in America and Russia wanted, for different reasons, Britain to repudiate Europe. As soon as Farage had helped to achieve this he was discarded as a worn-out puppet by the men who had promoted him.

Labour had no answers to these problems. Instead Labour was busy turning in on itself, trying to regain popularity in an impossibly short time-frame after the ejection from office in 2010.

Ed decided that a major reform of the Labour Party constitution and rule-book would help Labour back to power. The way forward was to distance Labour from the trade unions. It was true that in no other left party in Europe or in countries influenced by British political traditions, like Australia or Canada, did trade unions have the institutional role they had in Labour in Britain.

Labour's constitution had a bizarre system for electing a leader. Forty per cent of the vote went to trade unions, thirty per cent to MPs, and thirty percent to constituency rank and file members or those in outfits like the Fabian Society which were affiliated to Labour. So this meant in 2010 I had had four votes – as an MP, as a trade union member, as a Labour Party member in Rotherham, and as a Fabian Society member to elect the new Leader. But my vote as an MP was worth 30,000 votes more than the one vote cast by party members. For Labour Party anoraks and infighters this was indefensible. As indeed it was. But did it matter to voters? The Labour Party thought changing its internal rule book would be welcomed by the electorate, which couldn't care less.

It was a sensitive point for Ed as his brother David had won more votes amongst MPs and rank-and-file members, and Ed was the leader only thanks to the trade union block vote. In addition, the trade unions provided about one third of Labour's annual running costs and added in millions at the time of a general election.

The obvious answer which just about every other democracy in the world – other than the United States – had already grasped was that a democracy should pay for its democracy. A strictly controlled and limited amount of public funding should be made available for the conduct of democracy and to terminate the money that rich individuals or trade unions could give to their favoured parties.

I had been arguing this nearly all my political life including as a minister. But my Labour comrades stuck to trade union funding with even Robin Cook resisting public money paying for a functioning democracy. Instead, we had to sit through endlessly boring fund-raising dinners for rich donors who as soon as Labour looked like losing power switched to their natural Tory home.

Ed and his team were too nervous to support reform of political financing. Instead he sought to appear a radical reformer by removing all rights for trade unions and MPs and enshrining the OMOV principle – One Member, One Vote – for electing a new party leader and other Labour Party decisions. Paid-up party members would vote. So too would "registered" supporters, an ill-defined category and trade union members who had declared themselves to be supporters of the Labour Party.

It was a dramatic reduction in trade union power. Finally after more than a century the leader of the Labour Party and putative prime minister would be elected by individual votes of equal weight and worth. It seemed to be the culmination of three decades of campaigning to reduce trade union power and the influence of the left.

Miliband's reforms led to many thousands of 'supporters' who would join just to vote to elect the leader but not do any work to win elections. Many individual Labour Party members were as hostile to the 1997-2010 Labour government and Tony Blair as my generation had been to the 1974-79 government and Jim Callaghan. They had quit the party in disgust over Iraq or what they saw as right-wing policies. Now they could rejoin for a nugatory fee and take their revenge by voting for a leader of their WhatsApp groups dreams.

## 2015

The year the Corbyn era began. The new rule change imposed by Ed Miliband and extended by the acting Leader, Harriet Harman, allowed anyone who paid £3 to vote for the next leader of the Labour Party. The Labour leader was now to be chosen by people who had no previous connection to the party, no understanding of its history, no experience of why it failed to be elected between 1979 and 1997, and no commitment to working at the grass roots for Labour. It was the apotheosis of One Member One Vote which anti-left Labour bigwigs has been touting since the early 1980s as the magic solution to block a left takeover.

Now OMOV was to deliver Labour into the hands of a clique, many of whom had supported parties other than Labour or foreign governments opposed to democratic socialist values, indeed to democracy of any sort.

There are no magic solutions in politics. No mechanical voting system that produces any desired result. All politics is about education, education, education working to educate the party and then wider voters. In an ironic reversal of fortune the preferred system of Labour right-wing reformers in the 1980s and 1990s to keep at bay the militant left – OMOV – was to rise up and impose Jeremy Corbyn on Labour.

In 2015, Ed Miliband, who represented the continuation of Blair-Brown New Labour by other means was rejected at the ballot box. Ed Miliband and Ed Balls lost twenty-six seats – including that of Ed Balls in Yorkshire – and Labour's share of the votes slumped to thirty per cent.

Worse in some respects for the broader non-Tory coalition was the fate of the LibDems who saw forty-nine of their fifty-seven MPs lose their seats as voters expressed their anger at 'Sir' Nick Clegg, 'Sir' Vince Cable, 'Sir' Ed Davey and other MPs, and at them having spent five years as junior assistants to David Cameron and George Osborne's policy of austerity which increased poverty and cut public services.

**Lesson 46.** *Labour needs allies to reduce number of Tory seats. In 1950 the Liberals stood in 475 seats and won 2,621,487 votes, about a quarter of the Tory total. This gave Labour a narrow majority. Attlee then called an election in 1951 and Liberals contested only 109 seats and won 730, 546 votes, about a quarter of their vote tally in 1950. Those other 1,900,000 votes went to Tories. So Labour benefits from a strong Liberal (today LibDem) or Green votes in as many constituencies as possible. LibDem voters are basically Tories who read the Guardian and shop in Waitrose. Nonetheless Labour needs the strongest possible LibDem (or possibly the Green) party to work to win Tory seats that won't come to Labour.*

Clegg's Faustian pact of selling his party's soul to the Tories left millions of LibDem voters confused and demoralised. It guaranteed David Cameron's win in 2015. Clegg's decision to make the LibDems the Tory helpmates drove Labour further to the unelectable left as all hope evaporated of a broad left-liberal-centre movement – not a formal coalition but the kind of togetherness that we saw between Blair and Ashdown in the 1990s, and which was common enough in progressive politics across the Channel.

So Jeremy emerged. He faced opposition from three stalwart Blair-Brown era middle-ranking ex-ministers Yvette Cooper, Liz Kendall and Andy Burnham. All were likeable, fluent enough on television, all associated with modernising New Labour ideology, Oxbridge graduates who had been political aides. The massive influx of new members into the Labour Party did nothing for them. This was the real entryism that took Labour to the left far more effectively than the efforts of other entryist parties like Militant or organisations like the Campaign for Labour Democracy. It was an emotional evangelical movement that found, if not their Messiah at least their John the Baptist, in Jeremy Corbyn.

I had known Jeremy sort of all my political life as we are the same age. He was there in the background of politics during the Callaghan government. Did I see him on the Grunwick Picket line? Or on the Anti-Nazi League executive? He certainly was opposed to nuclear weapons though I don't think I ever encountered him at European Nuclear Disarmament events. END was as opposed to Soviet nuclear weapons as those possessed by Britain or the US.

Combatting Stalinism was never a Corbyn priority and when he became leader two of his closest aides, Seumas Milne and Andrew Murray, one a veteran *Guardian* journalist, who often published me when running the *Guardian's* Comment section, and the other a trade union official and Communist Party member, were both open apologists for Soviet communism. They both came from elite, privileged British upper-middle-class family backgrounds, educated at private schools – in Seumas' case the super-elite Winchester. They were friendly, polite and always good company.

I never crossed swords with Jeremy and always found him unfailingly courteous. He voted consistently in the Commons against EU Treaties in the same lobby as many a Little Englander Tory, but that was in the tradition of a Denis Healey or Peter Shore and of 'socialism in one country' economic nationalism, not the dislike of EU citizens working in Britain that motivated so many others. He also supported any campaign to replace the existing Labour leader with someone more to Jeremy's liking.

> **Lesson 47.** *Labour should split the post of party leader and party candidate for 10 Downing Street. The German Social Democrats do this. Corbyn was the choice of the new party members who wanted ideological rhetoric but were not interested in making any compromise to win power. However, he was utterly unelectable. Many members of the Labour Party knew this but the shadow cabinet Corbyn appointed formed a protective shield around him instead of being honest with themselves and politely suggesting he stand down to be replaced by a Labour PM candidate who would stand a better chance.*

His disloyalty was serial but no one much bothered as he was so marginal and in personal terms genial enough. He was a moralist, not a Marxist, a preacher more than a political leader, a one-man home to lost or unpopular causes which he espoused when others turned away. Hence his talks with Sinn Fein based on his belief in a united Ireland, an honourable if contested political aim. It brought him tabloid press condemnations but before long the John Major government was doing the same thing. The Palestinian cause is worthy of support as are the needs of people in countries like Nicaragua or Venezuela to live free of oppression. Jeremy never drew a distinction between supporting a cause and endorsing some of its uglier proponents, who in the case of Islamists are Jew-haters and called for the destruction of Israel, or in the case of Latin America were politicians who denied women's rights or often were as corrupt and vicious as their opponents.

Jeremy was easily elected leader of the Labour party in September 2015. Six months previously I had published a book, *Brexit. How Britain Will Leave Europe*. It was written in 2014 and posited the thesis that if David Cameron's promised referendum were to take place there would be only one likely outcome, a vote against Europe.

I had hoped it might get some play in the election debate in the months leading up to David Cameron's victory. There were one or two nice reviews and an interview in the *Observer*. I gave a copy to Jim Naughtie, a friend, then in his last period as a presenter on Radio 4's *Today* programme. He turned a few pages, saw the news value of a former Europe Minister known to be a strong pro-European admitting that if it came to a referendum the anti-Europeans would win. 'We'll definitely get this on, Denis,' Jim said.

Nothing happened.

A little-known fact is that no matter the status and popularity of a well-known TV or radio current affairs presenter they decide very little of what appears is a programme or who gets interviewed. *Today* was being edited by a right-wing Tory. My hope of making an argument that electing David Cameron would ensure a referendum that would in turn take Britain out of Europe, got no traction. There were many other programmes: Sky, Channel 4 News, ITN. But other than LBC no one gave me much space for my warning that the Cameron referendum would turn into a lie-filled celebration of populist anti-immigrant emotion.

One just had to tot up the newspapers by readership to see the massive imbalance against Europe. Even the *Guardian,* which carried weekly bromides against Europe from star columnists like Sir Simon Jenkins and Canon Giles Fraser, now launched a campaign shaped by its rising young left-wing columnist, Owen Jones, who was close to Corbyn. Owen called for a left-wing Brexit, a "Lexit" as he baptised it, and the term "Lexit" became fashionable in the *London Review of Books* as a jejune leftist version of what the hard anti-Europeans of the right had been campaigning for all this century.

As I took my book from conference to conference, from think tank to think tank, as I gave copies to friends in the shadow cabinet, the French and German ambassadors, retired senior diplomats, the big names setting up the Yes vote campaign I found no audience at all. There were friendly pats on the back, acknowledgements that I had good arguments and perhaps, after so many years of writing and thinking about European politics, some experience in this field, yadda, yadda, yadda, but everyone was convinced that Cameron would win and Britain would never vote to cut links with Europe.

For Jeremy Corbyn and his new team of insiders there was no enthusiasm for Europe. Jeremy had visited nearly every capital in Latin America and much of the global south. He travelled more often to Gaza than to Brussels or Strasbourg. But he knew little of Europe and cared nothing about the EU as presently constituted. Above all the Labour luminaries who did speak up for Europe – Tony Blair, Peter Mandelson, David

Miliband, Douglas Alexander –constituted the very Labour Party that Jeremy had opposed and voted against in his thirty-two years as an MP. And from the ideological point of view of his inner team of advisors Labour pro-Europeans were as bad as or even worse than Cameron and Clegg.

I was full of foreboding as the year ended. George Osborne, reconfirmed as Chancellor, announced a fresh round of £20 billion cuts in public services. The City and financial pages roared him on. I just saw the plebiscite coming up fast next year as the moment when so many would take their revenge on an elite of rulers and money men who had left too many without hope or a sense that Britain belonged to all its people and not just a small caste at the top of the nation.

# 2016

The year of Brexit and Donald Trump. The Siamese twins of populist, post-truth right-wing nationalist populism. In 1958, John F Kennedy had written a book, *America, a Nation of Immigrants*. Now the United States elected a president whose first act was to attacks immigrants and refugees in the United States. At home, a populist plebiscite won based on appeals to reject European citizens living and working peacefully in Britain as well as contributing to British wealth creation and tax revenues.

The most successful Leave campaign poster showed a snaking queue of Middle Eastern-ish men and women, with the implication they were all about to descend upon Britain. The photo was taken in the Balkans far from British shores, but the message of hate was the same as Donald Trump's.

I just felt sad. All my warnings that Brexit would take place ever since I first used the word in 2012 and reinforced these warnings in my 2015 book *Brexit: How Britain Will Leave Europe* were turning out to be true. The campaign to persuade Britain not to be duped by the promises of the anti-Europeans was hopeless. Add frustration to sadness.

Nonetheless, it was good to be back in harness even if I knew our horse would not win. I wrote and spoke as much as I could and did a great deal of TV and radio debates about Brexit for French and other foreign media.

Our biggest problem was complacency. On the day of the plebiscite, the 23rd June 2016, I bumped into Professor Anand Menon of Kings College, London on the way out of Broadcasting House. I'd known Anand for years. He organised an impressive team of academics at Kings College, London to comment on the referendum in the months before the vote. I asked Anand what the result would be.

'I know the English,' he replied without hesitation. 'They will bottle it. They don't have the nerve to vote to leave,' he said with all the assurance of a top professor. He was in good company. On the same day, Peter Kellner, one of the best number-crunchers on British politics for decades, a founder of the successful polling outfit, YouGov, and a man whose insights into politics especially on the centre-left have been widely hailed, tweeted that the result would be 55-45 in favour of Remain.

Andrew Cooper, a close confidante of David Cameron (who

gave him a peerage), and another political insider who had gone to make money via setting up a polling firm, Populus, was one of the trio that headed the official Stronger In campaign. On 22nd June he told both his fellow Stronger In directors that Remain would easily win and a No 10 official working on the campaign to keep the UK in Europe told me that the same confident, but utterly wrong message was conveyed to the Prime Minister.

I was left dumbstruck at how wrong-headed these clever, influential 'experts' could be. Had any of them, I wondered, ever knocked on doors in the last decade and asked people their views on Europe? I had spent nearly two decades as an MP watching the slow rise of anti-European politics. It subsumed all the dislikes many ordinary people in Britain had. Dislike of foreigners; dislike of the business elite who attended Davos to explain why their wealth could best be guaranteed by inducing poverty in the populace; dislike of the Tory and LibDem ministers who had imposed austerity, tripled student fees and failed to bring in labour market measures to control or even know the number or whereabouts of the European citizens working in Britain. This was the moment of revenge for forgotten, taken-for-granted-England.

It was about England too. Scotland and the six Irish counties of the UK voted for Europe. So too did big cities, university towns, Asian voters and young people. But huge swathes of middle class, middle England had been fed on a daily diet of anti-European propaganda by their papers, the *Telegraph* and *Mail*, and guided by the BBC *Today* programme, which on Europe sounded like Radio *Spectator*. They could now take their golf-club and saloon-bar prejudices and express them via the ballot box.

Angela Merkel had opened the doors of Germany to one million mainly Arab or North African Muslim immigrants fleeing the wars and violence of the failed states of Libya and Syria. The decision of David Cameron and William Hague to unleash another round of regime-change-type interventions in Muslim nations in 2011 had made the mass movement of people worse than the Iraq war in the previous decade. Worse, at least in terms of its impact on Europe. The right-wing refugee-hating papers like the *Sun* and *Daily Mail* portrayed these pathetic asylum-seekers as a mortal threat to Britain. It helped create the atmosphere for the Brexit vote.

It certainly didn't help that the prime minister, David Cameron, was an unconvincing advocate for EU membership. I had taken part in most of the Commons debates on Europe in which he spoke as MP, leader of the Tory Party and then prime minister. Cameron never had a good word to say about Europe. His tone when discussing Europe was sneering, dismissive, condescending, patronising and above all, like William Hague, hostile to the arguments for Europe advanced by many in the Conservative Party. Cameron's words to persuade voters to stay in Europe rang hollow and unconvincing. The official Remain or Yes Campaign was run by an assortment of public relations firms working for UK-based global corporations and a shopkeeper who had been the boss of Marks and Spencer. His main claim to fame was to be a recipient of a public protest by Jeremy Paxman, the BBC's star political interviewer, that the underpants he'd bought from Marks and Spencer had so little elastic in the waistband they kept falling down.

Tony Blair made a speech here or there or wrote something in favour of Europe. So did his press *consigliere*, Alistair Campbell. When Alistair was in Downing Street he called in Robin Cook's special advisors and told then 'to get all the pro-European shit out of Robin's speeches.' What goes around comes around. Labour's failure 1997-2010 to make a case for EU membership with their voting base was part of the reason for the Brexit vote in 2016. Gordon Brown wrote a 350-page book *Britain: Leading, Not Leaving: The Patriotic Case for Remaining in Europe*. It was published a few weeks before the referendum by a Selkirk publisher. As always with any writing by Brown the book was solid, fact-based and well-argued. But it came out too late to appear in many bookshops and had very little impact.

At least Tony, Alistair and Gordon were out there fighting against the isolationist and neo-xenophobia of the Brexit camp. The new Corbyn-led Labour Party regarded Blair as the devil incarnate due to the Iraq conflict and refused to listen to him on Europe. During the thirteen years of Labour government, after an initial enthusiasm for reversing some of the more stupid of John Major's policies on Europe, Labour ministers kept presenting EU membership as a problem to overcome not a source of added value to a Britain that otherwise would have been more alone and marginal.

Corbyn kept well away from the campaign. Jeremy had refused to appear on platforms with David Cameron and Nick Clegg to argue for a Yes vote. He also refused to appear on a pro-EU platform with Tony Bair and Gordon Brown and Neil Kinnock despite Gordon urging him to drop such sectarianism and speak with fellow Labour Party leaders. I went to one rally in London which was billed as a major Jeremy speech in favour of voting Remain. It turned out to be a call for better air quality in London. There were some vague words about staying in the EU to uphold better environmental standards but a vigorous appeal to Labour voters to defeat UKIP and Boris Johnson it wasn't. Labour MPs who were anti-European like Kate Hoey or Gisella Stuart got far more publicity than any member of Labour's shadow cabinet. In the final few weeks of the campaign, fifty per cent of Labour party members did not know the stance of the Labour party on Brexit.

In the confusing weeks and months after the referendum result Corbyn and Labour were left helpless, unable to offer any national leadership. They had never thought through a *policy* on Europe. Instead they had a *wish list* for Europe that would offer jobs and protect trade union rights and the environment but not be an open border social market to increase Europe's economic strength in face of the United States and the rising economic might of China. Nothing wrong with wish lists. But it reminded me of my grandson's wish list for Santa. He wanted an eagle.

At the Labour party conference the young stars of Ed Miliband's shadow cabinet all came up with their own schemes on how the new prime minister, Theresa May, should respond to Brexit. Examples included Rachel Reeves, Chuka Umanna and the newly elected Stephen Kinnock, son of Neil. Stephen had won a south Wales seat and worked for the World Economic Forum in Davos, and his wife was briefly a social democratic prime minister of Denmark. What they all had in common was an acceptance that Britain should not challenge the referendum vote. I was puzzled by this. Of course, one accepted the vote just as one accepted the vote of any democratic ballot box exercise.

But throughout all my life one lost vote did not mean giving up. As my old friend, David Davis, liked to say: 'A democracy that cannot change its mind ceases to be a democracy.'

I thought the narrowness of the result and clear evidence of outside interference meant that the vote of just over one third of the total British electorate could indeed be challenged.

> **Lesson 48.** *Thought-out positions on constitutional questions have always been missing from Labour's political tool-box. Absent a written constitution there is little intellectual or academic or journalistic work of value on constitutional issues. The Brexit referendum result was a fundamental change in the rights of all British citizens – their constitutional status and rights - as well as economic relations and international treaty obligations. From now on Labour needs to think about such constitutional questions.*

My position was made easier by the decision of Theresa May, the prime minister, to leave the centre ground. She moved her position close to that of Nigel Farage and filled her cabinet with UKIP fellow travellers. She made a foul xenophobic speech to her Tory party conference in which she described as 'citizens of nowhere' those who believed that people could co-exist, live and work together within a democracy like Britain, even if they came from different nations.

I gently mocked all these newly minted Labour grandees and their desire to endorse the referendum result as 'Red UKIP.' This was a play on what was called 'Blue Labour,' a concept advanced by one or two professors who thought that the best way for Labour to win back working-class votes was to adopt Tory policies and right-wing nationalist protectionist and chauvinist mood music.

The Labour Party conference was at sixes and sevens without leadership of any sort. I had no expectation that Jeremy Corbyn would be able to offer leadership but I did hope some of members of the shadow cabinet, especially those who had entered parliament in 2015 with a reputation for not wanting to have a rupture with Europe, might be able to articulate more sensible views.

But in the six months after the June plebiscite this was not to be. Indeed, victory for Donald Trump in the United States, and his celebration with Nigel Farage and Michael Gove of the double Brexit-Trump victory seemed to point in the other direction. Boris Johnson even proposed the new hard-right racist president should receive the Nobel Peace Prize! In the closing years of my political life I resolved to keep arguing, writing, campaigning and speaking for a return to common-sense, middle-of-the-road European politics.


## 2017

All this year I still could get little idea of what Labour now stood for. Jeremy and shadow cabinet members went through the motions in the Commons. The left columnists like Owen Jones, Rafael Behr, Stephen Bush and others wrote about Labour but there was no story, no narrative, no well-chosen epigrams that conveyed what Labour *raison d'être* was in the nation.

Corbyn was clearly no intellectual, no shaper of ideas into a theory and then policy proposals that made political sense. He was adrift over Brexit. Everyone was coming to terms with the referendum. Only thirty-six per cent of the registered electorate voted to break links with our neighbours. But this fact was lost in the non-stop invocation of the Brexit win. Labour MPs were confused and divided over how to respond to the vote, as were the trade unions and the left opinion formers. It was no secret that Corbyn did not like Europe.

Now Corbyn was faced with Labour MPs who split in many different camps over Brexit. As he had never thought about Europe and always preferred causes in the global south to collaborating with the democratic left in Europe, he had no clear policy path to follow. Instead he took the easy way out of just insisting that Labour wanted a social justice, pro-worker, pro-jobs, pro-green, pro-peace Europe. Who could oppose such an idealized left, green and pacifist European Union? But it was not on offer from the 27 sovereign national government many headed by socialists or with left parties in coalition who decided EU policy.

**Lesson 49.** *It is always easier not to have a policy as policies, other than those supporting motherhood and apple pie, rarely produce unanimity in politics. But Labour's failure since 2016 to have any kind of policy on Europe after the plebiscite result just leaves voters puzzled and confused.*

He was rescued by Theresa May. A general election is always a defining moment in politics. Most internal party differences fade or are put on hold for the duration of trying to win.

Like Ted Heath's 'Who Governs' election of 1974, Theresa May's 2017 election was pure opportunism. She clearly hoped to capitalise on Brexit but still refused to reveal what kind of Brexit she wanted. This played into Corbyn's hands as Labour was badly divided over Brexit.

It was a boring, endless election. I campaigned in as many seats as possible and was struck by the personal hostility to Corbyn. In Tooting, a safe Labour seat, a man pulled down a bedroom window to shout at me as I knocked on doors across the street for Labour. 'I'll vote Labour when you get rid of that fucking communist, Corbyn,' he yelled.

That was on the first day of the campaign and I discounted it. Yet again and again wherever I asked people to vote Labour the question of Corbyn came up. For the new members who had flocked into Labour paying a £3 membership fee, Jeremy was a kind of secular saint. He was speaking a gospel truth, light years from the cautious, reasoned policies of Ed Miliband, let alone the unmentionable Tony Blair or the forgotten Gordon Brown.

I found no enthusiasm for Theresa May. But there was active dislike and contempt for Jeremy Corbyn. I went to work in two seats held by pro-European women MPs who were friends, Emma Reynolds in Wolverhampton and Mary Creagh in Wakefield. Here the rejection of any idea of Corbyn being in No 10 was palpable and freely expressed. Both seats had seen a clear majority for Brexit but the two MPs, women of principle, insisted that Brexit would do damage to the local economy unless carefully handled.

Both Emma and Mary were frightened they might lose their seat. Corbyn's fence-sitting on Brexit with the surreal proposition from his Brexit spokesman, a senior QC, that Labour would negotiate a 'jobs-first' Brexit, without challenging the concept of amputating Britain from Europe, was utterly unconvincing and exposed these two fine young politicians to more and more criticism locally.

In the end Mrs May's hopes of making this a Brexit election did not work. She actually won the election with 317 seats against Corbyn's 262. But she did not have an overall majority and had to make a pact with an extreme Ulster unionist protestant party to have a slim majority in the Commons.

In comparison, Corbyn was treated as a conquering hero with crowds at the Glastonbury festival and at any Labour event for the next two years chanting, 'Oh, Jeremy Corbyn,' as if he were the Messiah. At the Labour Party conference, the chant of 'Oh, Jeremy Corbyn' was endless.

Going into the hall there were stands of t-shirts on sale with Corbyn's face on them. This cult of personality was disturbing. The first time I'd been a delegate at a Labour Party conference was in 1973 and in those forty-four years I'd never seen t-shirts on sale with the leader's face on them, like Che Guevara or Hugo Chavez. Tony Benn was once the darling of left Labour but no one produced t-shirts with his face and pipe clenched between his teeth.

I bumped into Jon Lansman, the leader of Momentum, which was organising a parallel conference and asked him if this cult of personality was wise. He smiled and shrugged his shoulders as if it was unavoidable. The buzz in the conference was like that before winning in 1997. It seemed churlish to point out that Labour had fifty-five fewer seats than the Tories. What was missing was any discussion of the elephant in the room: the two great bulwarks of Labour's victory twenty years previously – a large phalanx of Scottish seats and fifty to sixty LibDems seats – were missing.

Corbyn's Labour Party existed in its own time warp. The rest of Europe appeared not to exist. Momentum had invited Jean-Luc Mélenchon, a flamboyant French leftist who had broken with the Socialist Party and launched his own left party, which then split the French left asunder and handed an easy victory to the ex-banker, Emmanuel Macron. The *New Statesman* gave him a glowing profile-interview. However Corbyn's Labour had no interest in what was happening amongst other democratic left parties elsewhere in the world. In that regard, Corbyn's Labour party was exactly like all his predecessors.

There was nothing intellectually exciting about Corbyn's Labour. There were the rather obvious policies like re-nationalising the railways or the post office which not many could object to, although there was no evidence that Whitehall bureaucrats were better at delivering rail or postal services. Books appeared by younger journalists and academics on the rebirth of Labour under Corbyn. However elections deliver the only verdict that matters in a democracy. The people of Britain did not want a Corbyn government.

As so often in the past Labour stuck with a loser leader while the Tories were moving to replace their loser, Theresa May.

# 2018

I couldn't get a feel of Labour in this third year of Brexit. I went to meetings in Hyde Park and elsewhere addressed by Jeremy Corbyn where they chanted, 'Oh, Jeremy Corbyn,' like the monks at my school softly singing their appeal to God as they waited for the Saviour to return to earth. I was fed up with the duopoly of politics. No 1 issue – Brexit. No 2 issue – the character of Jeremy Corbyn. The rest of the world and Britain's pressing needs didn't exist.

There was so much that felt bad. On every street corner of London, outside supermarkets, tube stations, on every second tube journey in the carriages themselves there were homeless people. Central London and my two stamping grounds of Clapham Common and Pimlico had more homeless than I had ever seen in my life outside of the global south. As I walked along Clapham High Street there were men and women lying on cardboard, just sleeping out in the cold and rain.

Yet a quick foray to the City or Mayfair and I was with the richest of the rich in the world. Dinner parties in Kentish Town, Islington, Hampstead or Kensington, and I was sitting with friends who were all on the left: QCs, editors, writers, think-tankers, TV and radio journalists, many proud of their left-liberal pedigree, all on six-figure incomes and living in houses worth more than a million. No one who spoke for us in the High Command of the Labour Party could articulate specific, concrete, implementable proposals for finding resources to deal with this shaming poverty all around us.

2018 was election year for bigger local government councils including all those in London. Eight years into an unpopular Tory government Labour could reasonably expect to win control of Barnet Council in North London where the Conservatives clung on by just one seat. My local council, Westminster, was a taller order as the Tories had a substantial majority. But Westminster had voted massively against Brexit in 2016. Might Labour profile itself as the pro-European party and pick up some council seats in London boroughs that had voted against Brexit?

As ever I liked going out canvassing with our Labour candidates, but a cold electoral truth soon revealed itself. We knocked on doors on the open balconies of blocks of council flats – pretty solid Labour territory in the past. But they were empty or had people living in them who were not on the electoral register. Many had poor or no English. Immigrants or asylum seekers who had managed to get into Britain and now worked anywhere, for anyone, at any pay rate in London's cash-in-hand deregulated labour market. This was the new working class, the 21st century lumpen proletariat, the Deliveroo bikers, the pre-dawn cleaners of London's offices, the day-hire labourers, the women in nail bars or keeping hole-in-the-wall fast food parlours open for most hours of the day.

The trade unions, now mainly based in the public sector where recruitment, organisation and representation were regulated, did not exist for this new proletariat. Trade union leaders always had words to tell Labour: what to do or how its members should react to Jeremy Corbyn and the clique around him. But what was missing was the energy, resources and leadership to go out and recruit the new workers of Britain as their trade union forebears had done 100 or more years ago.

Lesson 50: *Labour needs to recognise that as the world changes, so too does the nature of work. If Labour is to be the party of the workers (as opposed to being one of generalised social equity and social justice), then it has to recruit new kinds of followers, creating strategies that include them and proposing policies that match their realities.*

We did street stalls along the busy shopping street of Warwick Way and Tachbrook market. One Saturday morning, a man of about sixty walked past us with his laden Tesco bag. He paused to look at Labour Party activists handing out leaflets, put down his shopping bag for a moment, shook his head sadly and said: 'I'm very sorry. I can't vote Labour. I'm Jewish you see.'

I did not bother to enter into a discussion or try to persuade him. In the minds of many, probably the majority of Jews in Britain, the Labour Party was now seen as hostile to Jews, their identity and core beliefs. Labour shadow cabinet members led by a lawyer who had never held elected office, Shami Chakrabarti, who had produced an eccentric stream-of-consciousness report with references to her personal experiences, as if she were Jewish, exculpated Corbyn. She kept appearing on TV and radio to deny that Labour had an antisemitism problem. Corbyn made her a peer and a shadow cabinet member though she had no record of Labour Party commitment or activism.

The trouble was that very few Jews in Britain – other than

Corbyn groupies – believed this defence. It made shadow cabinet members look at best disingenuous, at worst unwilling to deal condignly with the rabid Jew hate on social media, shared or re-posted by Labour members, elected officials and activists.

**Lesson 51.** *Labour must never, ever allow itself to be contaminated by accusations of anti-Semitism. We must be inclusive to all peoples.*

I hoped some of these problems might be discussed when the Labour party held a Saturday afternoon session before the May 2018 local elections. The event was presided over, not by the leader of the Labour group of councillors, but by the Labour parliamentary candidate. The Reverend Steven Saxby was very much a red reverend. He was a curate in Walthamstow, an associate of George Galloway, led the faith division of the union Unite and was a fully paid-up member of Momentum.

As we all settled down to discuss how Labour might win Westminster Council seats Steven turned it into some kind of evangelist rally. It was made all the more a moment of religious-political ecstasy when Jeremy Corbyn quietly came into the hall. The buzz and fervour of our Messiah being amongst us was palpable. As always, Jeremy just quietly sat down and waited for his turn on the agenda.

The Revered Saxby opened it by introducing an American campaigner for Bernie Sanders who was running for the Democratic nomination against Donald Trump in 2020. The American let us into the secret of the advance of Bernie Sanders. 'Friends, we do something I can really recommend to you. We go and talk to people on the doorstep. We knock on doors and have face-to-face interactions with voters to get them to vote for us.' There was a sweet innocence in this young American revealing the secret of successful campaigning to fifty or sixty Labour activists who had been knocking on doors for decades.

Sensing this part of the afternoon service wasn't quite working out, the Red Reverend tried another tactic. He took the microphone and like a TV evangelical he walked around asking selected speakers to say what Labour should do to win in Westminster.

I was midway down the hall in a gangway seat and suddenly Saxby put the microphone under my nose. He didn't really know who I was as I had avoided playing the ex-MP and kept myself in the background at meetings preferring to be out on the streets talking with voters.

'What should we do to win Westminster for socialism?' he asked.

I made a short statement. 'Well, Steven, the big thing Labour has going for it in Westminster is that this area had the largest number of anti-Brexit voters in the country. So we should focus on the damage that will be done to London across the board under Tory Brexit plans and make clear a Labour-led Westminster Council would join with Sadiq Khan in opposing Tory plans to cut us off from Europe.'

By now, Jeremy Corbyn had turned around as he recognised my voice and the fact I was speaking clearly and to the point. He gave a half-smile as if to say, 'Oh dear, not more European stuff from Denis.' As always with Corbyn the innate politeness of a properly brought-up middle-class provincial lad meant he just smiled and turned away. Not for him the get-down-and-get-dirty hashing out of differences.

Jeremy's presence and Stephen's preaching made little difference. Labour gained just three more seats on their 2014 tally, leaving Westminster firmly in Tory hands. Indeed, the Labour councillor for the Churchill ward where I lived defected to the Tories who promised him money for some project or maybe a good place on a committee.

Normally after a decade of national government by one party (and the LibDems had lost their identity as the Tories swallowed them up) one would expect the main opposition party to win lots of council seats and control of councils. Yet in London, with its ranks of Labour MPs, a Labour Mayor, and councils like Barnet with a one seat Tory majority, voters refused to support Jeremy Corbyn's Labour despite Jeremy being a London MP for more than three decades. In Kensington despite the outrage over the local Tory council's handing for the Grenfell fire disaster which led in 2017 to Labour winning the Commons seat, Labour gained only one extra councillor.

What was going on? What messages were voters sending us? And could Labour listen and learn? Or was it all too late?

# 2019

Apotheosis. I joined the Labour Party after a defeat in 1970 that soon became a win in 1974. Now I had to live with one of the saddest, shabbiest, sickening years in Labour history culminating in a big triumph for the most shallow, cynical, dishonest Tory politician in the party's 300-year history. His deputy at the Foreign Office was the Tory MP Sir Alan Duncan who recorded in his diary in September 2017 that Johnson 'is a clown, a self-centred ego, an embarrassing buffoon... an international stain on our reputation... selfish, shameless.' And that's what a life-long Eurosceptic Tory MP thinks of his new party leader and prime minister.

Thanks to Labour and other opposition parties Boris Johnson became the prime minister with a mandate to make my country weak, xenophobic and regarded with pity and increasing indifference around the world.

Early in the New Year I went to Newport for the funeral of my friend, Paul Flynn. We had both been on the Council of Europe. Paul was one of the most original of any Labour MPs I served with. Paul was his own man, a big-hearted generous Welsh intellectual with a deep musical voice that commanded the Chamber of the Commons. He was on the left, or perhaps more accurately, he was a propagator of radical values and ideas that emanate in Wales from Lloyd George, through Nye Bevan and Neil Kinnock, and in MPs like Ann Clwyd. Welsh radical politics have been transformational for Labour and Liberal politics and it is surely no accident that there is no big Tory in history who hailed from Wales.

The funeral in Newport Cathedral was a gathering of men in black suits from Labour and the trade unions, some women, the deep voiced preaching of a eulogy from a bishop, and the sheer joy of a Welsh choir.

Then suddenly, from the middle of the congregation,

up rose Jeremy Corbyn to deliver a tribute. It was well done. Jeremy's praised Paul's opposition to war but did not – rightly – claim him as a Corbynite. He told jokes at his own expense about Paul.

It was short and to the point and the Labour faithful liked the tribute. I sat thinking that this could be a new role for Corbyn. He was never going to lead the party to power but perhaps Jeremy could be the 'Eulogiser-in-Chief' for his generation of MPs as they died off one by one.

Afterwards he waited outside the cathedral with just one aide, as approachable as ever. He greeted me warmly. I said how much I, as well as all current and former Labour MPs who were present, enjoyed the tribute.

'Oh, thanks very much, Denis. Err, I didn't say anything wrong on Europe, did I?'

'No, Jeremy,' I told him but failed to add, 'The problem is that you have never said anything right on Europe.' But it was a funeral and it was decent of Jeremy to have come from London to pay tribute to Paul.

The opposition to the hard Brexit line of Theresa May, and behind her Boris Johnson and other UKIP fellow-travellers amongst Tory MPs, was growing. Up to a million people marched through London to demand the right to have another say on Brexit. After all, Boris Johnson, had written in the *Daily Telegraph* in June 2016 just after the plebiscite, 'I cannot stress too much that Britain is part of Europe – and always will be. British people will still be able to go and work in the EU; to live; to travel; to study; to buy homes and to settle down. There will continue to be free trade and access to the single market.' The pro-Brexit Dominic Cummings had earlier called for a second, confirmatory referendum.

Corbyn and the Labour leadership were paralyzed. As hundreds of thousands marched in London – as joyous a demonstration I've ever taken part in since 1968 generation marches and rallies in London against the Vietnam war and apartheid – there was no sign of a single senior Labour MP, let alone the party leader or members of the shadow cabinet.

I was just baffled at the political stupidity of this. Here was the pulsating energy of young people, eighty per cent of Labour Party members were in favour of a new referendum. And this time it could be ring-fenced against Russian and other social media interference that would allow all British citizens to vote fairly and cleanly.

The May-Johnson version of Brexit was that of UKIP, the BNP, Donald Trump, Rupert Murdoch, the *Daily Telegraph* and *Express* and every known foe of progressive politics in Britain. So where was Jeremy and the shadow cabinet? One positive outcome of Brexit was the rise of new younger journalists. Some like Ash Sarkar, described herself on social media as, 'Anarcho-Fabulous. Luxury-Communist. Walks like a supermodel.' Which was certainly a little different in style from my generation of left-wing campaigning women journalists. Sensibly, Ms Sarkar, a strong fluent journalist, has changed her twitter handle after Corbyn led Labour to destruction. But her language reflected the enthusiasms of an intellectual elite swept away by the Corbyn moment that was not grounded in any electoral reality.

The majority of next generation of opinion-formers on the left was clear that isolating Britain from Europe was a reactionary, nationalist populist project. Yet the Labour leadership seemed incapable of articulating that simple fact. I tried to persuade trade union contacts after 2016 that the damage done to jobs, incomes and worker rights by Brexit would be a major blow to trade union strength. Instead, the main industrial and public service unions joined with the CBI and the British Chambers of Commerce in pulling a Brexit duvet over their heads and wishing the problem would just go away.

I was back where I had begun in the early 1970s, with Labour unable to offer any leadership on the Europe question. My part of the Labour family until I became an MP was the trade union movement. It was now absent without leave on the battlefield of my country's future.

A brand-new weekly political newspaper, *The New European*, had emerged from the Brexit plebiscite. As a child of print media, it was a joy to feel real printed pages in my hand instead of the endless scrolling on a computer or iPhone screen. I thought it would last a few weeks but years after Brexit it was still on sale in supermarkets and WHSmiths. It mixed news reports and invective against the Johnson-Farage double act, but added excellent cultural and sporting history coverage of Europe, today and yesterday.

The *Independent* campaigned for a new referendum but the *Guardian* and *New Statesman* had no clear intellectual or policy line on Brexit and reflected the confusion and multi-faceted, often contradictory line of the Labour shadow cabinet.

The old military adage of *Order. Counter-order. Disorder.* applied to Labour on how to respond to Brexit. Unions do respond to leadership but Corbyn offered none. Andrew Adonis, a Labour peer and former cabinet minister, had thrown himself whole-heartedly into the campaign to allow a democratic say on the final deal once it was known, as had been promised by Leave campaigners in 2016. Writing in *The New European*, Adonis argued that Labour's shadow cabinet spokesperson on Brexit 'did not want to change the weather. Since 2016, he had been a Brexiter... he talks about getting the best Brexit deal, not stopping Brexit.'

I thought this was hard on Sir Keir Starmer who had never been involved in Labour politics until entering the Commons in 2015. He was a QC well versed in arguing what his client wanted. But his client, Jeremy Corbyn, didn't know what he wanted, or if he did, kept it a secret.

The category error made by some in Labour in this period was to assume that any seat that voted Brexit in 2016 was lost to Labour unless it embraced the nostrums of the anti-Europeans. In truth in most of safe Labour seats – now dubbed 'red wall' seats – Labour often only got half the votes or even less. Under the First Past the Post system for elections to parliament, a winning candidate could get as little as twenty-five per cent of all votes cast provided they had one vote more than the other candidates. So even in safe Labour seats in England a majority of votes could go to opponents of Labour – Conservatives, UKIP, BNP, Independents, LibDems. To say a seat voted Brexit meant it was automatically lost to Labour was untrue. The majority of *Labour* voters in these seats were opposed to Brexit and wanted their democratic right to be heard again and respected.

No one in the shadow cabinet, let alone Corbyn and his team, was ready to make this argument. Labour paid a price in the European Parliament elections in May 2019. Corbyn's approach to Europe led to half of Labour's twenty MEPs being defeated while the pro-EU LibDems, Greens and SNP made gains.

This major defeat for Labour was lost in the domestic news of a number of Labour MPs resigning from the Party in protest against Labour's failure across a range of issues from anti-Semitism to foreign policy. I would have begged them to stay, hold their noses, see out the doomed Corbyn project and wait for sense and a hunger for power to emerge.

I knew first hand the frustration of seeing my beliefs not taken up by the Blair-Brown governments: workplace democracy, a reform of media ownership and an ending of the dependence on donations from the super rich. But strategic patience is needed in politics. When I began arguing for an end to whites-only journalism in Britain or for Freedom of Information legislation it took years, decades even, to see policy demands become practice or law or just accepted as normal. Walking out of Labour made no sense.

Some joined the LibDems like Chuka Umunna. He was selected to be the LibDem candidate in the constituency where I lived in central London which had a comfortable Tory majority. If he'd bothered to ask me, I could have told him he was wasting his time. I had every sympathy for Luciana Berger, a Jewish Labour MP, who was subjected to unacceptable anti-Semitic abuse by Labour leftists in Liverpool where she was an MP. Other Jewish women Labour MPs like Ruth Smeeth and the veteran, indefatigable Margaret Hodge also suffered 1930s style anti-Jewish abuse. It was horrifying and disgusting.

But the Labour leadership refused to offer nothing other than token suspensions and initiating disciplinary action.

I am not Jewish and no supporter of the right-wing nationalist government of Benjamin Netanyahu. I had, however, chaired a Commons Commission on Inquiry into Anti-Semitism which led me in 2008 to write a book, *Globalising Hatred. The New Antisemitism*. The affinities, identity and fears of Britain's Jewish community could not be ignored. For decades many Jews had found their party in Labour and saw it contrast to the Tory right which fawned upon Arab dictatorships whose media and ministers openly indulged in anti-Jewish language.

Now the Corbyn leadership had ruptured that relationship between Labour and Britain's Jews. I wrote an article in *The Times* explaining how Corbyn could make amends with symbolic visits to Auschwitz or Yad Vashem, the Holocaust memorial centre near Tel Aviv. But I was wasting my time.

The Tories had finally got rid of Theresa May and turned to their Brexit hero, Boris Johnson. All he wanted was an election to confirm the 2016 plebiscite. Labour under Corbyn was by now unelectable. The LibDems had an odd leader who said his version of religious belief prevented him from condemning aspects of homophobia. The Scottish Nationalists were growing in support by confirming the wish of Scots as expressed in the 2016 referendum to stay linked to Europe. Between them, Labour, the LibDems and the SNP had enough votes in the Commons to deny Johnson a majority for his election, which required a change in the law to do away with the law stipulating a five-year fixed term parliament.

Then Jo Swinson, a forty-year-old Scottish LibDem MP

who had taken over the leadership of the party in July after the debacle over her predecessor's views on gays, suddenly announced she would become prime minister if a general election was called. It was nonsense and instead of saying so and continuing to deny Johnson his election, Corbyn also embraced the idea of general election which took place in December.

> **Lesson 52.** *In politics, as in war, never do what the enemy wants you to do. The Tories wanted Labour to support abolishing the nuclear deterrent. The Tories wanted Labour to raise taxes on working people to pay for public sector wages and projects. If it is clear the Conservatives want Labour to adopt such proposal perhaps it should give pause for thought. In October 2019 Boris Johnson wanted a general election. Why did Labour grant his wish?*

I could not believe the stupidity of this error. Locked in his cage of no general election with Corbyn holding the key, Johnson was erratic and angry and unable to explain any other reason why he should be prime minister, other than to deliver for Nigel Farage and the anti-European ideology forged this century.

I campaigned in different seats. The venom against Corbyn was off the wall. In a freezing, blinding, winter rain I walked the streets of Wolverhampton with Emma Reynolds, a young MP with a big future in Labour. Our eyes were wet with rain but also with tears as we knocked on door after door and were told these Labour households would never vote Labour as long as Corbyn was our candidate.

I knocked on doors in seats we won like Putney or held like Canterbury and in Bristol. I was with old comrades like Don Brind and Giampi Alhadeff. We had been joined in common progressive international politics for forty years. No one said a good word about Boris Johnson or any aspect of the Tory Party platform. It was Corbyn, Corbyn, Corbyn. We sat in misery at the sad, bad state of our party.

I began my life in Labour believing that ideas, policies, values, vision should matter in politics. Now in the fourteenth general election campaign I'd taken part in, the question of the leader, the person you put forward to be prime minister, was all important.

All politics is personal. We stuck with Jim Callaghan and Gordon Brown as prime ministers when it was clear they were going to lose. We stuck with Michael Foot and Neil Kinnock when it was clear they were unelectable. Labour could, only two or three times in its more than a century of history, produce a leader who was a winner. But Labour preferred to be led by losers whose language pleased the faithful rather than embrace progressive reform and renewal. Jeremy Corbyn again proved this iron law of Labour history as we gave Johnson his victory.

# 2020

So once again a new start for Labour. How many such fresh beginnings since I first joined the Party in 1970? We seem to lurch from one side to the other, stop and start, leaving party members and voters politically sea sick from the changes in direction and new faces on the bridge of the good ship Labour.

Yet Jeremy took his time in leaving. Books were produced by a new generation of fine young political journalists about the Corbyn years. But even before they were on sale the names of the personalities and the endless infighting in Labour during the Corbyn era were hard to recall or get worked up about. There were ugly leaks from within the Labour Party head office about the handling of the anti-Semitic poison that had been allowed to fester. There was a pointless leadership campaign as the only possible winner was Sir Keir Starmer.

Every other Labour leader since 1906 had spent many years in the Commons, had written and spoken extensively on politics, adapted their positions to new circumstances (with the exception of Corbyn) and taken part in bruising internal Labour party battles.

Sir Keir was quite different. He had never sought election until inheriting Frank Dobson's safe Camden seat. He had never taken part in any Labour party battles. He was a loyal local Labour man in Kentish Town, the ward I once chaired. Until he was put into the shadow cabinet by Corbyn he had no profile other than being one of a good number of liberal-left barristers who pleaded in court for honourable causes often linked to human-rights campaigns overseas. As the government's chief prosecutor under both Labour and Tory governments he was a senior civil servant and could not participate directly in party politics.

All these attributes made his election as party leader a foregone conclusion. A left-over from the Corbyn years, Rebecca

Long-Bailey, who faithfully embraced every nostrum that had led to the 2019 election defeat, was the candidate of the left but Sir Keir was easily elected.

His calm, organised barrister-style advocacy was in strong contrast to the emotional, exaggerated bombast of the new prime minister, Boris Johnson. Both men faced the double 'Brovid' challenge of the Covid Pandemic and what I defined in a new book, *Brexiternity. The Uncertain Fate of Britain* as the unending question of Europe. Neither the referendum in 2016, nor Johnson's election win in 2019, nor the two formal treaty agreements between the UK and the EU agreed by the end of 2020 and endorsed by votes in the Commons and the European Parliament in 2021 had properly answered it.

Covid and Brexit dominated the first period of both Sir Keir Starmer and Boris Johnson's leaderships. The extraordinary number of deaths in Britain, especially amongst the elderly and those entrusted to care homes, was shameful. There were horrifying stories of corruption as people with contacts with Tory ministers and MPs were awarded lucrative multi-million pound NHS contracts to import masks or gowns from China at inflated prices and became rich in the process.

The Commons became a shadow of its normal self with benches empty and Johnson and Sir Keir facing off from the Dispatch Box with no MPs behind or in front of them or to their sides.

Sir Keir as a seasoned QC more than held his own in exchanges with the prime minister who had never mastered the Commons either in his first period as an MP or after he returned following eight years as Mayor of London. Yet in the more than

100 wider polls on voting intention carried out during the year only five showed Labour in the lead over the Tories. By March 2021, the Tories were often leading Labour in opinion polls on the intention to vote at the next election despite the damning record of the Johnson government in having the highest level of deaths from Covid in Europe.

This was offset by the success of the NHS operation to vaccinate the nation which was a major World War 2 type mobilisation. Organized and delivered by the public sector not-for-profit National Health Service, it stood in stark contrast to the Boris Johnson's management of the pandemic when decisions leading to avoidable deaths were delayed and endless scandals about multi-million-pound contracts were awarded to individuals with good connections to Tory ministers or to Johnson himself.

There was a row when Corbyn was suspended as a Labour MP after a damning report by the Equality and Human Rights Commission which said Labour had been guilty of 'unlawful acts' in its handling of complaints into anti-Semitism when Corbyn was leader. His supporters on Labour's ruling National Executive Committee mobilised to get him reinstatment as a Labour MP.

Sir Keir then said the Labour Party whip in the Commons would not be restored to Corbyn. The bitterness and division were out in the open. I attended the All Members' Meeting in my own constituency party where members passed a motion praising Corbyn and calling for his full instatement. The atmosphere was rancorous. Crude personal insults were made. Hate was in the air.

The new Labour leader carefully avoided saying anything about Brexit. He instructed Labour MPs to vote for the deal Johnson concluded with the EU. It was the first trade deal in British history which sought to reduce – not increase – commercial possibilities for the UK's economic actors. Labour remained divided as the pointless recriminations about the handling of the Europe question since 2015 droned on and on.

Some argued that Sir Keir's policy of 'Speak No Europe. Hear No Europe. See No Europe' made tactical sense. It was accepted by the party which had given up thinking about Europe. But it left the millions of Labour supporters opposed to Tory-UKIP isolationism without a voice to speak for them in the main opposition.

In the 1950s Harold Wilson wrote a book *War on Want* which developed the concept of international aid culminating in the creation of the Department for International Development (DfID) in 1997. Boris Johnson abolished DfID in 2020 folding it into the Foreign Office and cut the aid budget by nearly a third. Britain would no longer have an independent ministry to help combat world poverty. Wilson said in his period of leadership before winning in 1964 that 'the Labour Party is a crusade, or it is nothing.'

Anyone can point to the gap between such rhetoric in opposition and the brutal realities of compromises in power. Nonetheless, the left and progressive souls in Britain as well as most Labour party members do want some inspiration, some metaphor of a hill to climb or of evils to conquer, as Beveridge had laid out in his 1944 vision of the Welfare State. Labour's 1997 manifesto was full of progressive pledges on a legal minimum wage, guaranteeing European social rights, creating a national network of early years centres, putting men and women in police uniforms back on the streets, creating a separate Department of State for overseas aid and legislating to make 0.7 per cent of the GDP to help the poorest of the world. There was much pragmatism but little to excite the soul.

In 2021 and thereafter, Labour would also have to fashion an answer to the question of Scotland. Sir Keir's shadow cabinet team had several competent and intellectually focused MPs but they came from the southern half of the United Kingdom. Scotland, which gave us Keir Hardie to Gordon Brown, has been a large part of the Labour mix for over a century. Yet it seemed to no longer to exist in the wider British Labour party as it entered the third decade of the new century.

Across Europe, Labour's sister parties headed or are represented in various types of coalition governments. Progressive politics represented by the Greens or more left-wing parties also won seats in parliaments. The idea, much touted by English academics like Professor Matthew Goodwin that rightist, often-racist, nationalist populists were on an unstoppable march to dominate politics in Europe, turned out to be wrong. They were not able to break through into governing power and during the Covid pandemic their Donald-Trump-like nostrums about how to handle the virus failed to impress or convince. Trump's defeat at the hands of the pragmatic centrist can-do Joe Biden suggested the democratic world was not turning to the populist identity politics and cultural warriors of the rightist think-tanks and their journals.

So if Labour is again to form a government, can it do so

without any alliance or arrangement with other non-Tory parties, notably the Scottish nationalists? Scottish identity populists are as righteous in their dislike of union with England and Wales as English Tory nationalists are in their dislike of union or partnership with the independent sovereign nations of Europe.

Yet the example of continental Europe suggests that the 20th century centre-left political parties were unlikely to win enough votes to form a majority government. Coalitions, arrangements and understandings with other parties were needed to keep the right in opposition. Was Britain so different?

A set of elections in May 2021 for major cities in England, the Scottish parliament and Welsh Assembly, councils in small cities and big towns showed both Labour and Tories losing and winning seats. However a big tactical error was made by the Labour leadership in holding a by-election in Hartlepool on the same day. The Labour MP there had resigned over allegations about sexual behaviour. Without any consultation with local Labour Party members, the Labour machine in London imposed an MP who had lost his seat in 2019. There was a reservoir of 10,000 voters who had supported the Brexit party in 2019 and were never going to vote Labour.

Boris Johnson had a 36 hours of triumphant headlines when the Tory candidate inevitably won the election. As results came in from Scotland where the Scottish Nationalists and Greens won a majority for holding a secessionist referendum, and Wales where the Labour first minister was popular and professional, it was clear that voters were not endorsing the prime minister as they had in the parliamentary bye-election.

Of the twelve big city elections to choose mayors, Labour won nine of them including London and Manchester.

The Labour leader then bizarrely decided to use the by-election defeat as a reason to seek the demotion of his deputy, a popular and effective communicator, a woman who had left school and had a child aged fifteen and was a grandmother at 37. Labour MPs and members were baffled at the decision to turn the by-election defeat into a week-long saga about internal Labour leadership turmoil.

Political commentators including most sympathetic to Labour were aghast. The talk was about the need for a new Leader with senior Labour figures calling for a new leader. Once again Labour seemed to be looking at a long period in opposition especially as there seemed little hope of winning a solid number of parliamentary seats in Scotland.

All the old formulae resurfaced. Labour should move to the centre, to the right said some, to reconstruct itself from top to bottom, said some. No, said others, Labour should become again a working class party and move to the left. The Labour Mayor of Manchester said Labour was too 'London-centric,' forgetting perhaps that it was seats in London that helped Labour have the numbers it did in the Commons.

There was an endless incantation that Labour 'had to accept Brexit and move on.' But others were not certain that Labour, adopting the language of Nigel Farage and ignoring the clear difficulties so many economic sectors from the fishing industry to City financiers were facing, was a magic solution.

On the eleventh anniversary of Labour being ousted from power in 2010, the future was bleak. Political pendulums always swing. Yet it was far from clear where the push or political energy would come from to get the electoral pendulum to Labour at an election in 2023 or 2024.

My story might as well end there. I have no crystal ball and in my fifty years of Labour Party activism just eighteen have been spent under a Labour government and during five of those eighteen years, 1974-79, Labour was in an unhappy de facto coalition with other parties, the Liberals in Britain and the Social Democrats in Northern Ireland.

I must accept my share in the responsibility for those thirty-two years of Tory rule. I believed passionately the leftism of my early Labour years in the 1970s and into the 1980s would be rewarded at the ballot box. It wasn't. I hoped I might transfer some of the good practice I had learnt from working with progressive politicians and unions in Europe 1979-1994 but I was unable to find many, if any, in Labour interested in such reformist radicalism.

I have enjoyed every moment of political activity and being in Labour has given me so many friends, so many possibilities, and so many chances to promote the values and ideals that matter to me.

Am I in the end a failure? I failed to keep my country in Europe even if Ireland has kindly given me European citizenship thanks to my Donegal grandmother. I failed to get Labour to take seriously progressive policies and social and economic practice in other countries. I failed also to keep my own financial records in order and was duly punished for my stupidity. Enoch Powell once said all political careers end in failure. I prove his point.

But not quite. After I left Oxford I could have stayed in the BBC and polished seats to a big salary and giant pension pot. I might have followed other friends to the Bar and become one of the millionaire QCs driving around in a Porsche. Or into banking and financial services and made loadsa money.

Instead, I have had the best life I could have wished for, engaged in fighting for good causes I think worthwhile and making friends who are as warm and witty to be with today as they were when all of us were younger.

I had the honour to be an MP and minister in a Labour government that was one of the best reformist administrations to be seen globally even if it made one or two big mistakes, including the giant error of invading Iraq. I saw a South Yorkshire town, laid to waste by the cruelties of the Thatcher years, see investment in public services that helped the very youngest to those in the closing years of their lives. Along with many many others, I was part of making that happen.

So yes, politics has been a worthwhile life. And I would not have swapped it for anything else on offer.

Now the torch is passed to a new generation. I wish them all luck and better outcomes than I or my generation have achieved. If in 2070, some older Labour MP reflects on his or her half century in politics beginning today I just hope, despite the fun and enjoyment and satisfaction I have had from political engagement, she or he will have spent more time in government and less time living under Tory rule.

**Part 3:**
# 12 STEPS TO MAKE LABOUR ELECTABLE

As a final sign off here are 12 lessons I've learnt.

1. Don't stick with a loser as leader. I have no idea what the mechanism is but the plain fact is that Labour has kept on as leader on Prime Minister a man (so far never a woman) when it became clear as the nose on our faces that he was not going to win an election. There is no guarantee that a replacement will be a winner but there'll a better chance of winning than with a guaranteed loser. Removing a loser is something Labour needs to learn about.

2. In opposition behave like a government – measured, responsible, representing a broader national interest. In government the party should behave like an opposition: challenging managerial government-accepted wisdom, coming up with new policies, being a home to argument and debate.

3. Establish a story – the famous narrative. The French word *l'histoire* means both story and history. Labour should seek its own story as the vector of some of the best things in British history – standing with Churchill to defeat Hitler, being firm on Soviet and Chinese communist tyranny, the founder of the free national

health service. Then present new policies as the continuation of that story-history. It should be stirring and passionate while grounded in a proven track record. It answers the question of *Why vote Labour* at a non-manifesto level.

4. Abolish the annual conference. There is no greater waste of money than this outing for tired vanities and show-boating. No other democratic left party indulges in the annual week of drink and clichés. Instead, hold regional or thematic conferences and gatherings where Labour lays out its policy on a rolling basis and where new voices and talent emerge. Politics is about education. Labour should learn how to be teachers again.

5. Hire the smartest journalists around to be the party's chief media person. She should be across all media not just the Westminster lobby pack, though they need careful schmoozing and flattery and occasionally some menace. Labour had two media chiefs of genius in my time – Peter Mandelson and Alistair Campbell. Only the best will do. Try and move Labour out of its analogue old-age home. Most of us receive our news via the net (the *Guardian's* actual sales are under 100,000 but millions many of them overseas read it online), FaceBook, free giveway papers, twitter, YouTube or other net platforms. Brexit was won by lies on the net. Labour really has to move out of 20$^{th}$ century media management structures it still uses and into the digital age.

6. Avoid single authors or intellectuals who write one book which then become modish. Single club golf never works. Anthony Crosland or Stuart Holland were mighty intellectuals in their time as are Thomas Piketty and Mariana Mazzucato more recently. Labour policy must be the outcome of team work, tested rigorously. Big intellectuals can offer big ideas but they need to be folded into a broader process of policy development.

7. Teach everyone who will speak for Labour in public – on the doorstep, on councils, in the Commons, on TV or radio the ancient art of rhetoric and good English prose. The mumble and bumble of Labour speakers on the media or the incantation of slogans is deeply unpersuasive.

8. Bring in age or term limits for MPs. The number of Labour MPs this century over the usual retirement age of 65 has been embarrassing. This is hard on MPs with a sense of destiny and who want to go on forever but voters like to see a party continually renewing itself and new voices allowed to emerge.

9. Be seen where people are: sporting occasions, the theatre, music festivals, rural shows, village fetes. Tweets by MPs are mainly flatulence. Just being out and about, organising street stalls, outings for the elderly or for children from poor backgrounds will do far more to promote Labour.

10. Elect the shadow cabinet. The centralisation of shadow cabinet members under the choice and control of the Labour leader may suit party managers and the Leaders Office but it reduces MPs to crawlers.

11. Always have two or three shadow cabinet members who have written proper books. The British love reading, admire authors and respect someone who has made the effort to get facts and ideas into order in a book.

12. Create an international department, properly staffed and financed (from democratic funding of democratic politics) to hold regional education workshops on best government practice by sister parties and progressives around the world. There should be someone in the leader's office who can read and speak at least two foreign languages. Act local. Vote national. Study global.

Good luck.

# Acknowledgements

This book reflects so many conversations with Labour comrades and with friend from other parties whose comments on Labour can often provide insight that we Labour Party members are to defensive about. It is also based on work with and many conversations with progressives in parties and trade unions in many parts of the world. My heartfelt thanks to you all. A big thank you to publisher Katie Isbester of Claret Press and to Benjamin MacShane for text editing.

Claret Press shares engaging stories about the real issues of our changing world. Since it was founded in 2015, Claret Press has seen its titles translated into German, shortlisted for a Royal Society of Literature award and climb up the bestseller list. Each book probes the entanglement of the political, the historical and the everyday—but always with the goal of creating an engaging read.

If you enjoyed this book, then we're sure you'll find more great reads in the Claret Press library.

Subscribe to our mailing list at **www.claretpress.com** to get news of our latest releases, bespoke zoom events and the occasional adorable photo of the Claret Press pets.

Lightning Source UK Ltd.
Milton Keynes UK
UKHW011959150821
388856UK00001B/6

9 781910 461532